Learning Critical Reflection

Experiences of the Transformative Learning Process

Edited by
Laura Béres and Jan Fook

LONDON AND NEW YORK

First published 2020
by Routledge
2 Park Square, Milton Park, Abingdon, Oxon OX14 4RN

and by Routledge
52 Vanderbilt Avenue, New York, NY 10017

Routledge is an imprint of the Taylor & Francis Group, an informa business

© 2020 selection and editorial matter, Laura Béres and Jan Fook; individual chapters, the contributors

The right of Laura Béres and Jan Fook to be identified as the authors of the editorial material, and of the authors for their individual chapters, has been asserted in accordance with sections 77 and 78 of the Copyright, Designs, and Patents Act of 1988.

All rights reserved. No part of this book may be reprinted or reproduced or utilised in any form or by any electronic, mechanical, or other means, now known or hereafter invented, including photocopying and recording, or in any information storage or retrieval system, without permission in writing from the publishers.

Trademark notice: Product or corporate names may be trademarks or registered trademarks, and are used only for identification and explanation without intent to infringe.

British Library Cataloguing in Publication Data
A catalogue record for this book is available from the British Library

Library of Congress Cataloging-in-Publication Data
Names: Béres, Laura, editor. | Fook, Jan, editor.
Title: Learning critical reflection : experiences of the transformative learning process / edited by Laura Béres, Jan Fook.
Description: 1 Edition. | New York, NY : Routledge, [2019] | Includes bibliographical references and index. | Identifiers: LCCN 2019015667 | ISBN 9781138491304 (paperback) | ISBN 9781138491298 (hardback) | ISBN 9781351033305 (ebook)
Subjects: LCSH: Social service. | Social workers--Training of.
Classification: LCC HV40 .L373 2019 | DDC 361.3072--dc23
LC record available at https://lccn.loc.gov/2019015667

ISBN: 978-1-138-49129-8 (hbk)
ISBN: 978-1-138-49130-4 (pbk)
ISBN: 978-1-351-03330-5 (ebk)

Typeset in Bembo
by Taylor & Francis Books

Learning Critical Reflection

Learning Critical Reflection documents the actual learning experiences of social work students and practitioners. It explores how a more in-depth understanding of the process of learning, combined with an analysis of how to critically reflect, will help improve the learning process.

The contributors are all professionals who have learnt, in a formalised way, how to critically reflect on their practice. They speak in depth, and with feeling, about their experiences, how downsides and upsides worked together to transform the way they understood themselves, their professional identity, and their practice. Existing literature about critical reflection is reviewed, identifying the details of learning, and pulling no punches in recognising the difficulty and complexity of becoming transformed through this learning process. The editors of this book also contribute their own reflections on learning how to teach critical reflection and include the findings of a research study conducted on students' learning.

Edited by two experienced educators, this book showcases the process of learning, from the perspective of the learners, in order that educators and students, managers, supervisors, and frontline practitioners alike, may make the most of opportunities to critically reflect in both educational and workplace settings. It should be considered essential reading for social work students, practitioners, and educators.

Laura Béres is Associate Professor in the School of Social Work at King's University College in London, Ontario, Canada. She is known internationally for her work on narrative practices, spirituality, and the intersection of these areas with critical reflection on practice.

Jan Fook is currently Professor and Chair of the Department of Social Work at the University of Vermont. She has held professorial positions in Australia, Norway, Canada, and the UK in both Social Work and Education. She is most well known internationally for her work on critical social work and critical reflection.

Contents

List of illustrations	vii
List of contributors	viii

1 Learning critical reflection   1
   LAURA BÉRES AND JAN FOOK

SECTION I
Developing an appropriate learning culture and strategies to support the critical reflection process   21

2 Critical acceptance: A pathway to critical reflection on practice   23
   TONYA SALOMONS

3 The energising experience of being nonjudgmental in the critical reflection process   34
   STEPHEN LAWLEY

4 Finding exception: Application of narrative practice in professional critical reflection on practice   44
   NATE MEIDINGER

5 Learning how to be reflective   55
   HELEN HICKSON

vi Contents

SECTION II
The changes made from the learning process

67

6 From 'imperfect perfectionism' to 'compassionate conscientiousness'
REBECCA DONATI

69

7 Confronting the role of my identity as a mother in my social work practice
JACKIE SCHINDLER

79

8 Critical reflection on practice: Reflecting on confidence and group dynamic
ASHLEY ELSIE-MCKENDRICK

90

9 Deconstructing 'pretty'
JASMYNE LENNOX

102

10 Social worker well-being and critical reflective practice
FENIX CORNEJO

106

SECTION III
Research and reflections on learning and teaching critical reflection

121

11 Reflections on learning as a teacher: Sharing vulnerability
LAURA BÉRES

123

12 Researching the learning experience of critical reflection
LAURA BÉRES AND JAN FOOK WITH NATE MEIDINGER AND
TONYA SALOMONS

139

13 Conclusion: Issues in teaching and learning critical reflection
JAN FOOK AND LAURA BÉRES

154

14 Resources for learning and teaching critical reflection
LAURA BÉRES AND JAN FOOK

165

Index

176

Illustrations

Figures

14.1 Simple reflection loop   173
14.2 From domination to hegemony   174

Table

10.1 Keywords and phrases related to learning critical reflection   114

Boxes

14.1 Exercise in developing critically reflective questions   165
14.2 Critical reflection 'cheat sheet': Pointers for facilitators   169
14.3 Possible critically reflective questions, which can be asked using different theoretical frameworks   171
14.4 For a university setting: Clarifying what makes this *critical* reflection (usually using PowerPoint slides)   173
14.5 Considerations for a university course   175

Contributors

Fenix Cornejo, MSW, MPA, is a qualified social worker who has worked professionally in Los Angeles, California since 2005 and London since 2007 (in various statutory settings including adult's and children's social care. She recently moved into workforce development and currently works as programme manager for the Step Up to Social Work programme and supports social work education in the West London Alliance and the West London Teaching partnership. Fenix has a degree in Sociology from the University of California, Irvine and a dual Master's degree in Social Work and Public Administration from the University of Southern California, School of Social Work, USA. She is currently finishing an MSc in Advanced Social Work (Practice Education) from Goldsmiths University of London, UK.

Rebecca Donati, BA, BSW, MSW, is a recent graduate of the Master of Social Work (MSW) programme at King's University College at Western University, Canada. Previously at this institution, she attained a Bachelor of Arts (BA) degree with a Major in Sociology and Minor in Psychology and a Bachelor of Social Work (BSW) degree. She has completed placements in probation and parole, women's community work, and health care. She is hoping to work in the area of clinical counselling while also pursuing her interest in research and macro level advocacy.

Ashley Elsie-McKendrick, BSW, MSW, RSW, completed both her BSW and MSW at King's University College at Western University, Canada. Ashley's previous work experience, as well as both her placements during her BSW and MSW, were in clinical practice settings. Critical Reflection on Practice (CRoP) helped shape Ashley's learning during her MSW and clinical placement at a community counselling agency. CRoP gave Ashley the opportunity to practice from a holistic and ethical place that has inspired her to incorporate elements of CRoP in her ongoing practice. After completing an advanced intern programme, Ashley recently started her own private practice alongside part-time work in a community counselling agency.

Helen Hickson, BSW, Master of Professional Practice Development (Critical Reflection), Ph.D., is a social worker, researcher, and educator with a long-standing interest in rural communities and sustainable models of service delivery in rural Australia. She has strong leadership skills, with foundations in corporate governance, stakeholder engagement, financial management, strategic leadership, and health service commissioning.

Stephen Lawley, MSc, MSc, studied politics at University of Warwick, UK, before obtaining an MSc in International Development at University of Birmingham in 2011. He worked in supported housing for people with mental health problems before working in a homelessness assessment and reconnection hub in west London. He trained and qualified as a social worker after completing the Step Up to Social Work course in 2016–17 in the London borough of Brent. In this programme he participated in monthly critical reflection groups with other students and an advanced practitioner. He has been employed in a care planning team in Brent children's services since May 2017.

Jasmyne Lennox, BSW, currently works for Headspace Youth Early Psychosis programme in Perth, Australia, as a case manager. She studied a Bachelor of Social Work at the University of the Sunshine Coast, Queensland, Australia.

Nate Meidinger, BSW, MSW, RSW, is a graduate of the School of Social Work programme at King's University College at Western University, Canada. His past social work experience includes work in child protection, front-line mental health support, and mental-health counselling. Nate's current area of practice interest is exploring ways to enhance the ongoing development and resilience of social work students and professionals through Critical Reflection on Practice. He has recently begun a social work position in a local family health team.

Tonya Salomons, BSW, MSW, RSW, completed her Master's in Social Work at King's University College at Western University in London, Canada. Tonya was first introduced to Jan Fook's work on Critical Reflection on Practice in her graduate studies. One of the highlights of her graduate studies was travelling to the UK with Dr. Béres, presenting her thoughts about Critical Reflection on Practice from a learner's perspective at a seminar organised by Jan Fook, and meeting with social work practitioners in the UK. Since her exposure to Critical Reflection on Practice Tonya has committed to applying this approach to her ongoing practice, and has recently begun work as a community mental health worker in the Toronto area.

Jackie Schindler, BSW, MSW, recently graduated with her MSW from King's University College at Western University, Canada, where she studied as a part-time mature student. She has commenced a career as a child protection worker as she is passionate about working with vulnerable individuals impacted by poverty and addictions. Fook and Gardner's model of Critical Reflection on Practice provided her with the opportunity to acknowledge and explore why, as a self-identifying feminist, she was ashamed and felt the need to hide the presence of her maternal identity in her social work practice.

Chapter I

Learning critical reflection

Laura Béres and Jan Fook

Why this book?

Both of us are experienced educators who have worked with critical reflection for several decades, with students at different levels, with practising social workers, and in different countries and fields of practice. We have witnessed people coming to new understandings, transforming old ways of thinking, and being able to develop meaningful insights directly from their own experiences. From our perspective, being part of this learning experience can be very moving, sometimes exhilarating, and can make us feel imbued, as colleagues, with a sense of compassion and empathy, with those who are critically reflecting on their, sometimes fraught, experiences. Yet whilst transformative learning of this type is generally regarded as overwhelmingly desirable, we have also observed first hand some of the anxiety and resistance, and indeed loss, involved in making the often fundamental changes called for in transformative learning. Exactly what are the emotional and cognitive experiences which take place for learners in becoming more critically reflective? Although we have discussed many aspects of these experiences with our own learners, we became curious about documenting these in a more systematic and holistic way, from their own perspectives. Laura embarked on teaching a whole semester module (13-week academic term) on critical reflection in a newly refocused graduate programme, and her students produced some very thoughtful and insightful thinking on their personal learning experiences. This inspired us to contact other learners who had learned to become critically reflective through a range of other programmes. The result is this book.

Many professions now require a reflective, reflexive, or critically reflective ability (Stedmon & Dallos, 2009). There is a plethora of literature which argues for the value of reflection (e.g. Gardner, 2014) and indeed outlines and describes many different models and strategies for teaching it (e.g. Watson & Kenny, 2014). However, there is less literature which questions its value and/or attempts to research its efficacy (Fook, Collington, Ross, Ruch, & West, 2016). In this book, we do not argue for the value of critical reflection, suggest models for its practice, or provide evidence for its value. Rather, in a reflective manner, we seek to provide illustrations of the experience of learning to be critically reflective from different perspectives and to allow readers to make up their own minds as to the upsides and downsides of the experience. In some ways, however, trying to assess the contribution to learning of critical reflection through a simple binary polarisation of upsides and downsides does not seem to do the experience justice. How all aspects of the learning experience integrate to create new meaning and ways of thinking and acting is something which can perhaps best be illustrated through the narratives of learners themselves. We are, therefore, interested in presenting *experiences* rather than *outcomes*.

A third reason we wanted to produce this book was to showcase the experience of people for whom critical reflection is 'done to'. Most of the literature is written by educators or researchers, i.e. people who are usually in a position of authority in attempting to make others reflective, usually, because it is a requirement of the educational programme they are providing. Given that reflection is in some ways something which can best be undertaken on a voluntary basis (Finlay, 2008, p. 15) it is a great irony that its learning is required on a nonvoluntary basis. We were, therefore, interested not so much in the perspectives of educators and authorities but of those being subjected to the learning. For example, what is the influence of power dynamics in these scenarios?

In this chapter, we will give a brief overview of different approaches to critical reflection and a brief description of the model of critical reflection being learnt by the contributors in this volume. We will also review some major learning and teaching issues covered in the literature on critical reflection and discuss our own approach to teaching and learning. We also include a brief overview of the way critical reflection was taught in the programme in which the majority of contributors participated. For those who did not participate in this programme, we have asked that they include a brief description of how the model was learnt in their respective chapters. This will hopefully provide enough background context.

Issues involved in learning and teaching critical reflection

Defining critical reflection?

There seems to be general agreement that there are a number of different terms associated with the concept of critical reflection and that this can also lead to confusion and lack of clarity about what is meant by the term. (Saric & Steh, 2017). Indeed, this is a common criticism of the idea of critical reflection (Ixer, 1999). This, of course, does not mean that critical reflection is a meaningless term, but it does mean that it is important to clarify what it means in both theory and practice. Some of the associated ideas include reflection, reflexivity, and reflective practice (Fook, White, & Gardner, 2006; Ixer, 2011). We will discuss briefly our understanding of these in this chapter. There is also popular usage of the term 'reflection' to denote simply 'thinking about' something, and it is important to note at the outset that we regard reflecting as a *particular* form of thinking. In addition, there are many different suggestions for how critical reflection should be practised and, indeed, many different theoretical frameworks underpinning these. Moreover, meanings and definitions and, indeed, even how the purpose of critical reflection is perceived differ according to different academic disciplines (van Beveren, Roets, Buysse, & Rutten, 2018).

It is important to acknowledge the contribution of early philosophers as far back as even Socrates who spoke of 'the examined life for ethical and compassionate engagement with the world and its dilemmas' (Nussbaum, 1997), while Laura has examined what more recent philosophers Heidegger and Gadamer might contribute to our understanding of reflection (Béres, 2017b). Within the field of education, Dewey's understanding of reflection as 'learning from experience' (1933) forms the backbone of most ideas of reflection today, but the ideas have been reworked constantly over the last few decades and are especially dominated by the 'reflective practice' approach developed by Schön (1983). How and whether reflection is 'critical' is also another contentious idea, as sometimes, 'critical' is taken as meaning 'negative' rather than in its more academic sense of denoting a critical theory perspective on how power is created and maintained in personal experience and social arrangements (Brookfield, 2016). Of course, critical reflection is also closely associated with Mezirow and Associates' (2000) notion of 'transformative learning', which entails a deep change of perspective.

Given this abundance of different theories, meanings, and practices, we have decided to work with a model of critical reflection, which attempts to integrate these different perspectives into a framework and model based on a clear articulation of fundamental principles that are relatively and commonly held between different perspectives. This model was first developed primarily based on postmodern and critical perspectives (Fook, 2002) but has been further developed using additional theoretical frameworks (e.g. Fook & Gardner, 2007). We will elaborate on the actual theoretical underpinnings and the practical process further on, but at this point, it is helpful to state how we define critical reflection in a way, which integrates different perspectives: critical reflection involves learning from and making deeper meaning of experience through a process of unsettling and examining deeply hidden assumptions in order to create better guidelines for action and so improve professional practice and develop a more ethical and compassionate stance. It is informed by a reflexive awareness of how the whole self influences knowledge-making and behaviour by an appreciation of the link between language and power, an understanding of how personal experience is also social and political, and how individual beliefs can be changed in order to contribute to socially just change.

The experience of learning reflection and issues involved

In a very engaging way, Jeffrey Baker (2013) describes how he enthusiastically introduced critical reflection to his 'bright and plucky public sector' team, only to slowly witness their increasing 'cringe' from taking part. He notes that in the unsettling of assumptions 'there is the experience of uncertainty, of *not* [italics added] knowing [. . .] and the possibility that aspects of our professional selves, our practice and its context will be revealed as problematic or troubling' and, furthermore, that in this loss of innocence may be the realisation that 'solutions to dilemmas may not be readily forthcoming' (p. 17).

These kinds of sentiments are echoed in a classic article by Stephen Brookfield (1994) in which he outlines the 'dark side' of critical reflection. It is important to note what the 'dark side' is here, as Brookfield's is one of the few pieces of work, which attempts to detail the experience of learning and interpreting learning from the perspective of the learners themselves. Brookfield notes five main themes in the experience. First, there is a sense of 'impostorship', that participating in critical thinking is, itself, an act of bad faith given the act of criticising the contexts and structures, which in fact maintain yourself as a learner. This is related to the second theme of 'cultural suicide', which involves recognising that being critical of, and challenging, conventionally agreed assumptions risk putting the learner out of step with colleagues and cultures in which they are also invested and which have sustained and may also continue to sustain them on some levels. The third theme is that of 'lost innocence', which involves the uncertainty (as mentioned by Baker previously) caused by moving from more certain universalistic ways of being and knowing to more dialogical and multiple understandings. Fourth is what Brookfield terms 'road running', that is, the incrementally fluctuating flirtation with new modes of thought and being. The concept of road running is quite apt, as it vividly captures the sense of uncertainty intertwined with excitement and apprehension, which trying on new ideas can induce. There is also the sense of feeling 'unfaithful' to old, tried, and tested ideas. Lastly, he describes the theme of community, which incorporates the idea of the importance of having a support group for those engaged in a critical process.

It would, of course, be inaccurate to suggest that these downsides are the abiding experience of reflection, as most of the literature written by students of reflection dwells on the transformative outcomes of their learning (e.g. Hickson, 2011; Pockett & Giles, 2008). In addition, even to conceptualise the experience of critically reflective learning as either having 'upsides' or 'downsides' is, perhaps, quite erroneous, as, in fact, upsides may also have downsides and vice versa. It may be their coexistence, which is crucial to learning how to become transformative. This idea recurs throughout this section, because it may be that the downsides actually lead to the upsides (e.g. being vulnerable may lead to change, and it is only in being vulnerable that change can be attained). Another example would be that of uncertainty, as it is through being uncertain that improvements might be made. In this section, we wish to pinpoint a little more, what actual detail regarding the challenges is inherent in the transformative learning experience. As a follow on from that, it will be important to note what safeguards need to be built into the critically reflective learning process in order to capitalise on its transformative aspects. Many suggestions are made along these lines from the contributors. In addition, we outline these in the model of critical reflection, which we use.

It is instructive to note here that, historically, it may have been the intellectual and cognitive aspects of transformative learning, which were emphasised (see, for example, Mezirow & Associates, 2000). However, more recently, there has been very appropriate recognition of the emotional aspects of the experience (McManus, n.d.). Saric and Steh (2017, p. 79) give a helpful overview of the ways in which emotions can affect critically reflective learning. First, emotions may constitute one of the motivations for engaging in reflection, as it is often unsettling, perplexing, or discordant experiences, which trigger the impulse to reflect. People may be left with feelings of anger, disappointment, frustration, regret, or distress or, perhaps, even wonder and feel the need to explore the experience to understand it better. In this sense, these triggering emotions can also become part of the reflective experience, as the connection between these feelings and the deeper assumptions or beliefs held by the person need to be better understood in order to understand the whole experience. Secondly, the experience of reflecting may become emotional in and of itself as other unpredicted emotions may surface or as long-held views are shaken. This is, of course, to be expected if the experience being reflected upon is personal. Sometimes, as well, the experience itself may not have been shared with anyone else before, so the more public act of reflecting in a group may engender its own set of emotions. Lastly, the longer-term implications of the reflective learning can also be emotional, as learners redevelop their thinking and actions to incorporate newly developed emotional responses.

Some quotes from critically reflective learners interviewed by Helen Hickson (2013) illustrate more about the experience of learning to critically reflect. One spoke of how assumptions about learning are challenged:

> we often think that learning is something that should be linear – they teach it, we learn it, and away you go. With critical reflection you are learning a way of thinking, but it's not always clear where you are going and what is at the end. People are sometimes impatient and get lost and frustrated, because they want to know where they are going, and I guess that's the very nature of it. People also need to understand that they may experience some personal discomfort and vulnerability thinking about assumptions and values and where they came from.
>
> (p. 62)

In a response from another participant, Hickson (2013, p. 63) draws out the idea of 'spiraling', which, rather than just going around in circles and ending up in the same place, describes a sense of going around in circles but, at the same time, going deeper. Through this process, participants particularly became aware of themes of resistance and acceptance. It was helpful to explore her assumptions about these themes in her own critical reflection process. She describes the overall experience of critically reflective learning in this way:

[I]t feels a bit like the eye of a cyclone – where it is calm, but you seem to go around and around but always come back to the central themes. And I wonder what creates this? Is it a life experience that keeps bringing us back to a similar place, and no matter what happens this central theme is going to be there? I have used critical reflection with lots of different groups and different people but I often end up back in familiar territory – the common denominator is me.

(p. 63)

Saric and Steh (2017, p. 79) also draw attention to how confronting what is less well-known about oneself has the potential to shake the foundations of one's identity. In our own experience in conducting critically reflective groups, we do find that this is one of the biggest challenges for learners, as it is not generally expected that focusing on professional learning may involve needing to remake one's identity. For example, Jane was used to thinking of herself as a 'bad' manager, because she felt she had mishandled supervision of a case where a client died and could not shake the feeling of failure. She did not undertake critical reflection in the expectation that she would revise her own identity but simply hoped that she would better understand why she felt this way. In the process, though, she questioned deep assumptions about the nature of 'bad' management and revised her own thinking about management to become open to the possibility that she could be a 'good' manager (Fook, Royes, & White, 2017). Whilst this may be seen on one level as a 'good' outcome, the experience is not without its stresses. Making such a drastic change in identity may also involve reworking other personally held narratives, which have served to solidify the old identity.

Vulnerability and uncertainty can play a constructive role in motivating learning (Hickson, 2011). It may, of course, as suggested earlier, also be that being vulnerable is a crucial aspect of critically reflective learning, because being vulnerable goes hand in hand with being open to change (Fook & Askeland, 2007). These concepts also suggest that risk needs to be taken in order to make gains and suggest that the more risk that is taken, the more likelihood there will be of making learning gains. Laura explores more of this link between vulnerability and authenticity within the educator and transformative learning in Chapter 12.

Finlay (2008) discusses the risky aspect of undertaking critical reflection. She helpfully details the different types of risks, which may be involved. First, there is an ethical aspect to the risk. Some of this has already been outlined in relation to the emotional aspects we discussed earlier, but she very appropriately emphasises potential ethical concerns involved if critical reflection acts like 'emotional dynamite' in exploding learners' preconceptions (Finlay, 2008, p. 10). This can be particularly problematic if facilitators are unable to help, or are inept at helping, to deal with such fallout. The expertise and sensitivity of the learning facilitator become crucial, and, of course, this is not always easy or possible to control. In this sense, there is a risk of critical reflection being handled unprofessionally. There is, therefore, the risk of harm (both emotional and reputational) being done to participants. This may further be exacerbated if the reflection takes place in a political environment of victim blaming, as may be the case if an organisation wishes to shift responsibility for poor standards of professional practice to individual practitioners or even supervisors. Lastly, she mentions the issue we have noted earlier of the potential contradiction between requiring reflection (which also involves assessing it) and the importance of the reflection being undertaken voluntarily to maximise the capacity to be open to change.

Another factor in critically reflective learning may be that change itself can involve loss, and, therefore, a tendency to resist the change. As mentioned previously, if the change involves a change of a long-held identity (Saric & Steh, 2017), or of long-held and fundamental beliefs, then there may be an understandable tendency to resist or defend. The loss of long-held beliefs or identities may involve the questioning of narratives or ways of thinking, which have been developed as a result of traumatic or life-changing events or of events, which occurred some time ago and have also been formative of whole sets of beliefs and lifestyles. To expect these to change, especially without necessarily having something with which to replace them, involves a good deal of trust, optimism, and creativity. It is, therefore, highly understandable that there may be a tendency to resist making these changes, as opposed to unequivocally embracing the potential opportunities. McGregor (2008) compares the stages of the grieving experience with the stages of transformative learning, effectively underlining the emotional challenge involved.

Writing within a Brazilian context in the same volume of work, Traverso-Yepez (2008) elaborates on how the context (both the immediate learning context and the broader societal context) plays a role in creating challenges for transformative learners. Clearly, the immediate context needs to foster openness to learning, but sometimes, the challenge of addressing broader social and political changes can feel overwhelming. The theme of the importance of context recurs repeatedly. It is important to note that it is all aspects of context, which are crucial: political, cultural, organisational, and professional. Bekas (2013) notes how critical reflection can be easily disrupted by work environments, which are rule-bound. Fook (2012) discusses the different types of learning, professional and workplace cultures that can undermine or work against the willingness and ability to reflect. These internalised cultures include needing to be seen as 'the expert' (someone who has extra knowledge and skills), 'the manager' (the person who can 'fix it' and suggest solutions), 'the evangelist' (someone who has 'seen the light' and wants to advocate this as the 'solution' to anything), 'the victim' (someone who has a vested interest in being seen as powerless and not responsible for the situation), and/or 'the technician' (someone who believes that there are technical 'answers' to every problem and cannot recognise the role of different beliefs or assumptions in creating situations). Many workplace and professional cultures unwittingly encourage these ways of thinking, and critically reflecting, especially in a group environment, can be seen as a forum for demonstrating these perspectives in a competitive way. Unfortunately, all these ways of thinking work against critical reflection by discouraging openness, implying judgements, reinforcing power differences, encouraging passivity, or placing value on purely technical solutions.

Helyer (2015) also notes the problem of making judgements, which can be a strong deterrent to reflect. Judgements can be made by others, assumed to be made by others, or made by oneself, and it is this culture, endemic in both workplaces and broader settings, which can inhibit reflection. For this reason, Fook and Gardner (2007) argue for the need to develop a 'critically accepting' learning climate to facilitate critical reflection. Much, of course, has been written about 'blame' cultures inherent in child protection services and how working in such an environment induces stress and anxiety (Munro, 2011). Ferguson (2013) reemphasises the need to create a nonjudgmental environment for critical reflection in statutory services. Other aspects of the cultural environment, which can constitute a challenge to critical reflection, include how reflective learning can become 'opportunistic and discretionary' (Bekas, 2013), or, indeed, can also be used as a tool of oppression (Brookfield, 1995) and demoralistion.

On a more practical level, some students noted a dislike of journaling. However, Tsang (2009) admits that although she thought that journaling was time wasting, she, in fact, came to recognise that reflecting in this way actually saved her time in the long term. Presumably, it also depends on how students are asked to journal and how the journaling is used to aid reflection. Some learners also note a problem with trying to learn or use different models of reflection (Middleton, 2017) and how a more open-ended approach can work better. On a more positive note, Cairney (2015) argues for the positive use of narratives in a relational way to enable critical reflection. We will develop this idea more when elaborating on the narrative aspects of the model of critical reflection we have adopted.

Our approach to teaching/learning

Given that we have both been engaged in learning and teaching critical reflection for some time, we have both reflected on our own approach to teaching and learning and how it has been influenced by this experience. Laura discusses in Chapter 12 her enjoyment of catching and examining her previously taken-for-granted assumptions but also acknowledges how this might not always be an enjoyable experience for everyone. As a social worker whose career began in direct counselling practice settings, as someone who continues to provide psychotherapy on a part-time basis in addition to holding a full-time academic position, and as an educator who primarily teaches direct practice courses, my approach to teaching cannot help but be influenced by my approach to counselling. I describe myself as a narrative therapist/practitioner

(Béres, 2014; Béres, Bowles, & Fook, 2011) and as committed to maintaining congruence between my various roles as educator, researcher, and psychotherapist. For me, this means putting into practice the philosophical and political underpinnings of narrative therapy in the classroom: unsettling the position of expertise and attempting to create a nonhierarchical classroom context of equality, which values students' experience and voice. This is not always straightforward or unproblematic, which I also reflect upon in Chapter 12. These commitments within my teaching practices were also influenced by pursuing a Ph.D. in Critical Pedagogy and Cultural Studies, where I was not only introduced to Jan's work on critical social theory and social work for the first time (Fawcett, Featherstone, Fook, & Rossiter, 2000; Fook, 2002) but also to the work of Paulo Freire (1972), and Henry Giroux and Roger Simon (1989), to name a few. Critical pedagogy, much like transformative learning, suggests that education cannot be neutral and nonpolitical and must support the analysis of social structures of domination and control. All of this together has resulted in me attempting to always be transparent about my power in a classroom setting, attempting to use that power ethically, and supporting students in accessing and using their power also.

For Jan, the experience of learning how to reflect through teaching has been a long and revealing road. I have always espoused social justice ideologies in relation to teaching, and so, I tried to devise ways of teaching reflection, which modelled this as closely as possible. Early on, I realised that it did not seem fair to expect students to do something I didn't, so I always tried to model my own personal reflection before expecting learners to do so. This was intentional in setting up a climate of collegiality, but it also forced me to experience the vulnerability and uncertainty, which I expected them to embrace. I found that reflecting on my own experience with a group of learners meant that I did not know what they would raise, or what feelings of my own would surface. This was especially the case when I used to reflect on an incident in which issues of race, and potential racism towards myself, were factors. These happen to be issues, which for me (as a person of Chinese descent raised in a predominantly white society) were relatively unexamined. They had the potential to cause me distress, and what was even more distressing was discussing them in a forum with my own students. This experience, of often feeling 'out of control' as an educator and of exposing myself to people who were not officially my equals, meant that I had to trust them. It also confronted me with the question of what learning and teaching actually meant and to question why the two concepts were habitually separated. What I, of course, discovered, which is what many participants in my critical reflection workshops say, is that I constantly learnt about myself even whilst facilitating reflection for other people. Teaching and learning are not mutually exclusive categories. Learning is essentially a social and relational process, which, in some ways, is what it is in 'real' life. It occurs through interaction and dialogue. So, the lines between 'learner' and 'teacher' are much more blurred for me now, although I realise that as the 'teacher', I

10   Laura Béres and Jan Fook

am more responsible for creating an environment to enable learning than the 'learners'. This conception of teaching as 'creating a learning environment' sits well with a non-'banking' notion of education (Freire, 1972). I see teaching and learning as not being about directly imparting facts or skills but creating an environment, which enables learners to be open to change. In this process, I also ensure that they have an environment, which encourages and supports them to name, develop, and practise the kinds of knowledge and skills they believe are relevant. I have elsewhere developed in detail what this 'critically accepting' environment should look like to enable critical reflection (Fook & Askeland, 2007; Fook & Gardner, 2007). We will say a little more about this when we discuss the model of critical reflection used by the contributors to this volume.

Overview of an integrated model of critical reflection

In this section, we outline the model of critical reflection we mentioned earlier. This model has been used by all the contributors in this book. This model has been developed using the major different frameworks for reflection and so aims to integrate these different perspectives and theories. There are basically five different frameworks, which underpin different approaches to reflection: reflective practice, reflexivity, post-structural thinking and postmodern narrative practice, critical social theories, and spirituality. It is perhaps useful to point out that the addition of spirituality as a fifth framework is relatively new and was not present in the Fook and Gardner (2007) resource handbook, which was used as one of two textbooks within the Canadian course Laura taught. This means that within the chapters written by Laura and former students of that course, there will only be mention made of four theoretical frameworks, although spirituality was discussed. We will briefly outline each of the five frameworks that follow and in so doing will effectively discuss some of the definitions of these different terms as they relate to critical reflection.

Reflective practice

Most of the current interest in reflection stems from the work of Donald Schön (1983) who developed the concept of 'reflective practice'. Reflective practice is based upon the idea that there is often a large gap between what professionals say they do (their espoused theory) and what they actually do (their practice). Schön posits, however, that there is an implicit theory embedded in what people do, because they are assuming certain ideas upon which they base their practice. Practice can, therefore, be made better by professionals becoming aware of these embedded assumptions and, thus, improving their practice by bringing it more into line with their desired espoused theory. Thus, 'reflective practice' is practice, which is improved through a process of bringing to awareness the hidden assumptions that might be causing practice to work at cross-purposes with the espoused theory. The strength, therefore, of the reflective practice approach is its emphasis on the improvement of practice. This appears to be the prime understanding of reflection in social work circles. Another strength of the reflective practice approach is that it gives a clear starting point for the practice of reflection – the uncovering of embedded or hidden assumptions.

Reflexivity

There is also much criticism of the reflective practice approach as being relatively superficial and theoretically weak. It does also, of course, leave out the value dimension mentioned earlier. In theoretical terms, there are other concepts, which provide more substance to the idea of critical reflection. For instance, the concept of 'reflexivity' is also referred to in tandem with the idea of reflection. Reflexivity as a term arises from social science research traditions. It refers to the ability to factor in awareness of oneself as a creator of knowledge or the lens through which one's world is seen and evaluated. It relies on an understanding of how knowledge is socially constructed but also extends to the material and emotional aspects of who we are as human beings and acknowledges that these aspects also play a part in influencing the types of knowledge we create, what we think is important, and the interpretive frameworks we use. To be reflexive, therefore, is to be aware of who we are as whole human beings and how this influences the way we think and behave. Being *reflexive* is, therefore, an important aspect of being *reflective*, in that, we need to be aware of how we as social individuals might have a tendency to maintain certain biases or preferences in the assumptions we make about our world and the people in it.

From a reflexivity point of view, then, reflection involves being aware of who we are (physically, psychologically, historically, socially, and culturally) and how this influences the hidden assumptions we make.

Post-structural thinking and postmodern narrative practice

Post-structural ways of thinking are useful in reflection, particularly because they draw attention to the language we use and how we construct very fundamental ways of thinking because of this. From a post-structural standpoint, the language we use has a role in creating and maintaining knowledge and power, as it is often the dominant groups whose language (and corresponding perspective or worldview) is used. Also, this way of thinking about how language use and power are connected points to the idea that any one way of talking about something is, in fact, only one of a range of possible 'stories' or 'narratives', i.e., it is that person's way of constructing how they talk about their experience. In this sense, stories are neither necessarily true or false but are simply told that way in order to convey the sort of message that a person wants to convey about their experience. There might always be other types of language which could be used, other themes which could be emphasised, and other bits of the story included. What the person chooses to focus on, and how they choose to frame the experience, is an important source of reflection. Although it is important to stress that critical reflection is not about engaging in therapy, we have found that some of the theoretical and practical ideas within narrative therapy (White, 2007; White & Epston, 1990) are useful in thinking about how stories are constructed and how they impact the person telling a story. Nate Meidenger discusses these ideas further in Chapter 4. However, at this point, it may be useful to at least consider how a story is made up of a series of events linked over time according to a theme and that as some events are chosen to become part of a particular story, other events are ignored or 'unstoried'. These previously unstoried events, which White calls 'unique outcomes', drawing upon Goffman's work (White, 2007), can offer the possibility of developing an alternative and preferred story. For instance, someone might be recounting a story of how they believe they are a 'bad' social worker, providing descriptions of events of which they are unhappy, but there are almost always more accounts of practice events, which they would be more likely to describe as 'good'. This highlights how, initially, someone might continue to think in terms of binaries and good or bad practice, but there are many possible storylines that could be strung together by linking together events that could fit somewhere on the continuum between bad and good.

Post-structural theory points to some specific common ways of constructing our knowledge, which are often embedded in our thinking. An example of these is constructing 'one truth', i.e. the idea that there is one 'right' perspective and that any contradictory ones must be wrong (often when constructing a social work assessment, we are striving to put forward this 'one truth'). Another common construction is the tendency to categorise social phenomena into 'binary opposites' or 'forced choices', as touched upon previously. These occur when we divide the whole population of something into only two categories, and every example must belong to one or the other (e.g. male and female). In a 'forced choice' scenario, the categories are often constructed so that they are, by definition, mutually exclusive (e.g. 'bureaucrat' or 'professional'). The problem with binaries, of course, is that there are many experiences or phenomena, which are either left out or do not fit at all. Life and people are often much more complex, and it is this complexity, which is left out. This makes it very difficult to practise in responsive ways if the situation itself is defined too simply or rigidly.

Post-structural thinking is vital to reflection because analysing our thinking from the point of view of the language we use, how it constructs our knowledge/reality, and how it creates certain power relations is a relatively clear way to identifying some of our underlying assumptions and what we might want to change. Questioning why we use certain words, terminology, or phrases, and exposing the biases inherent in these, is called 'deconstruction', and it is by deconstructing the language we use, and the stories or narratives which we tell about these experiences, that we can begin to understand more about our own experiences and how we might want to 'reconstruct' them in order to make our desired changes or improvements.

Using a post-structural framework, then, critical reflection involves being able to deconstruct the narratives we use and to become aware of how we maintain and create power through the language (and implied assumptions) we use. This enables us to reconstruct these narratives along more empowering and preferred lines (Fook, 2016).

Critical perspectives

Critical perspectives involve the major tenets of critical social theory, which emphasise the connections between personal experience and the social/political world. In particular, they detail how individuals can hold social beliefs, which have political functions that ironically may work against the best interests of the individual. An example of this 'hegemony', 'false consciousness', or 'ideology' might be a working-class person who will not consider attending university, because they believe that 'people like them' do not have the ability to study at higher levels. Understanding the link between personal and social beliefs is important in that it gives a starting point for individuals to change specific beliefs of theirs, beliefs which perform social functions, in ways which work against their own interests or serve to maintain social inequalities. This function of critical reflection has been termed 'ideology critique' (Brookfield, 2009). This is similar to the older concept of consciousness-raising, whereby individuals became aware of how some of their beliefs might be self-defeating, because they primarily functioned to preserve the social order and keep them 'in their place'. Clearly, some post-structural thinking is also critical in that it also emphasises the link between power and the knowledge that individuals construct. The idea that knowledge is socially constructed, and therefore changeable, is central to a critical perspective.

Critical perspectives are based on an analysis of how power is created and maintained socially and structurally (which includes an understanding of personal beliefs and agency in this context) and, therefore, how social inequalities are maintained. There is, therefore, a strong social justice and social change value inherent in critical perspectives. This adds the important value dimension in critical reflection, which is perhaps less obvious in some of the other theoretical frameworks.

Critical reflection, from the perspective of critical social theory, then, is a reflection on personal experience based on an analysis of the creation and operation of power in society, which perpetuates inequalities. It focuses on uncovering hidden assumptions about power, exposing how they might unwittingly contribute to power inequalities, so they can be changed in order to develop practice, which is more socially just and equitable. Reflection is critical if it is based on a critical analysis, which provides a basis for addressing social justice.

Spirituality

Over the past several years, both of us have separately started to focus more on the role of spirituality both in professional practice and also in the process of critically reflecting on that practice (Béres, 2018, 2017a, 2017b, 2013; Fook, 2017; Gardner & Béres, 2018; Rogers & Béres, 2017). We include a spirituality perspective, not in the sense of formal religion or dogma, but more in the sense of valuing and honouring what gives people a sense of meaning and purpose. A good definition of spirituality is the following:

> Spirituality is a distinctive, potentially creative and universal dimension of human experience arising from both within the inner subjective awareness of individuals and within communities, social groups and traditions. It may be experienced as relationship with that which is intimately 'inner', immanent and personal, within the self and others, and/or as relationship with that which is wholly 'other', transcendent and beyond the self. It is experienced as being fundamental or ultimate importance and is thus concerned with matters of meaning and purpose in life, truth and values.
>
> (Cook, Powell, & Sims, 2009, p. 4)

This clarifies how, for some people, their spirituality and what gives them meaning and purpose may involve involvement in a religious group and belief in the Divine, but for other people, it will not.

Hunt (2016) describes the focus on 'ultimate questions' involving meaning and values: Who am I? Why am I here? And what am I supposed to be doing? She also mentions the more immaterial and mystical aspects of spirituality. As Canda puts it, spirituality is about 'the human quest for personal meaning and mutually fulfilling relationships among people, the nonhuman environment, and, for some, God' (Canda, 1988, p. 243). Unfortunately, this has meant social workers and psychotherapists, who are more likely to be less religious than their service users (Holloway, 2007; Pargament, 2011) have been challenged recently in developing skills in discussing and reflecting upon spirituality and religion.

Sheldrake (2013) introduces another way of conceptualising spirituality as an integrating factor in life and as a stance of attending to 'life as a whole.' (p. 3). He also clarifies how spiritual traditions do not 'exist on some ideal plane above and beyond history. [They . . .] reflect the circumstances of time and place as well as the psychological state of the people involved. They consequently embody values that are socially conditioned' (p. 12). His comments resonate with our approach to integrating the spiritual perspective into the critical reflection process, since this contextual understanding of spirituality is consistent with our commitment to examining the impact of social structures. This also means that we are approaching the study of spirituality not as if there is only 'one' correct religious truth that must be supported but rather that each person in their own unique context will develop their own sense of meaning and purpose, even if involved in a traditional religious community.

From a spiritual perspective, critical reflection might be defined as a process of examining experience in order to identify and articulate those previously hidden values and commitments, which have provided meaning to life while also making deeper and perhaps transcendent meaning of 'life as a whole'. Refection is critical if and when it allows deeper and transcendent meaning.

A process for practising critical reflection

The first absolutely necessary condition for critical reflection is a learning environment, which facilitates reflection. A reflective learning culture is usually not mainstream. Many workplaces are putting increasing emphasis on measurement and task performance, which seem to fly in the face of a reflective way of being. Therefore, it is crucial for effective reflective learning to create an alternative 'microculture'. I (Jan) have termed this alternative learning culture 'critical acceptance' (Fook & Askeland, 2007). It denotes a nonjudgmental, open learning culture, which aims to use dialogue to assist people to reflect on their own experience and to arrive at their own understanding rather than having other people's beliefs imposed on them. The aim of a critically accepting learning environment is to create a space, which is safe enough so that it encourages self-challenge and self-learning. In this culture, the aim is to assist people to 'learn how to learn' rather than simply accept new viewpoints without going through a process of developing these for themselves. The culture of critical acceptance also involves principles of being able to listen; hear multiple and sometimes contradictory viewpoints; focus on ideas and thinking which are underneath the superficial, 'presenting' or 'problem' story; and a non-blaming reflexive and responsible awareness.

There are a particular skill and art to engaging in reflective dialogue in a critically accepting environment. It involves asking reflective questions (of others or yourself) in order to open up people's thinking in a way, which does not imply or enforce one's own existing particular perspective. It also involves close listening in order to develop further questions and dialogue to take the reflection to deeper levels. This type of dialogue takes much practice, particularly since the aim of the dialogue is to keep the way open to discovering new perspectives. This process has been likened to 'co-research' (Fook, 2011) where the aim of the dialogue is a joint discovery of fundamental and possibly new meanings, which have not been identified or articulated in this way before. This process also shares much in common with good therapeutic dialogue even though, as stated previously, the purpose of critical reflection will be different than the goals of therapy.

The process is normally conducted in small groups (but this can be adapted to self-reflection, or reflection on a one-to-one basis, for example, with a supervisor/supervisee). This has been documented in detail elsewhere (Fook & Gardner, 2007).

16 Laura Béres and Jan Fook

First, each member of the group is asked to choose an incident (an event, which they experienced) that they want to learn something from (and are prepared to share). This is often called a 'critical incident', that is, an incident, which was critical or significant to them. Their 'story' or description of this incident provides the raw material for reflection on their experience of this event. They are asked to describe:

1 Why they chose the incident (i.e. why it was 'critical' for them)
2 The context of the incident
3 A raw description of the incident without reflection as much as possible

They may write the incident down before presenting it to their group or speak from notes about it.

The critical reflection dialogue process is then structured in two stages aiming ultimately to help the reflecting person develop the deeper meaning of the experience and to remake new guidelines. In the first stage, each person reflects on their experience (incident) focusing only on unearthing the deeper assumptions of which they were formerly unaware. They are asked not to make judgements of them at this stage but just to sit with them and develop a feel for whether these ideas do seem to be congruent with how they believe they think. Members of the group engage in dialogue with the person, asking questions deliberately designed to help them reflect and unearth the deeper meaning. This might involve questions like: 'What are you assuming about your own power? I wonder what you were feeling and what that says about your fundamental values?' At the end of this stage one reflection, they are asked to try to sum up what they will take away to reflect on further: what has stood out for them about their main assumptions and where they feel they have gotten after this first stage of reflection. They are then asked to reflect further on these main ideas, which have arisen after they leave this first stage. This first stage might be likened to a form of 'deconstruction' where participants are digging underneath the original story of their experience to discover the more hidden ideas, which have constructed it.

In the second stage of the reflection process, each person presents their further reflections on the main assumptions, which arose from the first stage. The purpose of this stage is to remake their understanding of their experience given their new awareness and to turn this learning into a new framework, including new guidelines for action. It is in this second stage that the person remakes the fundamental meaning of their experience. They are able to do this, because, in the first stage of reflections, they became aware of really deep or taken for granted beliefs or values. Once they become aware of these, they are often led to reframe or reinterpret earlier experiences in line with these values. This second stage might be likened to a form of 'reconstruction' whereby participants are putting their own story back together in the way they wish to construct it, based on a new awareness of their fundamental ideas or meanings. Often, it is also helpful to reframe this new meaning by putting a name to the new 'theory' they have created.

Stages one and two are kept deliberately separate, since stage two often feels more 'solution-focused' (although it isn't). It is important that stage one avoids jumping to 'conclusions' or 'answers' as this can close down further reflection and derail a person's ability to arrive at a new understanding. Stage two, however, is important in bringing the reflection to a point where it is clear enough for the person to be able to take away some clearly labelled ideas for further reflection. Stage two in this sense is not 'closure' but is about moving the reflection to a point where some fundamental meaning is articulated well enough to allow more focused further reflection. Normally, stages one and two would be separated by about a week or at least half a day if possible.

Overview of book and chapters

The first section of this book is made up of four chapters, which focus on the development of an appropriate culture for, and strategies to support, the critical reflection process. Chapters 2 and 4 are written by former Master of Social Work students who learnt critical reflection in a required graduate level 13-week course in a Canadian university, which Laura facilitated. Chapter 3 has come about by reflecting upon learning the process as a social work student in London, England, whereas Chapter 5 was written from the perspective of learning how to integrate critical reflection in a managerial/leadership context in Australia.

The second section of the book is made up of five chapters, which focus on the learning process and the changes that occurred as a result. Chapters 6, 7, and 8 were also as a result of learning critical reflection in Laura's 13-week course, whereas Chapter 9 is as a result of having been involved in an academic course regarding critical reflection in Australia and creating a short video of a spoken-word poem as part of a reflection for an assignment. Chapter 10 is as a result of being involved in critical reflection groups within a London borough in England.

The third and final section of this book is about research and reflections about learning and teaching critical reflection. In Chapter 11, Laura describes her process of learning how to teach critical reflection through describing the process and results of having critically reflected upon two incidents, which she experienced as 'critical' during the first year she taught the new 'Critical reflection and appraisal of practice' course in the Canadian university context. She concludes her chapter by adding a further level of reflection and learning, which came about from having recently completed teaching the course for a second time. In Chapter 12, we report on the small-scale research project, which was conducted within, and about, the Canadian course, and in Chapter 13, we present concluding remarks about the themes presented in this book. Finally, we also provide some resources in Chapter 14 to assist with both learning and teaching critical reflection.

References

Baker, J. (2013). Cringe-ical reflection? Notes on critical reflection and supervision in a statutory setting. In J. Fook & F. Gardner (Eds.), *Critical reflection in context* (pp. 117–126). London: Routledge.

Bekas, S. (2013). Critical reflection: A sound foundation for learning and practice in Psychiatry. *British Journal of Psychiatry*, 19(5), 320–328. doi:10.1192/apt.bp.112.011064

Béres, L. (2013). Celtic spirituality and postmodern geography: Narratives of engagement with place. *Journal for the Study of Spirituality*, 2(2), 170–185. doi:10.1179/jss.2.2. h84032u7246xg776

Béres, L. (2014). *The narrative practitioner*. Basingstoke: Palgrave Macmillan.

Béres, L. (Ed.) (2017a). *Practicing spirituality: Reflections on meaning-making in personal and professional contexts*. London: Palgrave MacMillan.

Béres, L. (2017b). Maintaining the ability to be unsettled and learn afresh: What philosophy contributes to our understanding of 'reflection' and 'experience'. *Reflective Practice: Multidisciplinary and International Perspectives*, 18(2), 280–290. doi:10.1080/14623943.2016.1269003

Béres, L. (2018). How travel might become more like pilgrimage: An auto-ethnographic study. *Journal for the Study of Spirituality*, 8(2), 160–172. doi:10.1080/20440243.2018.1523048

Béres, L., Bowles, K., & Fook, J. (2011). Narrative therapy and critical reflection on practice: A conversation with Jan Fook. *Journal of Systemic Therapies*, 30(2), 8–97. doi:10.1521/jsyt.2011.30.2.81

Brookfield, S. (1994). Tales from the darkside: A phenomenography of critical reflection. *International Journal of Lifelong Education*, 13(3), 203–216. doi:10.1080/0260137940130303

Brookfield, S. (1995). *Becoming a critically reflective teacher*. San Francisco, CA: Jossey-Bass.

Brookfield, S. (2009). The concept of critical reflection: Promises and contradictions. *European Journal of Social Work*, 12(3), 293–304. doi:10.1080/13691450902945215

Brookfield, S. (2016). So what exactly is critical about critical reflection? In J. Fook, V. Collington, F. Ross, G. Ruch, & L. West (Eds.), *Researching critical reflection: Multidisciplinary perspectives* (pp. 11–12). London: Routledge.

Cairney, K. (2015). *Critically reflecting on critical self-reflection: An examination of students' experiences and professional development in a human service practicum course* (Unpublished thesis). University of Guelph, Guelph, Canada.

Canda, E.R. (1988). Spirituality, diversity, and social work practice. *Social Casework*, 69 (4), 238–247. doi:10.1177/104438948806900406

Cook, C., Powell, A., & Sims, A. (Eds.) (2009). *Spirituality and psychiatry*. Glasgow: RCPsych Publications.

Dewey, J. (1933). *How we think: A restatement of the relation of reflective thinking to the educative process*. Boston, MA: D.C. Heath & Co. Publishers.

Fawcett, B., Featherstone, B., Fook, J., & Rossiter, A. (2000). *Practice and research in social work: Postmodern feminist perspectives*. London: Routledge.

Ferguson, Y. (2013). Critical reflection in statutory work. In J. Fook & F. Gardner (Eds.), *Critical reflection in context* (pp. 83–92). London: Routledge.

Finlay, L. (2008). Reflecting on 'reflective practice'. Retrieved from www.open.ac.uk/opencetl/sites/www.open.ac.uk.opencetl/files/files/ecms/web-content/Finlay-(2008)-Reflecting-on-reflective-practice-PBPL-paper-52.pdf

Fook, J. (2002). *Social work: Critical theory and practice*. London: SAGE.

Fook, J. (2011). Developing critical reflection as a as a research method. In J. Higgs, A. Titchen, D. Horsfall, & D. Bridges (Eds.), *Creative spaces for qualitative Researching* (pp. 55–64). Rotterdam: Sense Publishers.

Fook, J. (2012). Challenges of creating critically reflective groups. *Social Work with Groups*, 35(3), 218–234. doi:10.1080/01609513.2011.624375

Fook, J. (2017). Finding fundamental meaning through critical reflection. In L. Béres (Ed.) *Practicing spirituality: Reflections on meaning-making in personal and professional contexts* (pp. 17–29). London, United Kingdom: Palgrave MacMillan.

Fook, J., & Askeland, G.A. (2007). Challenges of critical reflection: 'Nothing ventured, nothing gained'. *Social Work Education*, 26(2), 1–14. doi:10.1080/02615470601118662

Fook, J., & Gardner, F. (2007). *Practising critical reflection: A resource handbook*. Maidenhead: Open University Press.

Fook, J., Collington, V., Ross, F., Ruch, G., & West, L. (2016). Introduction: The promise and problem of critical reflection. In J. Fook, V. Collington, F. Ross, G. Ruch, & L. West (Eds.), *Researching critical reflection: Multi-disciplinary perspectives* (pp. 1–8). London: Routledge.

Fook, J., Royes, J., & White, A. (2017). Critical reflection. In M. Chambers (Ed.) *Psychiatric and mental health nursing: The craft of caring* (3rd ed.) (pp. 117–126). London: Routledge.

Fook, J., White, S., & Gardner, F. (2006). Critical reflection: A review of current understandings and literature. In S. White, J. Fook, & F. Gardner (Eds.), *Critical reflection in health and social care* (pp. 3–20). Maidenhead: Open University Press.

Freire, P. (1972). *Pedagogy of the oppressed*. Harmondsworth: Penguin.

Gardner, F. (2014). *Being critically reflective*. London: Palgrave Macmillan.

Gardner, F., & Béres, L. (2018). Social work and spiritual care. In. L.B. Carey & B.A. Mathisen (Eds.), *Spiritual care for allied health: A person-centered approach* (pp. 94–112). London: Jessica Kingsley Publishers.

Giroux, H.A., & Simon, R.I. (1989). *Popular culture, schooling, and everyday life*. South Hadley, MA: Bergin and Garvey.

Helyer, R. (2015). Learning through reflection: The critical role of reflection in work-based learning (WBL). *Journal of Work-Applied Management*, 7(1), 15–27. doi:10.1108/JWAM-10-2015-003

Hickson, H. (2011). Critical reflection: Reflecting on learning how to be reflective. *Reflective Practice*, 16(6), 829–839. doi:10.1080/14623943.2011.616687

Hickson, H. (2013). Learning critical reflection for professional practice. In J. Fook & F. Gardner (Eds.), *Critical reflection in context* (pp. 57–67). London: Routledge.

Holloway, M. (2007). Spiritual need and the core business of social work. *British Journal of Social Work*, 37(2), 265–280. doi:10.1093/bjsw/bcl014

Hunt, C. (2016). Spiritual creatures? Exploring an interface between critical reflective practice and spirituality. In J. Fook, V. Collington, F. Ross, G. Ruch, & L. West (Eds.), *Researching critical reflection: Multidisciplinary perspective* (pp. 34–47). Milton Park: Routledge.

Ixer, G. (1999). There's no such thing as reflection. *The British Journal of Social Work*, 29 (4), 513–527. doi:10.1093/bjsw/29.4.513

Ixer, G. (2011). 'There's no such thing as reflection' ten years on. *The Journal of Practice Teaching and Learning*, 10(1), 75–93. doi:10.1921/jpts.v10i1.238

McGregor, S.L.T. (2008). Transformative education: Grief and growth. In M. Gardner & U. Kelly (Eds.), *Narrating transformative learning in education* (pp. 51–73). New York: Palgrave Macmillan.

McManus, J. (n.d.). A new wave of sensation: The critical role emotions play in critical reflection. Retrieved from pdfs.semanticscholar.org/4cc7/9d92e6772eab30a f3b8360185860a278c265.pdf?_ga=2.169721513.92170630.1515491864-449003615. 1515491864

Mezirow, J. and Associates (2000). *Learning as transformation*. San Francisco, CA: Jossey Bass Inc.

Middleton, R. (2017). Critical reflection: The struggle of a practice developer. *International Practice Development Journal*, 7(1). doi:10.19043/ipdj.71.004

Munro, E. (2011). *The Munro review of child protection*. Norwich: The Stationery Office.

Nussbaum, M.C. (1997). *Cultivating humanity: A classical defence of reform in liberal education*. Cambridge, MA: Harvard University Press.

Pargament, K.I. (2011). *Spiritually integrated psychotherapy: Understanding and addressing the sacred*. New York: Guilford Press.

Pockett, R., & Giles, R. (2008). *Critical reflection: Generating theory from practice*. Sydney, Australia: Darlington Press.

Rogers, M., & Béres, L. (2017). How two practitioners conceptualise spiritually competent practice. In J. Wattis, S. Curan, & M. Rogers (Eds.), *Spiritually competent practice in health care* (pp. 53–69). Boca Ratan, FL: CRC Press.

Saric, M., & Steh, B. (2017). Critical reflection in the professional development of teachers: Challenges and possibilities. *CEPS journal*, 17(3), 67–85. Retrieved from http s://ojs.cepsj.si/index.php/cepsj/article/view/288

Schön, D. (1983). *The reflective practitioner*. New York: Basic Books.

Sheldrake, P. (2013). *Spirituality: A brief history* (2nd ed.). Oxford: Wiley-Blackwell.

Stedmon, J., & Dallos, R. (2009). *Reflective practice in psychotherapy and counselling*. Maidenhead: Open University Press.

Traverso-Yepez, M. (2008). Examining transformative learning amidst the challenges of self-reflection. In M. Gardner & U. Kelly (Eds.), *Narrating transformative learning in education* (pp. 157–171). New York: Palgrave Macmillan.

Tsang, A. (2009). Reflective learning as a student and an educator: Connecting the scholarship of teaching and learning. *International Journal for the Scholarship of Teaching and Learning*, 3(2), 1–4. Retrieved from https://files.eric.ed.gov/fulltext/EJ1136746.pdf

van Beveren, L., Roets, G., Buysse, A., & Rutten, K. (2018). We all reflect, but why? A systematic review of the purposes of reflection in higher education in the social and behavioral sciences. *Educational Research Review*, 24, 1–9. doi:10.1016/j. edurev.2018.01.002

Watson, G., & Kenny, N. (2014). Teaching critical reflection to graduate students. *Collected essays on learning and teaching*, 7(1), 56–61. Retrieved from https://ir.lib.uwo. ca/ctlpub/10

White, M. (2007). *Maps of narrative practice*. New York: W.W. Norton.

White, M., & Epston, D. (1990). *Narrative means to therapeutic ends*. New York: W.W. Norton.

Section 1

Developing an appropriate learning culture and strategies to support the critical reflection process

Chapter 2

Critical acceptance
A pathway to critical reflection on practice

Tonya Salomons

I am a critical thinker. At least that's what I like to think about myself. I like to think I move beyond implicit assumptions to get to the heart of the matter. While I like to think I am a critical thinker, I have learned that my critical thinking very rarely turns into critical action. It was not until my very first day of studies at the graduate level that I began to understand that there is so much more to unsettling deeply held and often unconscious beliefs than a desire to think upon them critically.

Being part of a Critical Reflection on Practice (CRoP) class made me realise what I had previously considered critical thinking was really what my professor aptly named, 'navel gazing': reflecting for the sake of reflecting but not actually doing anything with any conclusions I may have come to. I must admit to a certain level of scepticism about CRoP. What was going to be different about this approach than my own thoughts and ideas about critical thinking? Along with this scepticism came a healthy dose of fear – fear of unpacking my assumptions that were going to occur as well as fear of the group process in which this unpacking would happen.

Any process in which one unearths deeply entrenched assumptions, whether right or wrong, positive or negative, has the potential to begin a process in which change is inevitable. I am not a fan of change; in fact, I am quite comfortable with the status quo. Change requires bravery, a vulnerability in which I am not always willing to engage. For this particular class, I could see embracing change would also mean embracing a group process; specifically, being part of a group that had the potential to be rife with interpersonal conflict.

The group in which I found myself came as a surprise to me. There is a larger story that speaks to why I found myself participating with my group that will be explored later in this chapter. Simply put, I was asked by those in my group who had already decided to work together to engage in CRoP with them. There was a past, negative history between myself and three other members of the group, which made my decision to join the group a difficult one. This history included interpersonal relationships marred by conflict – conflict that was largely based on assumptions and judgement. Despite a potentially acrimonious situation, I found myself engaging in CRoP with this group, and to my surprise, I watched myself being profoundly impacted by the experience.

Since my initial experience with CRoP had the very real potential to be negative, it begged the question: Why did this process work for me and other members of my group? It is my belief that the functionality of our group was successful because of what Jan Fook and Fiona Gardner (2007) call an 'atmosphere of critical acceptance' (p. 79). While critical acceptance is vital to the critical reflection process, in that it is essential for creating space for change, it can also impact the level of change one might experience and how this change can be enacted throughout one's professional practice. In this chapter, I will explore my own experiences as a graduate student engaging in the process of CRoP. I will also describe key themes related to critical acceptance and, through an overview of my critical incident, show how critical acceptance provided the impetus for change – moving beyond thought into action.

Fear of the critical reflection on practice process

Social workers, not unlike many other professionals, often struggle with what is commonly known as imposter syndrome, and I was not immune to its effects during my academic experience and field placements. My scepticism of the critical reflection process, the group work, the act of unearthing my assumptions, and wondering how others might perceive me as I shared my critical incident all came with a healthy dose of fear. At the root of this fear was the notion that, perhaps, I did not have what it takes to be a social worker and having to share my sense of inadequacy with members of the group whom I did not feel comfortable increased my anxiety about the process and disclosing my critical incident.

The process of CRoP can be deeply unsettling. It requires an openness to 'confronting "sticking points" or previously unresolvable dilemmas' (Fook & Aga-Askeland, 2007, p. 521), which can produce fear and anxiety. According to Fook and Gardner (2007), fear is a common emotional experience for many participants who engage in the critical reflection process; 'the pressure – both internal and external – to be a perfect worker' (p. 5) often makes it difficult for participants to share their critical incidents. For some participants, perhaps, there is a fear of renegotiating what Stephen Brookfield (2009) calls the 'text of our lives' (p. 294), that is, how we make meaning of our understanding and our place in this world.

Regardless of where the fears come from, it is important to acknowledge that they will surface in the process of CRoP. Facing your fears in a group setting can often compound them, and this was certainly part of my own experience with CRoP. With this in mind, I turn to my involvement in a group setting and how engaging with CRoP could have been a negative experience.

The group

We all knew each other quite well prior to forming our in-class group. We had just spent the previous two years together completing a Bachelor of Social Work programme at a small liberal arts university college in Canada. Our cohort was relatively small and there was not a lot of room to hide. Two of the group members, after experiencing a close friendship during the third year, had a significant falling out, and one of the two started dating another member of the group. There was also another close friendship in the group that appeared to be exclusionary and elitist. Three members of the group had incredibly strong personalities that were often seen by others as hostile or overbearing. The difficulties some members of the group had experienced during the previous year meant that many assumptions and judgements were passed, which left me feeling betrayed. As a result, relationships were damaged and feelings were hurt. You can imagine my surprise, and fear, when I was approached by one of these people to join this group.

I sat with the question of joining them for a day or two before I gave my response. I had felt so betrayed by the events of the past year that I was hesitant to engage in such a vulnerable manner with them. While I struggled with saying yes, I also began to question and reflect on how this might be an opportunity to demonstrate a level of professionalism and collegial respect that was based on more than just assumptions and judgements. After all, what was I in a CRoP class to accomplish? My professor, knowing the events of the previous year, approached me about my level of comfort with joining the group. Her awareness of the situation and my trust in her ability to create a safe learning space helped to ease some of my anxiety in saying yes.

Unbeknownst to me, the other members of my group were also approaching the CRoP process from a desire to increase professionalism and move beyond any preconceptions they may have had from the previous year. What we did not know was how this attitude was beginning to lay a foundation for what is known as critical acceptance (Fook, 2012 p. 223; Fook & Aga-Askeland, 2007 p. 530; Fook & Gardner, 2007 p. 78). Critical acceptance, along with five key features that were evident in our group process, will be explored in detail in the following sections.

Critical acceptance: The art of critical reflection on practice in a group setting

As has been previously mentioned, the task of CRoP can be a deeply unsettling one and one that has the potential to go awry in an atmosphere that is less than supportive. In our desire to engage in the critical reflection process in a collegial and professional manner, we set out to incorporate a space that supported critical acceptance. According to Fook and Gardner (2007), critical acceptance is a 'group culture that aims to maximise feelings of safety and respect enough to support the challenges that will induce learning' (p. 79). I understood that in the retelling of my critical incident, I would face challenges and a level of discomfort in allowing myself to be vulnerable. Understanding the challenges for myself helped me understand that each of my fellow group members might also be experiencing the same discomfort and, in turn, would also be looking for safety and respect as they presented their critical incidents.

The respect we had for the profession of social work and our individual desire to feel safe and secure during the CRoP process became the foundation on which we built critical acceptance. From this foundation emerged a scaffolding that incorporated five key themes that I feel were paramount to our success with the process. These themes were: courageous communication, staying outside the story, emotional safety, honouring professionalism, and vulnerability. In retrospect, CRoP was not just about how we crafted questions that would begin to unsettle our assumptions, it was also about creating a space that allowed those assumptions to be brought to the light and transformed (Fook & Gardner, 2007, p. 49). Gillian Ruch (2016) also speaks to the importance of creating a climate of critical acceptance and writes that there is an 'importance of attending to process, as much as content, when engaging in critically reflective activities' (p. 25). In other words, the focus of our time together was less about our individual incidents but rather the environment in which we brought these incidents in order to engage in CRoP.

Courageous communication

In the CRoP process, someone needs to take the initial step and be willing to share their incident first. Within our group, that someone was me. I was afraid, and in a monologue, I wrote for a class presentation, I expressed it this way:

> I think I might be too self-conscious for this process to be of any benefit to me. What if I say the wrong things? What if they judge me? Will our past experiences get in the way?

While the other aspects of critical acceptance are vital to the process of CRoP, it is my opinion that courageous communication is the first priority of critical acceptance, since, without it, there would be no description of a critical incident with which to engage. According to Fook and Gardner (2007), there needs to be a desire to be fully engaged, not only to unpack a critical incident but also a 'willingness to hear and understand (not necessarily accept) alternative points of view or interpretations' (p. 81). This level of engagement can be difficult to accomplish.

Part of the CRoP process is about examining the language used to describe a critical incident in order to begin to unpack each incident. However, the importance of the way in which language is interpreted by the participants and the interpersonal dynamics inherent to the group process are also important

(Ruch, 2016, p. 27). The dynamics that preceded our involvement with CRoP were less than stellar. Our past experience with conflict leads to the next element of critical acceptance that was so vital to our critical reflection experience, that of staying outside the story.

Staying outside the story

Many social workers are problem solvers by nature. We chose a vocation as Stephen Brookfield (2009) indicates that 'appears irreproachable' as it is a vocation which is about 'answering a calling and being in service to clients' (p. 302). It is because of this assumption of irreproachability that social workers often feel as if attending to, and deconstructing, what might be perceived as failures in service, and competence is a personal reflection of their skills and abilities, which is why they may be wary of engaging in CRoP. I know this is how I felt when presenting a particularly sensitive critical incident. According to Brookfield (2009), these fears come from ideas with hegemonic underpinnings that imply a social worker must selflessly and without complaint meet the needs of individuals even if they feel it may be out of their scope and even at the risk of mental well-being (p. 301).

There is a vulnerability in sharing a critical incident, and it should be understood that the nature of CRoP is not just about rehashing the story of your critical incident. The vulnerability of sharing your story needs to be protected, and according to Fook and Gardner (2007), this is achieved through 'focus on the "story", not the situation,' or what they call 'staying outside the story' (p. 82). From my experience in learning CRoP, staying outside the story is achieved by being willing to have others delve deeply into the incident while simultaneously trusting that the listener is not going to give unsolicited advice. The questions that come from the other members of the group will be challenging but they are necessary for the deconstruction process. I was able to articulate the importance of staying outside the story during my in-class presentation about our group process:

> I put myself out there and it was such an incredibly powerful experience. They never questioned the validity of my story or what really happened, they only sought to understand the incident from my perspective. . . . The various paths they carefully led me down did not hold any one perspective to be the absolute truth; instead, they gave me an awareness of how trusting this process only served to increase my insight and strengthen my skills as a social worker.

Staying outside the story, then, is vital in the CRoP process, because it helps to move the reflection from simple storytelling to critical action. In other words, a myopic view steeped in assumptions – your own and those of others – impedes an individual's ability to realise and be open to other interpretations of their incident (Fook & Gardner, 2007, p. 83). Not only does staying outside the story provide a 'counter-hegemony' (Brookfield, 2009, p. 303), it also provides a climate in which honouring professionalism is possible.

Honouring professionalism

Social work has the unique perspective of needing to straddle maintaining professional fidelity with working within a context that is driven by societal norms and expectations. This creates a context of practice in which social workers 'experience considerable strain by maintaining loyalty to the profession' while attempting to satisfy 'managerial and marketised priorities' (Stepney, 2006, p. 1296). CRoP creates the space for social workers to understand their own assumptions, to 'unpack dominant discourses' (Morley, 2004, p. 299), and to make space for critical change.

Some of my experiences in social work education have been predicated on the idea that 'the personal is regarded as unprofessional' (Fook & Gardner, 2007, p. 79). In other words, objectivity is something to be edified and subjectivity is something to be eschewed. This perspective has a significant impact on the desire to open up about a critical incident that may have impacted the participant emotionally. Social workers work with people, and we are people, so it is a detriment to our profession to ignore what Barbara Heron (2005) calls our 'subject position' (p. 342). The idea of subject position is viewed through the Foucauldian lens, examining of power, and based on the fact that all individuals, no matter their social context or location, play a role in the creation of power. It also implies that 'individuals take up or identify with particular subject positions structured through relations of power and made available through different discourses' (Heron, 2005, p. 347). We cannot simply shake off our subjectivity; instead, we must address it and reflect upon it as part of critical reflection.

CRoP invites the professional to make room for their subjectivity and, in fact, suggests that leaving subjectivity out of the process impacts the ability for change to take deeper root. By only addressing the objectivity in critical reflection, we are fundamentally ascribing to further entrenchment of our implicit assumptions. The narrow view of ascribing only to objectivity also serves to hinder our responsibilities as practitioners to promote our 'individual learning and professional development' (Baldwin, 2004, p. 46), which can have a greater impact on how we collectively seek to improve the profession.

Allowing our subjectivity to surface and be examined and explored outside of our own internalisations has the potential to expose fears and emotions. In the context of CRoP, honouring professionalism in an atmosphere of critical acceptance creates space where the personal and subjective is respected as an important element of professional development. If, however, throughout the CRoP process, we aim to honour our professionalism by unsettling our assumptions about subjectivity, it is imperative that emotional safety is created. If we endeavour to create a space that fosters courageous communication, promotes staying outside the story, and builds up professionalism, we also need to be open to giving and receiving emotional safety.

Emotional safety

According to Fook and Gardner (2007), and as it relates to the subject position discussed previously, 'critical reflection relies on personal experience, which almost irrevocably involves an emotional experience' (p.80). The personal nature of CRoP is such that emotional safety is paramount. I was quite surprised by a particularly emotional moment I experienced in the midst of presenting my critical incident. Aside from being surprised by the emotional experience, I was equally surprised by the way in which my group handled it. I felt as if they held my emotions in their care and trust until I was ready to explore their greater meaning.

It was my emotions related to the experience of my critical incident that led me to a deeper understanding of my 'underlying assumptions and values' (Fook & Gardner, 2007, p. 134) that I might not have recognised had I not allowed those emotions to surface. Had there not been an understanding that I would be cared for and my emotional experiences honoured, I would not have been able to open up to this vulnerable process. The expression of emotions also speaks to the previously discussed ideas of subjectivity and professionalism.

Often within social work, there is an expectation that as a professional, my emotions should not be discussed or considered. Often, this expectation filters into the critical reflection process (Fook & Gardner, 2007, p. 5). I found the previous rationalisation to parallel my experience with critical reflection. When I first began to present my critical incident, it was noted that I had done so with a flat tone and affect. I remember thinking to myself as I recounted the incident that it was important to leave emotions out of the experience. Not only because I felt it was expected of me but also because of the audience to whom I was presenting my issue. Imagine my surprise when I found myself tearing up unexpectedly and without warning.

It was perhaps this dynamic of our critical acceptance that imparted upon me the degree of vulnerability that is required to engage in the process of CRoP. The process of critical reflection relies on 'transformational learning' (Fook & Aga-Askeland, 2007, p. 529) and is by nature vulnerable learning; therefore, each person involved in the process must be able to demonstrate 'emotional maturity' (p. 529). That is, a recognition that emotion is often a precursor to change (Fook & Gardner, 2007, p. 134) and that those experiencing the emotion and those receiving the emotion must allow the space for the feelings to be explored in order for the change process to begin.

Vulnerability

Of all the elements of critical acceptance that have been explored thus far, vulnerability is perhaps an overarching theme that encompasses them. The most impactful learning I received throughout this process is the idea that vulnerability was not something that undermines me as a professional (Fook & Aga-Askeland,

2007, p. 229). Instead, maintaining a vulnerable stance and creating space for it in my practice provided me with a sense of connection to courageous communication, staying outside the story, professionalism, and emotional safety.

According to Ruch (2016, p. 30), vulnerability has the potential to be facilitated within the group process. This means that the group provides a level of understanding that can support the concerns of the person sharing their critical incident and, thus, share the experience with them. Through this mutual experience, those within the group 'feel held and able to confront difficult experiences that previously might not have been acknowledged' (Ruch, 2016, p. 31) and, thus, use those difficult experiences to facilitate change.

Critical acceptance and critical reflection on practice: The personal

Following is an overview of the critical incident I chose to share with my group in order to provide some context for my experience in CRoP.

Overview of the incident

While working as a relief street outreach worker for an agency that supports individuals experiencing homelessness and addictions, I received a phone call from a participant who was expressing suicidal ideations. While on the phone with him, I assisted him in developing a safety plan, which included accessing an overnight stabilisation space that was run by a local mental health agency. When attempting to advocate on the client's behalf with the agency, they concluded that the client was not an appropriate referral. I have had a similar incident with this organisation in the past as it relates to this particular client so their refusal of service did not come as a surprise.

I continued to advocate for the client and attempted to confirm that, in general, suicidal ideation would be an appropriate referral for me to make. In the end, the agency refused service to the individual who ultimately attempted to take his own life. This resulted in me needing to escalate the situation to involve police and emergency services. This interaction left me feeling angry and frustrated as it appeared to me that the mental health agency based the decision not on the client's needs but on their judgements of him and his experiences with homelessness and addiction. When I attempted to debrief this incident with my employer, I felt as if I was unsupported and that my concerns with the partner agency's handling of the situation were not addressed.

The incident of my incident

During my recounting of the incident in a classroom setting and my answers to the questions posed by my colleagues, I expressed a lot of emotions including anger, feelings of powerlessness, frustration, and self-righteous indignation. I expressed disappointment at my employer's inability to properly support me during an incredibly stressful event. I was able to articulate how this event still affected me months after it occurred, to the point of loss of sleep.

Underlying the emotions related to my incident were my own fears of bringing this incident to my particular group to unpack. Among the themes of powerlessness and unprofessionalism that were uncovered were also themes of gender identity and power related to childhood trauma that I had thought I long dealt with. When those themes began to emerge, my initial reaction was to step away from the process, because uncovering ideas about masculine concepts of power meant providing personal history and background for my assumptions about power, a background that had the potential to be used to undermine my adequacy and ability to practise as a social worker. I was not necessarily uncomfortable with talking about assumptions; it was more with whom I would be sharing these experiences and that they would perceive me as unsuitable for the social work profession.

Without fully understanding how, or even that we were doing it, we, by tacit agreement, demonstrated a level of maturity, that is, a desire to move beyond our contentious history to work collaboratively within CRoP (Fook & Aga-Askeland, 2007, p. 224). This was a maturity that was not present in our interactions in the previous year. This was a collective shift that resulted in dialogue outside the critical incident presentations. Beyond the CRoP process, we committed to continued communication and dialogue that, in the end, supported our environment of critical acceptance and, thus, supported a fully engaged and positive experience with critical reflection.

Moving forward

I can now say that I recognise the privilege of engaging in CRoP with my particular group. In recognising the impact of the critical reflection process, I am attempting to move beyond what Harry Ferguson (2003) calls a 'deficit approach' (p. 1005). According to Ferguson, the deficit approach is one that focuses solely on the negative aspects of what is not being done without considering the learning that can come from acknowledging the deficits that exist (Ferguson, 2003, p. 1005). For me, the deficit was to focus on how much time each of us in the group had wasted in the previous year because of our assumptions and judgements about each other. In other words, if only we could have recognised the importance of this process sooner, perhaps we could have changed the conflict of the previous year. Instead, I chose to view the powerful way in which this process forced each of us to attend to the conflicts we were experiencing and unearth the judgements and assumptions to which we were clinging. I find it interesting to note that the very process of critically reflecting on individual stories was, in fact, what created the space for us to also critically reflect upon our interpersonal dynamics.

While I initially approached this process with doubt, I have learned to understand its value in enriching and informing my social work practice. I come to understand its value not only in the way that the process can provide me with different perspectives when working with clients but also in the way I approach working with colleagues. Conflict is bound to happen amongst colleagues. Being able to recognise that I possess the emotional maturity and courage to face those conflicts within a CRoP paradigm gives me confidence in my abilities as a social worker that I do not feel I had previous to this experience.

I recognise that I will be practising social work in a culture where critical reflection is often considered the least important facet of our jobs (Fook & Aga-Askeland, 2007, p. 525). However, the experience I had this year has raised an awareness that I have not only a personal responsibility but also a professional and ethical responsibility to engage in regular critical reflection, even if that means I need to seek the space outside my place of employment (Ontario College of Certified Social Workers and Social Service Workers, 2008, p. 12).

As a social worker, I need innovative ways to help understand my context of practice as the 'current theory base is not adequate for processing the dilemmas and issues' (Fook & Gardner, 2007, p. 3) I will face in my practice and the critical reflection process is one of those innovations. I also recognise that the social work community is a small one and, as such, I need to continue to build strong relationships with other social workers – those who share my unique perspective and understand the ethics to which I am bound. I realise that I cannot afford to alienate colleagues because of inaccurate assumptions or judgements.

Conclusion

Learning about and engaging in CRoP is an experience that I am not likely to forget any time soon. It was an honour and a privilege to move from past negative history into bravery with members of my group. Through the CRoP process, I feel as though I have the foundation to build a strong, authentic and change-oriented practice – one that is predicated on my ability to engage in accepting the unsettling of assumptions and embracing change. What makes this experience even more powerful is that it would have never happened if I had not first been willing to accept reconciliation as a precursor to creating a climate of critical acceptance. Not only do I have greater self-awareness and stronger connections with colleagues, I also feel I have the freedom to accept what Fook and Gardner (2007) call the 'ambiguity of practice' (p. 140), in that I can be more inclined to relinquish my role as problem solver and embrace the unknown of my implicit assumptions. It is my hope that with continued use of the CRoP process I will become more adept at understanding its intricacies and making it a regular part of my practice.

References

Baldwin, M. (2004). Critical reflection: Opportunities and threats to professional learning and service development in social work organizations. In N. Gould & M. Baldwin (Eds.), *Social work, critical reflection, and the learning organization* (pp. 41–55). Aldershot: Ashgate.

Brookfield, S. (2009). The concept of critical reflection: Promises and contradictions. *European Journal of Social Work*, 12(3), 293–304. doi:10.1080/13691450902945215

Ferguson, H. (2003). Outline of a critical best practice perspective on social work and social care. *British Journal of Social Work*, 33(8), 1005–1024. doi:10.1093/bjsw/33.8.1005

Fook, J. (2012). The challenges of creating critically reflective groups. *Social Work with Groups*, 35, 218–234. doi:10.1080/01609513.2011.624375

Fook, J., & Aga-Askeland, G. (2007). Challenges of critical reflection: 'Nothing ventured, nothing gained'. *Social Work Education*, 26(5), 520–533. doi:10.1080/02615470601118662

Fook, J., & Gardner, F. (2007). *Practising critical reflection: A resource handbook.* Maidenhead: McGraw-Hill.

Heron, B. (2005). Self-reflection in critical social work practice: Subjectivity and the possibilities of resistance. *Reflective Practice*, 6(3), 341–351. doi:10.1080/1462394050020095

Morley, C. (2004). Critical reflection in social work: A response to globalization. *International Journal of Social Welfare*, 13(4), 297–303. doi:10.1111/j.1468-2397.2004.00325.x

Ontario College of Certified Social Workers and Social Service Workers. (2008). *Code of ethics and standards of practice.* Retrieved from www.ocswssw.org/professional-practice/code-of-ethics

Ruch, G. (2016). Relational practices in critical reflection: The role of communication and containment. In J. Fook, V. Collington, F. Ross, G. Ruch, & L. West (Eds.), *Researching critical reflection: Multidisciplinary perspectives* (pp. 23–33). Abingdon: Routledge.

Stepney, P. (2006). Mission impossible? Critical practice in social work. *British Journal of Social Work*, 36(8), 1289–1307. doi:10.1093/bjsw/bch388

Chapter 3

The energising experience of being nonjudgmental in the critical reflection process

Stephen Lawley

As a student social worker on a work-based training course in London, England, I participated in a monthly, facilitator-led critical reflection group over a period of roughly one year. My experiences of critical reflection were extremely valuable to both my personal and professional development; I was able to practise and gain a deeper understanding of the core social work skills of exploratory, nonjudgemental questioning and reframing. Furthermore, my difficulties in allowing myself to be vulnerable within the reflective process highlighted assumptions underpinning my own view of a good social worker, which I have recognised the need to challenge if I am to practise in a way more consistent with my values. Finally, I found that my understanding of the social work role itself was checked, clarified, and reconsidered and that this was a thoroughly refreshing and energising experience. In this chapter, I will describe the process and structure by which I learned critical reflection before exploring my own learning experience and identifying important factors that contributed to critical reflection being a valuable part of my social work training.

Wider learning context: Critical reflection as part of a work-based training programme

Before discussing the process by which I learned and practised critical reflection, it will be helpful to describe the wider context of my social work training. I completed a work-based training programme, which lasted 15 months. The condensed time frame of this course compared to traditional social work training courses in the United Kingdom was made possible by undertaking university-based learning alongside work-based placements rather than completing these elements of the course separately. This training programme was run through a partnership between eight local authorities in London with approximately 30 social work students on the programme split between the local authorities and with whom each student undertook their two work-based practice placements. The work-based placements took place over a period of 13 months in total with the remaining months of the course comprised primarily of preplacement university-based learning and study. This training programme was specifically geared towards recruiting children's social workers, so the second and longest practice placement for all students was in a team within their local authority's children's services.

The critical reflection element of our social work training involved an initial critical reflection skills day attended by all students from each local authority, which took place prior to the work-based placements. This skills day introduced trainees to different ideas and theories of reflective practice and critical reflection and provided an opportunity to practise Fook's model of critical reflection as described by Fook and Gardner (2007) in small facilitator-led groups. At this very early stage in my experience of learning critical reflection, I was enthused by the underlying theory and ideas; in particular, those relating to the extent to which power is exerted through the use of language and binary positions in constructing phenomena (Fook, White, & Gardner, 2006). However, I found the initial experience of practising critical reflection difficult and, to some extent, bemusing. While I suspect that my tendency towards wanting to 'solve the problem' is not unusual amongst people practising critical reflection for the first time, it was my difficulty understanding the purpose of the reflective task that left me puzzled. This idea, and the shift in my understanding of the reflective task, is discussed in the following sections.

Following the initial skills day, regular facilitator-led critical reflection sessions were scheduled on a monthly basis whilst we were working in our practice placements. These took place in small groups at local authority level. There were four students within my group and an advanced practitioner who facilitated our sessions. Sessions would typically last for around three hours, and our group met around ten times over the course of our two practice placements. These sessions were scheduled a number of weeks in advance and our critical reflection group meetings became a protected time in our diaries, which became increasingly important given the work-based demands of our placements.

Critical reflection sessions: The structure and process of learning critical reflection

As outlined previously, my experiences of learning critical reflection stem predominantly from participating in a monthly facilitator-led critical reflection group alongside three other social work students completing the same programme as me. Here, I describe in further detail the structure by which we learned and practised critical reflection within these groups.

The first group session involved working through Moon's (n.d.) 'The Park' exercise, which helps to develop an understanding of the aims of critical reflection and to 'improve the quality of reflection' (p. 1). This graduated scenario exercise is based upon four different first-person accounts of the same incident with each account offering a gradual shift from a description of the incident towards deeper levels of reflection on the impact of the incident

(Moon, n.d.). This exercise was extremely valuable in helping me to understand that critical reflection is less about what happened and why it happened and more about exploring the impact of what happened and how we might reframe our understanding of the incident and its impact.

The typical structure for each group session (with the exception of the very first session) centred around one member of the group sharing their own reflective log, prepared in advance and of no more than one side of the paper in length, based on an experience within their practice placement. This 'critical incident' did not necessarily need to be a big or dramatic incident and could simply be a short conversation with a colleague, a training event we had attended, or an observation in the workplace. The key thing was that the incident had an impact on us and led us to think about it, consider it, and question it afterwards. After the person presenting their reflective piece had shared it, we would begin the process of critically reflecting on this experience, guided and supported by the group facilitator. The approach we used was developed by our facilitator as an extension of the Fook model and is comprised of five stages (A. Senafit-Wudasee, personal communication, June 17, 2017).

As outlined previously, in the first stage, the person presenting the reflective piece shares this with the other group members, who can then ask any clarifying questions to ensure they are clear on what happened in the incident described within the reflective piece. The next stage is that of critical reflection itself, with group members asking questions to assist the person presenting their critical piece with the reflective process. This part of the session would be the longest in duration, with participants seeking to assist the person presenting to identify and consider underlying assumptions, which may have informed their view on the incident and shaped its impact. In the third stage of the process, each participant would select three words to describe the presenting person's pre-reflection 'theory of practice', and in the fourth stage, each person would select three words to describe the presenting person's new theory of practice. This three-word summary exercise was a key part of our facilitator's extension of the Fook model of reflection (A. Senafit-Wudasee, personal communication, June 17, 2017) and offered an effective and interesting approach to helping the person presenting their critical incident to 're-label' their practice and summarise the reflection undertaken. The fifth and final stage, described as 'final learning points' (A. Senafit-Wudasee, personal communication, June 17, 2017) involved facilitator-led discussion of themes that had arisen during our reflection.

Developing skills of critical reflection

As alluded to previously, I initially found the idea of critical reflection itself to be quite challenging and counter-intuitive. This was in large part due to the difficulty of not following an urge to try to 'solve the problem' or to explain the critical incident being presented. The role of the facilitator was particularly valuable in helping to recognise and address this tendency, especially during our first group sessions. Encouragement to consider the phrasing and nature of the questions we asked during stage two of the critical reflection process was an effective method in developing our skills of reflection. It was striking how frequently we would ask the person presenting the reflective piece a closed question such as, 'Do you think that this happened because. . .?' The presence of the facilitator ensured this was recognised when it did happen and that we rephrased questions so as to open up avenues for the person presenting the reflective piece to explore rather than offering our own take on the incident and, thus, precluding their reflection.

As our critical reflection sessions progressed, our tendency to ask questions at stage three of the critical reflection process, which projected our own understanding of the person's experience, diminished, and we became more skilled in asking questions, which helped the person presenting the reflective piece to consider multiple perspectives. Examples of such questions include, 'How do you think person X felt?', 'I wonder why you interpreted. . .this way?', or, 'Is there any other way that you could have understood or interpreted this?'

Furthermore, I developed a greater understanding of how assumptions and perspectives are implicit within language. A practical point about how our critical reflection sessions worked is relevant here: As noted previously, our sessions centred around one of the group members bringing a reflective piece to the group. As well as reading through their reflective piece at the start of the session, that person would also distribute hard copies of their reflective piece to each group member. I found that being able to see the words and the language used within the reflective log was helpful in supporting me to recognise instances where wording or a phrase had been used, which conveyed certain assumed ideas without these being explained. These phrases or words would rarely be obviously contentious or remarkable; for example, it might simply be a repeated reference to 'my values' within the reflective piece, with little exploration of what constituted these values or the use of a metaphor such as 'I walked straight into the trap', where an understanding of what 'the trap' involves remains implicit. Having a hard copy of the reflective piece in front of me helped with being able to identify such phrases, which, in turn, offered fertile ground for critical reflection in stage three of the process; for example, by asking the person presenting their piece to describe their values or to tell us what they feel the 'trap' was that they fell into.

It was through the process of highlighting and questioning such assumptions that I began to recognise the wider applicability and importance of critical reflection skills to social work practice. Developing parents' insight into concerns around the care provided to their children, as a basis for achieving meaningful and lasting change, is a recurring challenge for professionals involved in child protection practice (National Society for the Prevention of Cruelty to Children, 2014). However, as noted by Broadhurst, Holt, and Doherty (2012), the tendency for professionals to adopt a position of 'epistemological privilege [through their] authority to define problems and actions' (p. 525) tends to negate the extent to which meaningful partnerships with parents can be formed and, instead, elicits 'significant resistance from service users' (p. 531). Conversely, higher levels of parental engagement with social workers are associated with parents feeling that they have expressed and discussed their experiences and views in relation to their family's difficulties (Butler, Ford, & Tregaskis, 2007; Gladstone et al., 2012).

The focus within the process of critical reflection on using an individual's own account of a significant incident as a starting point for bringing in multiple perspectives and the importance of the individual taking the lead in recognising and considering the assumptions, which may have underpinned their thought processes, is highly applicable to achieving more meaningful engagement and partnership working with families as part of child protection work. The idea that power-sharing, discussing incidents nonjudgementally, and letting individuals take the lead in defining problems and identifying solutions is well recognised, for example, within motivational interviewing, narrative practices, and Signs of Safety models (Hohman, 2012; Turnell & Murphy, 2014). However, my experiences of critical reflection were important in developing a practice-based understanding and appreciation of these skills and ideas.

It is important here to stress the difference between recognising the applicability of critical reflection skills and suggesting that child protection social workers should be practising critical reflection with service users. The latter is not my intention as it risks confusing the focus of the social worker's role, which is misleading and potentially unethical. However, as noted previously, the underlying principles of critical reflection are shared by and relevant to other theoretical models of social work practice. Furthermore, being able to sustain open questioning, which digs deeper into what someone is saying (and not saying) without introducing a judgement unnecessarily or prematurely, is an important but often absent social work skill. One of critical reflection's key tenets is the idea that 'we have to reflect on all those taken-for-granteds' (Béres, Bowles, & Fook, 2011, p. 91); achieving this with families is not straightforward and requires considerable skill and discipline on the part of the practitioner. I have heard it said that as social workers we have the potential 'to shift or to shatter' families who are often at their most vulnerable point when we enter their lives. The communicative skills we employ actively shape the outcomes we achieve, and developing a greater understanding of, and proficiency in, nonjudgemental exploratory questioning and discussion represents significant 'added value' that I took from the critical reflection sessions within which I participated as a student.

A further point worth making here is that throughout the reflective sessions, I felt more adept and comfortable when supporting other students with the process of reflection rather than when I was the one presenting my critical incident. I found it extremely challenging to write a reflective log to share with the group, and while this difficulty lessened over the course of the sessions and as I became more comfortable with the process and group environment, it did not completely subside, and I continued to experience some difficulty in creating these logs. This difficulty stemmed from the discomfort of sharing an experience, which I had not fully resolved myself. I was acutely aware of this difficulty when considering critical incidents to share, as I would have to actively stop myself from choosing incidents where I felt I could predict the course and likely outcomes of the critical reflection process. The learning from this 'reflection on reflection' is valuable as it offers greater insight into the difficulties service users experience when asked to explore in detail emotive incidents and issues, which they themselves have struggled to resolve or to frame in a way with which they feel comfortable. Furthermore, this learning has led me to consider the extent to which I am really able to promote values of power-sharing and participation in my own practice.

Models of child protection practice, such as the Signs of Safety approach, query the 'professional as expert' role, highlighting how this contributes to 'professionals taking upon themselves sole responsibility for analysing the problem of child mistreatment and generating solutions' and, in turn, repeatedly responding to problems with the same actions regardless of how ineffective these may be (Turnell & Edwards, 1999, p. 18). My difficulties in sharing responsibility for analysing, exploring, and reframing my own experiences during critical reflection sessions suggest that the assumption that good social workers need to have, or be perceived as having, all the answers, may underpin my own practice to a greater extent than I had previously been aware. Despite subscribing to values of participation, power-sharing, and meaningfully recognising the expertise of families and service users, my experiences of critical reflection highlighted barriers to realising these values in practice.

Social workers are frequently put in positions of potential vulnerability, where their actions, thought processes, and decision-making are subject to scrutiny in professional supervision and conversations with service users and other professionals. Seeing other students allowing themselves to be in this position during critical reflection sessions, being able to own and examine their vulnerability, and recognising it as an opportunity to learn and develop has helped me recognise that the ability to be 'professionally vulnerable' is, in fact, a strength, and developing this is essential to being a competent and reflective practitioner.

An energising process and the importance of protected time for uncertainty

I have previously noted that the monthly critical reflection sessions in which I participated along with other students in the local authority were scheduled in advance and treated as 'protected time' in our work diaries. This recognition of the importance of the sessions as part of our training was shared by each student as well as our managers, practice educators, and colleagues within each of our social work teams. This meant that our attendance of the critical reflection groups remained a priority even as our caseloads and the demands of our placements increased.

This protected time for critical reflection, in the midst of busy and demanding child protection practice, was incredibly valuable to my overall learning experience. Holland (2004) identified a 'natural human tendency to be "verificationists"', which, in child protection practice, can often mean '[forming] an explanation for a family or individual's circumstances early on in our contact with them' (p. 128). It is well-recognised that actively seeking evidence and opinions that challenge initial explanations is, therefore, an important part of skilful decision-making within this area of practice (Holland, 2004; Ruch, 2009; Taylor & White, 2006). Despite this recognition, the procedures through which child protection practice often operate can serve to restrict the available space in which practitioners can acknowledge and explore uncertainty in their assessments and decision-making. D'Cruz, Gillingham, and Melendez (2007) recognised this and highlighted 'the certainty that bureaucratic organisations strive for through the employment of procedural strategies to manage risk in the lives of clients' (p. 81).

While I regard myself as lucky in having completed my student training with the support of a team manager and practice educator who were reflective, approachable, and caring on a daily basis, it is perhaps, to some extent, inevitable that certain procedures and pressures within a large and busy local authority children's services department will push social workers towards expressing a heightened level of certainty in their assessments and case recordings. This is a recognition of the reality that case recording and assessment writing is generally completed through generic computerised systems under significant constraints of time pressure, which are likely to make it difficult to fully reflect the specific nuances and grey areas within each case or assessment process. Recognising this context is important in understanding the value of having scheduled and prioritised critical reflection sessions, as these not only permitted uncertainty but also, through the identification and exploration of missing perspectives, actively encouraged it. I found that having the space to recognise uncertainty and acknowledge the complexity of our work was vital in developing my professional resilience and refreshing my motivation for the role.

The nature of the reflective logs presented during our group sessions changed each month, but emotional responses of deflation, disappointment, and frustration in critical incidents were common themes. These emotions tended to stem from attributing the difficulties we experienced in achieving desirable outcomes in our casework to our own shortcomings as social workers. However, through the process of nonjudgemental critical reflection, we were supported to consider the complexity of our day-to-day work with parents, foster carers, young people, and other professionals whose decision-making and behaviour were contingent upon a number of unpredictable variables. Reflecting on incidents helped to recognise these variables and to challenge instances where the person presenting their critical incident had initially framed it in such a way that their own perceived professional weaknesses were unduly prominent. We were, thus, able to adopt more realistic and healthy perspectives on our own roles in affecting outcomes in complex circumstances, with greater recognition of the 'smaller wins' we may have achieved in the midst of difficult situations and, ultimately, we were able to recognise that a position of honest professional uncertainty was better than one of false certainty. It was this element of the critical reflection sessions which enabled me to reconsider and clarify my understanding of the social work role and led to the sessions having an energising and remotivating effect on my outlook and approach to practice.

Final thoughts: The value of critical reflection and the importance of a supportive organisational environment

In this chapter, I have considered my experiences of practising critical reflection as a student social worker and recognised how these helped to deepen my understanding of core social work skills, provided my fellow students and I with a valuable space to acknowledge uncertainty and explore emotions of deflation and frustration, and highlighted previously unknown assumptions, which underpin my practice and may pose a barrier to promoting the values to which I aspire as a social worker. It is clear to me that critical reflection had abundant value to my personal and professional development.

By recognising the value of participating in regular critical reflection, it is also possible to consider what would have been lost in its absence. Had I not had the opportunity to participate regularly in these sessions, I consider it likely that I would have found my social work training more stressful, that I would have felt less motivated for the role over time, and that I would have felt a greater sense of inadequacy within the role. For those of us participating within the critical reflection group, we regularly felt refreshed and reenergised after sessions, having been supported to question and reconsider the negative perceptions of ourselves that developed through the daily challenges of complex child protection work. Accordingly, we increasingly looked forward to our monthly sessions and were extremely grateful for the protected time given to critical reflection within our student placements.

Furthermore, in the absence of regular opportunities to deepen my understanding of the social work skills inherent within critical reflection, encouragement to reflect on all the 'taken-for-granteds' in our daily practice, and without being challenged to adopt a position of professional vulnerability, I would have been far less aware of barriers that I need to overcome to improve my own practice and avoid a repetitive and potentially oppressive approach to working with families.

As noted within this chapter, the students on my social work training programme were afforded the luxury of protected time for monthly critical reflection sessions, as well as sustained group membership over, and a consistent critical reflection group facilitator for, the duration of the programme. All these ingredients contributed significantly to our positive experiences of critical reflection. The protected time ensured that sessions took place and were prioritised despite increasing work-based demands within our placements, while the sustained group membership helped us all develop a sense of trust within the group environment and commitment to the critical reflection process, which was conducive to more meaningful critical reflection. This commitment was important not only in ensuring that we actively participated in sessions but also in ensuring that we each spent time preparing reflective logs when it was our turn to do so and develop the quality of these reflective pieces beyond a descriptive narrative of an incident or observation.

While I am not naïve to the challenges faced by any busy local authority in seeking to provide the experiences I had as a student social worker to social work practitioners more widely, with high staff turnover and the existing significant pressures on resources and time constituting the two most obvious of these challenges, it remains important to recognise that the value of critical reflection is unlikely to be realised without a genuine and sustained organisational commitment to its provision. Solutions to these challenges may not be easily achievable, but a starting point is a recognition that critical reflection requires time – time for learning the critical reflection process, time for the sessions themselves, and time for preparing reflective pieces in advance. In my experience, this time is a worthwhile investment in both promoting the well-being of the practitioner and enhancing the skill and quality of work with service users. A lot of the tasks that take up much of a social worker's time on a daily basis simply do not have this impact, and efforts to make space for regular critical reflection to take place as a priority over other tasks would, therefore, undoubtedly be worthwhile.

References

Béres, L., Bowles, K., & Fook, J. (2011). Narrative therapy and critical reflection on practice: A conversation with Jan Fook. *Journal of Systemic Therapies*, 30(2), 81–97. doi:10.1521/jsyt.2011.30.2.81

Broadhurst, K., Holt, K., & Doherty, P. (2012). Accomplishing parental engagement in child protection practice? *Qualitative Social Work*, 11(5), 517–534. doi:10.1177/1473325011401471

Butler, A., Ford, D., & Tregaskis, C. (2007). Who do we think we are? Self and reflexivity in social work. *Qualitative Social Work*, 6(3), 281–299. doi:10.1177/1473325007080402

D'Cruz, H., Gillingham, P., & Melendez, S. (2007). Reflexivity, its meaning and relevance for social work: A critical review of the literature. *British Journal of Social Work*, 37(1), 73–90. doi:10.1093/bjsw/bcl001

Fook, J., & Gardner, F. (2007). *Practising critical reflection: A resource handbook*. Maidenhead: Open University Press.

Fook, J., White, S., & Gardner, F. (2006). Critical reflection: A review of contemporary literature and understandings. In S. White, J. Fook, & F. Gardner (Eds.), *Critical reflection in health and social care* (pp. 1–20). Maidenhead: Open University Press.

Gladstone, J., Dumbrill, G., Leslie, B., Koster, A., Young, M., & Ismaila, A. (2012). Looking at engagement and outcome from the perspectives of child protection workers and parents. *Children and Youth Services Review*, 34(1), 112–118. doi:10.1016/j.childyouth.2011.09.003

Hohman, M. (2012). *Motivational interviewing in social work practice*. New York: Guildford Press.

Holland, S. (2004). *Child and family assessment in social work practice*. London: SAGE.

Moon, J. (n.d.). *An example of a graduated scenario exercise – 'The Park': A means of introducing and improving the quality of reflective learning*. Retrieved from www.cetl.org.uk/UserFiles/File/reflective-writing-project/ThePark.pdf

National Society for the Prevention of Cruelty to Children (2014). *Assessing parenting capacity: An NSPCC factsheet*. Retrieved from www.nspcc.org.uk/globalassets/documents/information-service/factsheet-assessing-parenting-capacity.pdf

Ruch, G. (2009). Identifying 'the critical' in a relationship-based model of reflection. *European Journal of Social Work*, 12(3), 349–362. doi:10.1080/13691450902930761

Taylor, C., & White, S. (2006). Knowledge and reasoning in social work: Educating for humane judgement. *British Journal of Social Work*, 36(6), 937–954. doi:10.1093/bjsw/bch365

Turnell, A., & Edwards, S. (1999). *Signs of safety: A solution and safety oriented approach to child protection casework*. New York: Norton.

Turnell, A., & Murphy, T. (2014). *The signs of safety comprehensive briefing paper* (3rd ed.). East Perth, Australia: Resolutions Consultancy.

Chapter 4

Finding exception

Application of narrative practice in professional critical reflection on practice

Nate Meidinger

Canada has experienced a profound shift in the past 50 years as changes to the social, political, and market environments have significantly impacted the way social services are provided (Pager & Shepherd, 2008). Factors, like pressures resulting from increased health care costs and service regulations, have reduced the amount of public funding allocated to social service programmes and have, in turn, increased the burden placed on social workers to provide comprehensive services with less available resources (Westhues & Warf, 2013). These pressures, which have in many ways prioritised 'cost-effectiveness' and expediency over the long-term well-being of clients, have forced practitioners into increasingly complex and emotionally exhausting practice situations. In these complex situations, many practitioners have indicated feeling powerless and uncertain in determining how to best support their clients (Heisz, 2016; Sergeant & Firth, 2005). For some, this uncertainty has led to regrettable practice decisions, which have negatively impacted the work environment and have led to increased anxiety and tension in the practitioner's personal and professional lives (Fook & Gardner, 2007, p. 9).

As mentioned in Chapter 1, Fook's model of Critical Reflection on Practice (CRoP) offers a helpful framework for practitioners to process critical incidents that have been emotionally and professionally challenging (Fook & Gardner, 2007). Through its process of identifying and exploring the hidden assumptions that influence practice decisions, CRoP has enabled professionals to foster an increased sense of control and intentionality in decision-making (Fook, 2002, p. 140). This increased control and intentionality is significant for practitioners, as studies have demonstrated that perceived control in the workplace can improve worker effectiveness and longevity while also protecting workers against burnout and emotional fatigue (Day, Crown, & Ivany, 2017; Fernet, Guay, & Senéca, 2004; Hu, Schaufeli, & Taris, 2017; Lizano & Mor Barak, 2012). With these benefits in mind, exploring ways to improve the implementation of CRoP in professional practice is a worthwhile pursuit that can enhance worker health and service proficiency.

In this chapter, I highlight how incorporating concepts from narrative therapy (NT) in the CRoP process can enhance group cohesion, member participation, CRoP effectiveness, and can empower reflecting participants in their reflective process. Through comparing these concepts with current practices used in CRoP, I highlight how adopting the therapeutic posture of NT can enhance members' ability to be supportive in the reflective process, how externalising conversations can increase space and safety in the group environment, and how absent but implicit questioning can enhance the exploration of participants' hidden assumptions and values. My interest in incorporating NT concepts with CRoP originates from a combination of learning NT and CRoP in my Masters of Social Work education as well as from personal conversations I have had with Jan Fook and Laura Béres regarding the challenges faced by individuals learning CRoP. In contrast to previous literature that has explored the theoretical similarities of NT and CRoP (Béres, Bowles, & Fook, 2011), this chapter takes a more direct approach in identifying how concepts and practices from NT can be interwoven with CRoP.

Critical reflection on practice

As described in Chapter 1, CRoP is a reflective model for developing professional practice through the 'unsettling and examination of fundamentally held assumptions about the social world' (Fook & Gardner, 2007, p.14). Informed by postmodern views that question the idea of 'one truth', CRoP emphasises the subjective reality of experience and helps direct practitioners' focus towards identifying the ways that individual and social discourses have influenced professional practice (Fook & Gardner, 2007, p.31). By identifying these discourses, practitioners can examine the factors that influence their practice and can evaluate whether these factors should be replaced, altered, or further incorporated into future practice experiences (p. 175).

An important component of facilitating CRoP is creating a collaborative group environment where reflecting individuals feel safe and supported in exploring their critical incidents (Fook, 2012, p. 223). Although CRoP can be applied to experiences of practice success and learning, critical incidents are often identified as experiences that have been 'puzzling, traumatic, or experiences [practitioners] thought could have been handled better' (Fook & Gardner, 2007, p. 77). The unsettling nature of critical incidents, combined with the pressure of reflecting in a group environment, can cause anxiety and discomfort for participants (p. 81). This is especially true for new students, who may mistake group questioning about critical incidents as a judgement about their professional competence or suitability. To address this concern, group members are encouraged to adopt a mindset of respect towards the reflecting participant's contributions in the CRoP process (Fook, 2012, p. 223). This can be achieved by members acknowledging that the contributions and perceptions a reflecting participant holds towards their critical incident have value and legitimacy based on the fact that they represent what the reflecting individual believes to be true (p. 223). Although these contributions may be at odds with the interpretations of other group members, respecting the reflecting participant's account of their critical incident can help to create the space and security needed for participants to feel safe in exploring their critical incident in further detail (Fook, 2012, p. 224).

Although group members often express support for creating a nonjudgmental, supportive environment in the CRoP process, a common challenge that is experienced by facilitators is the impulse for group members to look for blame or to give advice to solve the reflecting participant's critical incidents (Fook & Gardner, 2007, p. 98). Fook (2012) describes these impulses in terms of 'pervasive cultures' that practitioners adopt while critically reflecting and explains that these cultures often originate from practitioners' previous roles in helping professions (p. 228). For example, a common culture that is experienced throughout CRoP is when members become 'inner managers', who seek to control reflections by providing a logical explanation for how and why critical incidents occurred and how these incidents can be prevented in the future (Fook, 2012, p. 228). Although this approach would be helpful for a social worker working in a case management role, this is not helpful for the CRoP process, as it draws attention away from the reflecting participant's autonomy and self-discovery and, instead, places the focus on the group member and their ability to fix the situation.

Another pervasive culture that I experienced in a CRoP group I participated in was the culture of the 'inner victim'. Fook (2012) describes the inner victim as a culture that seeks to avoid discomfort by aligning with the account of a reflecting participants' critical incident to avoid any exploration of personal responsibility (p. 232). I witnessed this culture occur in my group when some members appeared to struggle with emotionally-charged accounts of reflecting participants' critical incidents. These group members responded to this discomfort by assuming a therapeutic role of consoling and explaining why the participants' critical incident was not their 'fault'. The problem with this was that it sidetracked the critical reflection process by shifting focus from the reflecting participant's exploration of their critical incident and directing focus to the supporting member's analysis of who was to blame for the incident. This not only impacted the mood and ability for the reflecting participant to become immersed in the reflective process, but it also diminished the willingness of members to explore their own critical incidents in depth. This is an important caution for new practitioners of CRoP to remember, as the effectiveness of group members' contributions can be significantly impacted by how effectively reflecting participants are supported in their process of reflection (Fook & Gardner, 2007, p. 132). For additional information regarding the pervasive cultures and disruptions that are common to CRoP groups, readers are encouraged to read Fook's (2012) article, 'The Challenges of Creating Critically Reflective Groups'.

The use of the narrative therapy concepts of therapeutic posture, externalising conversations, and absent but implicit questioning offer a unique expansion to the methods already used in establishing a safe and supportive group climate in CRoP. The following sections will highlight how narrative therapy aligns with CRoP and can enhance critical reflection.

Contributions from narrative therapy

Narrative therapy was one of the first therapies to effectively incorporate postmodern notions of truth into a systematic approach to address client concerns (Doan, 1997). Originating from the work of Michael White and David Epston, NT asserts that the stories individuals tell about themselves directly impact the way they view themselves and their interactions with the social world (Combs & Freedman, 2012). When problem-saturated stories are internalised, individuals may experience negative perceptions of themselves, and these perceptions can lead to undesirable and destructive behaviours and beliefs (White, 2007). Many of these internalised narratives culminate in critical incidents. To address these concerns, NT assists individuals in examining the language, meaning, and impact of problem storylines and helps to identify gaps, alternatives, and exceptions to problem narratives (White, 1991). By identifying gaps and exceptions to problem narratives, clients can adopt alternative ways of understanding concerns, which enables the integration of preferred ways of responding to, and understanding, challenges in the future (White & Epston, 1990).

The therapeutic posture of narrative therapy

One of the innovative aspects to narrative therapy is the therapeutic posture adopted by practitioners. Unlike structuralist-based therapies, which view an individual's presenting concerns as originating from individual deficits, narrative therapy explains that people are able to experience an identity separate from the problem by acknowledging that the 'problem [is] the problem; not the person' (White, 2007, p. 9). From this distinction, individuals can separate themselves from internalised problem-identities and can identify contributing factors that have influenced the creation of these problem narratives (White, 2007). In the CRoP group I participated in, it was surprising how often members attributed problems within critical incidents to their own personal faults. The prevalence of this association highlighted the valuable role that NT could fill within the CRoP model.

Another key concept of NT posture is the value placed on insider knowledge. Madigan (2011) explains that 'insider knowledge is what the person [client] has in his or her relationship with the problem because of lived experience' (p. 92). Rather than approaching problem narratives as an expert, NT practitioners identify the client as the author and expert of their story (White, 1991). The benefit of this approach is that it deconstructs typical notions of expertise and enables reflecting participants to feel an increased sense of autonomy and control over their narrative (Van Wyk, 2008 p. 265). The prioritising of insider knowledge is a useful concept to incorporate with CRoP, as it can safeguard against members who take an overly challenging stance in their questioning by giving ultimate authority to the reflecting participant. This increased control enhances individuals' ability to find new meaning in their critical incidents and to reauthor their experiences in a way that is better aligned with their personal values and goals for the future.

By identifying the client as the expert of their story, practitioners are freed from the need to be 'clever' (Béres, personal communications, April 27, 2017). As a result, practitioners can take a 'decentred but influential' role by authentically engaging with client stories and assisting in the construction of preferred narratives through helpful questions that explore gaps, meanings, and alternatives to the client's problem storyline (White, 2007, p. 39). In a decentred role, practitioners can maintain a curious 'not-knowing' stance towards client descriptions and can act as a mirror to ask questions to assist clients in identifying previously unidentified aspects of problem narratives (White, 1991).

Integrating the therapeutic posture of NT in CRoP provides several benefits to practitioners, including enhancing the parameters and accessibility of group participation and providing an alternative approach for individuals who are prone to slipping into solution-seeking.

A common challenge experienced by new CRoP participants is the tendency to get sidetracked by becoming too focused on asking the 'right' questions rather than being attentive to the words and gaps in the reflecting individual's critical incident (Fook & Gardner, 2007, p. 96). This preoccupation with asking the right questions is often due to the novelty of the CRoP process and practitioners confusing questioning through specific theories with the primary goal of creating a culture of thinking and exploration (p. 98). Through the therapeutic posture of NT, practitioners are able to conceptualise their role in the CRoP process as being curious and supportive collaborators. In this role, it is the goal of participants to remain authentically engaged and curious to discrepancies and hidden assumptions that may influence the reflecting participant's critical incident. This is helpful for the CRoP process, as it alleviates the stress and burden of practitioners feeling they must have a comprehensive understanding of the theories of CRoP and refocuses their efforts towards supporting individuals in the exploration of assumptions that influence their practice (Fook & Gardner, 2007). An additional benefit of adopting a curious and collaborative approach to CRoP is that it provides group members the space to become immersed in the process of exploring hidden assumptions, which can ease their entry into the CRoP process for their own critical incidents.

As previously stated, one of the most detrimental actions that can occur in the CRoP process is group members slipping into problem-solving (Fook, 2012). Due to the vulnerability that is required when exploring critical incidents in a group reflection, the act of group members giving advice and encouraging alternative ways to author critical incidents can act to diminish the autonomy and authorship of the reflecting individual. Fook and Askeland (2007), highlight that giving advice can negatively impact reflection, as it may be perceived as a form of judgment, implying that the way the reflecting individual handled their critical incident was 'wrong' (p. 530). The posture of NT is helpful for keeping individuals from slipping into problem-solving, because it emphasises the importance of using questions, rather than suggestions, to explore possible gaps and assumptions (Carey & Russell, 2004). By incorporating a decentred role, practitioners maintain a curious 'not-knowing' stance towards client descriptions in the hope of uncovering gaps and discrepancies in their identified critical incident (White, 2007). Any suggestions or inquiries that are made are filtered through the collaborative goal of helping the reflecting individual come to a new level of understanding about their critical incident.

By identifying the reflecting individual as the expert and author of their incident, group members are freed from the burden of needing to persuade reflecting participants to adopt a specific interpretation of a critical incident. Instead, group members are encouraged to focus on supporting participants through tasks such as normalising challenges experienced in critical incidents and questioning judgmental internalisations that prevent professional learning and growth (Fook & Gardner, 2007, p. 100). The benefit of adopting this therapeutic posture is exemplified in a critical incident I participated in, where a colleague indicated that he had 'failed' a client and that he felt a strong sense of guilt regarding this experience. Rather than suggesting alternative ways to interpret the experience or seeking to present clever questions to guide him to a specific answer, I employed a narrative posture and remained curious regarding alternative experiences where 'failure' had impacted his life. Through this line of questioning, my colleague was able to reflexively explore how internal and external influences contributed to his critical incident and how his sense of failure was actually masking a felt sense of helplessness that he attributed to his childhood relationship with his father. From this realisation, he was able to explore the different factors and influences that mimicked his childhood helplessness in his workplace and was able to identify alternative ways he could manage what he perceived as 'failure' in his future practice.

It should be noted that although CRoP shares therapeutic aspects often attributed to formal therapy, CRoP distinguishes itself from therapy in that problems are explored only in so far as they lead to increased learning about professional practice (Fook & Gardner, 2007, p. 197). Unlike traditional therapy that emphasises finding solutions or ultimate 'truths' to a presenting problem, CRoP identifies the process of learning as being more important than simple knowledge acquisition (Béres, Bowles, & Fook, 2011). One of the distinguishing factors between CRoP and typical forms of therapy is that CRoP does not require individuals to explore all facets of a critical incident to experience the benefit of this model. Instead, CRoP focuses on equipping reflecting individuals with tools that can be used to explore the internal and external factors that influence practice decisions and knowledge (Fook &

Gardner, 2007, p. 28). This is important for students to remember, as it highlights the importance of continually asking whether the content being explored has relevance to professional learning and growth and for group members to be reminded that questioning is useful only so far as it aids the reflective process.

Externalising conversations

When participants of CRoP bring forward critical incidents that contain traumatic and emotionally painful experiences it can be challenging for group members to know how to best support the reflective process (Fook & Gardner, 2007). As demonstrated in the example of my group members slipping into cultures of blame and placating, emotionally distressing material may compel members to try to fix or ease the emotional tensions experienced by the reflecting participant. This compulsion is especially common for those working in helping professions, as practitioners have been trained to take control in crisis situations and to strive to ease the suffering and emotional distress of clients (Hussein et al., 2015).

However, to effectively reflect upon critical incidents, members must be able to sit with emotionally uncomfortable material and must temper their desire to ease the reflecting participant's distress with the goal of increasing the participant's professional learning and growth (Fook & Askeland, 2007, p. 527). To achieve this balance, externalising conversations can provide a powerful tool to help separate individuals from their 'problems' and to create space for individuals to identify the actions, influences, and beliefs that sustain problem narratives (Madigan, 2011).

When individuals are faced with traumatic or emotionally charged situations, they may experience a totalisation and internalisation of labels associated with these events (Carey & Russell, 2004). This is commonly seen in the therapeutic setting when individuals come to therapy identifying themselves as 'worthless' or 'failures'. In CRoP, participants may also engage with totalising labels, identifying themselves as 'failures' or 'imposters' due to their critical incidents. White (2007) explains that when individuals internalise problem labels, their identity may become 'overwhelmed' and 'dominated' by these beliefs. One of the challenges that occur when these labels are internalised is that it becomes increasingly difficult for individuals to identify alternative perspectives to their problem identity. This can be disruptive to the CRoP process, as it may limit the ability for the individual to identify outside factors that may have influenced their critical incident. Through externalising conversations, individual identities are separated from individual problems in order to help create the necessary space for individuals to identify and explore alternative interpretations of problem narratives. A benefit of using externalisation in CRoP is that it allows individuals to suspend the emotional elements of critical incidents and supports the exploration of critical incidents in a more objective manner (Turns & Kimmes, 2014).

A common technique used in NT to facilitate externalisation is speaking about the problem in the third person 'it' and by characterising the problem as a separate entity such as 'failure' or 'sadness' (Carey & Russell, 2004). In CRoP, this can be achieved through questions such as, 'When failure starts to creep into your life, what sorts of things does it do?' or, 'Are there any other times where worthlessness has shown itself and started impacting your life?'. When problems are 'decentred' in a person's life, individuals can experience relief from the pressure of blame and can identify the ways that specific problems have manifested and are supported in daily interactions (White, 2007). At the core of the concept of externalisation is the ability to separate the person from the problem. When this separation is achieved, individuals can experience a renewed sense of confidence in their ability to explore challenging critical incidents and can feel more equipped when confronted with critical incidents in the future.

Absent but implicit questioning

'Everything that we see is a shadow cast by that which we do not see.'
Martin Luther King, Jr. (King, 1988, p. 54)

I chose this quote to begin the discussion on absent but implicit questioning because it encapsulates the reality that what practitioners see in practice is often only partial truths, or 'shadows,' of what is actually happening. Although these partial truths can provide enough information for us to make day-to-day decisions, they may also lead to overly simplistic or problematic understandings of situations. To move towards more detailed and comprehensive understandings, absent but implicit questioning helps individuals to identify what is missing in situations.

White (2007) describes the concept of absent but implicit questioning as the act of exploring the duality of meaning in language and words. White (2000) explains this, stating 'there is a duality to all descriptions. Descriptions are relational, not representational – they do not directly represent the things of the world' (p. 36). By labelling descriptions as relational, White highlights that all language and meaning is derived from contrasts and comparisons with things that are currently known. For example, when individuals identify that they feel 'worthless', absent but implicit questioning helps individuals to explore how they came to identify this feeling of worthlessness and what experiences and knowledge contributed to their understanding and interpretation of the word 'worthless'. In identifying experiences and knowledge that have influenced the meaning in language, absent but implicit questioning can help individuals have a greater understanding of the social forces, influences, and values that have contributed to their problem narratives (White, 2000).

In addition to exploring the experiences and knowledge that have contributed to the meaning of specific words, absent but implicit questioning also teaches individuals how to 'double listen' for implied meanings and discrepancies in problem narratives (White, 2000). In the case of someone describing themselves as feeling worthless, double listening would encourage individuals to explore the implied opposite of worthlessness and to identify where the individual's understanding of worth originates from. Through this exploration of the social, historical, and personal influences that contribute to understandings of worth and worthlessness, an individual would have opportunities to identify gaps in their understanding that could facilitate a reframing of problem narratives.

The use of absent but implicit questions is especially useful in CRoP, as it teaches members to listen for implied meanings and discrepancies in the language that is used to describe critical incidents. By identifying opposite or contrasting words, reflecting participants can explore where their values and beliefs originate from and how discrepancies between these values and the actions of the critical incident resulted in emotional discomfort. This ability to identify factors that influence critical incidents is helpful, because it highlights possible avenues for change or reframing in the future. This was demonstrated in my first CRoP group when a reflecting individual became fixated on complaining about who was responsible for their critical incident occurring. Rather than trying to identify who was most deserving of blame in the situation, absent but implicit questioning and double listening enabled our group to explore the values that were infringed upon through this individual's critical incident. By asking the individual to unpack where their concept of blame originated from, they were able to identify that their feeling of responsibility was influenced by their deeply held beliefs in justice and fairness. Although their initial complaint was focused on blame, their deeper assumption and concern was focused on their inability to control their critical incident and to ensure their client was treated fairly. From these discoveries, the reflecting individual was able to progress to stage two of CRoP and to identify how their thinking and practice had changed.

At the core of absent but implicit questioning is the ability for practitioners to listen *to* the language used while listening *for* the absent meaning behind these words (Béres, 2014). By identifying the absent meaning behind words practitioners can be taken from a place of the 'known and familiar' to a place that is unknown but possible to know (Béres, 2014; Carey, Walther, & Russell, 2009; White, 2007). Through this new knowledge, practitioners can develop practices and beliefs that are more in line with their values and can be better prepared to address critical incidents in the future.

Conclusion

As the complexity of challenges faced by practitioners increases, it is essential that the tools used by practitioners be capable of supporting professional development and growth in ways that are accessible, effective, and time-sensitive. CRoP is an excellent tool to aid practitioners in professional development and growth, as it provides a structured and supportive approach to evaluate critical incidents. The impact of this model can be further enhanced through the incorporation of concepts from narrative therapy, such as therapeutic posture, externalising conversations, and absent but implicit questioning. The marriage of narrative therapy with CRoP can result in greater group safety and cohesion, increased autonomy for reflecting participants, and enhanced ability to explore alternative interpretations of critical incidents. I would encourage CRoP participants to consider the benefits that narrative therapy can bring to the reflective process.

References

Béres, L. (2014). *The narrative practitioner*. Basingstoke: Palgrave Macmillan.

Béres, L., Bowles, K., & Fook, J. (2011). Narrative therapy and critical reflection on practice: A conversation with Jan Fook. *Journal of Systemic Therapies*, 30(2), 81–97. doi:10.1521/jsyt.2011.30.2.81

Carey, M., & Russell, S. (2004). *Narrative therapy: Responding to your questions*. Adelaide, South Australia: Dulwich Centre Publications.

Carey, M., Walther, S., & Russell, S. (2009). The absent but implicit: A map to support therapeutic enquiry. *Family Process*, 48(3), 319–331. doi:10.1111/j.1545-5300.2009.01285.x

Combs, G., & Freedman, J. (2012). Narrative, poststructuralism, and social justice: Current practices in narrative therapy. *The Counseling Psychologist*, 40(7), 1033–1060. doi:10.1177/0011000012460662

Day, A., Crown, S., & Ivany, M. (2017). Organisational change and employee burnout: The moderating effects of support and job control. *Safety Science*, 100(A), 4–12. doi:10.1016/j.ssci.2017.03.004

Doan, R.E. (1997). Narrative therapy, postmodernism, social constructionism, and constructivism: Discussion and distinctions. *Transactional Analysis Journal*, 27(2), 128–133. doi:10.1177/036215379702700208

Fernet, C., Guay, F., & Senécal, C. (2004). Adjusting to job demands: The role of work self-determination and job control in predicting burnout. *Journal of Vocational Behaviour*, 65(1), 39–56. doi:10.1016/S0001-8791(03)00098-8

Fook, J. (2002). *Social work: Critical theory and practice*. London: SAGE.

Fook, J. (2012). The challenges of creating critically reflective groups. *Social Work with Groups*, 35(3), 218–234. doi:10.1080/01609513.2011.624375

Fook, J., & Askeland, G.A. (2007). Challenges of critical reflection. *Social Work Education: The International Journal*, 26(5), 520–533. doi:10.1080/02615470601118662

Fook, J., & Gardner, F. (2007). *Practising critical reflection: A resource handbook*. Maidenhead: Open University Press.

Heisz, A. (2016). Trends in income inequality in Canada and elsewhere. In D.A. Green, W.C. Riddle, & F. St-Hilaire (Eds.), *Income inequality: The Canadian story* (pp. 77–102). Montreal, Canada: The Institute for Research on Public Policy (IRPP).

Hu, Q., Schaufeli, W.B., & Taris, T.W. (2017). How are changes in exposure to job demands and job resources related to burnout and engagement? A longitudinal study among Chinese nurses and police officers. *Stress and Health*, 33(5), 631–644. doi:10.1002/smi.2750

Hussein, S., Manthorpe, J., Ridley, J., Austerberry, H., Farrelly, N., Larkins, C., Bilson, A., & Stanley, N. (2014). Independent children's social work practice pilots: Evaluating practitioners' job control and burnout. *Research on Social Work Practice*, 24(2), 224–234. doi:10.1177/1049731513492859

King, M.L. (1988). *The measure of a man*. Minneapolis, MN: Fortress Press.

Lizano, E.L., & Mor Barak, M.E. (2012). Workplace demands and resources as antecedents of job burnout among public child welfare workers: A longitudinal study. *Children and Youth Services Review*, 34(9), 1769–1776. doi:10.1016/j.childyouth.2012.02.006

Madigan, S. (2011). *Narrative therapy*. Washington, DC: American Psychological Association.

Pager, D., & Shepherd, H. (2008). The sociology of discrimination: Racial discrimination in employment, housing, credit, and consumer markets. *Annual Review of Sociology*, 34, 181–209. doi:10.1146/annurev.soc.33.040406.131740

Sergeant, J.C., & Firth, D. (2005). Relative index of inequality: definition, estimation, and inference. *Biostatistics*, 7(2), 213–224. doi:10.1093/biostatistics/kxj002

Turns, B.A., & Kimmes, J. (2014). 'I'm NOT the problem!' Externalising children's 'problems' using play therapy and developmental considerations. *Contemporary Family Therapy*, 36(1), 135–147. doi:10.1007/s10591-013-9285-z

Van Wyk, R. (2008). Narrative house. A metaphor for narrative therapy. Tribute to Michael White. *Ife Psychologia*, 16(2), 255–274. doi:10.4314/ifep.v16i2.23815

Westhues, A., & Wharf, B. (2013). *Canadian social policy: Issues and perspectives* (5th ed.). Waterloo, Canada: Wilfrid Laurier University Press.

White, M. (1991). Deconstruction and therapy. *Dulwich Centre Newsletter*, 3, 21–40.

White, M. (2000). Re-engaging with history: The absent but implicit. In M. White (Ed.) *Reflections on narrative practice* (pp. 35–58). Adelaide, South Australia: Dulwich Centre Publications.

White, M. (2007). *Maps of narrative practice*. New York: W.W. Norton.

White, M., & Epston, D. (1990). *Narrative means to therapeutic ends*. New York: W.W. Norton.

Chapter 5

Learning how to be reflective

Helen Hickson

I've been a social worker for nearly 20 years, living and working mostly in rural and regional areas in central Victoria, Australia. I studied social work at La Trobe University then worked as a social worker for a few years before enrolling in a Master's programme majoring in Critical Reflection. This experience ignited my interest in reflective practices and, in 2013, I completed a Ph.D., which focused on exploring how social workers learn and use reflection. Although social work provides the foundation and professional framework that I use to inform my approach to work and life, much of my work experience has been in leadership and management roles rather than as a clinical social worker practitioner. In this chapter, I explain my pathway to learning and using critical reflection and use a case study to deconstruct my experience of introducing critical reflection to a group of executive level managers.

Learning to be reflective

My experience of learning to be reflective came after much searching. I stumbled across a half day 'Introduction to Critical Reflection' workshop while I was looking for professional development activities. I was curious about the nature of critical reflection and a little worried about what I might find if I thought too much about my practice. Of course, I was immediately drawn into the enticing pathways of being reflective not knowing where I would end up if I explored this or that (Hickson, 2011).

I studied Fook's (2002) model of critical reflection with Jan Fook and Fiona Gardner at La Trobe University in Australia. As part of a postgraduate Master's programme, I learned a two-stage model of critical reflection, which involved describing an unsettling experience, deconstructing and exploring assumptions, and reconstructing different ways to respond in the future (Fook, 2002). For me, exploring my assumptions was challenging and exhilarating, and I never cease to be amazed at the powerful transformation that takes place during critical reflection. I find critical reflection to be an engaging and useful way to deconstruct interactions and assumptions and to make meaning from experiences.

Since then, I have explicitly included the elements of critical reflection in my teaching and supervision of social work students at university and during field education (social work placements). I have worked outside the university environment for the past three years and established and maintained a group of critical friends who use critical reflection to deconstruct and explore assumptions and make sense of their experiences. I continue to hear the assumption that critical reflection is a 'social work thing'. In the literature, it is clear that critical reflection and reflective practices are embedded across most disciplines, although it can be called different terms, involve various steps and techniques, and have a variety of aims and intentions.

Exploring how social workers learn and use critical reflection

I completed a Ph.D. in 2013 (Hickson, 2013) that involved a research study with 35 participants to explore how social workers learn and use reflection. I found that there were a number of temporal opportunities that appear during a person's life that might stimulate an interest in reflective practices. For some people, this was something that was learned in childhood when they recall being asked to 'sit quietly and think about their behaviour' or was through being inspired in early childhood by a parent or educator who encouraged them to search for multiple meanings within a storybook or to consider how a storybook character might react or respond to a situation. This helped children to develop an awareness of different perspectives and multiple truths (Hickson, Lehmann, & Gardner, 2016). For others, learning to be reflective came later, after a critical life event, or particularly engaging reflective supervisor. Research participants consistently described a readiness that was necessary for the person to embrace the opportunity to engage with reflection. Although the precise nature of this readiness has remained elusive to me, it is clear that you cannot force someone to reflect on their practice if they do not wish to engage in the activity.

Case study: Critical reflection with an executive leadership team

During 2016, I had the opportunity to introduce critical reflection to a multi-disciplinary executive leadership team in a human service organisation in Victoria. This team of about 15 people included the CEO, executive directors, and managers. About half of the group had previously worked in clinical roles in health or allied health disciplines (such as nursing, podiatry, social work, and occupational therapy), and the other half had finance, governance, or business background. The organisation was a startup company that had been in operation for about one year and was set up as a medium-sized, not-for-profit entity.

I was employed as a manager by the company and was a participant in this team.

The newly established executive team was looking for an approach to support better communication and to be more explicit about deconstructing assumptions. The team was geographically dispersed and gathered once a month for a face to face meeting. There was agreement that it would be good to introduce elements of being reflective and to reflect on the outcomes of previous decisions. I suggested critical reflection as a framework for exploring assumptions, and I described the theory and the practice of the approach. Rather than seek to introduce the two-stages of Fook's approach (as described in Fook & Gardner, 2007), I suggested that we start by inspiring a sense of curiosity and willingness to develop a shared understanding and shared learning space about the challenges and opportunities in the organisation. This was based on the various professional backgrounds of the participants and the sense that reflective practice was a very new concept for some participants, and I wanted to start small and get buy-in then expand as required. Although all participants indicated that there were support and commitment to participate in reflective conversations, it was not clear whether participants were ready to reflect on their interactions and deconstruct assumptions.

Being ready to reflect is an important aspect that needs to be considered, and knowing if you are ready can mean different things to different people. Readiness (Yip, 2006) is a sense of preparedness to engage with uncertainty or change whether it is to start a new job, a new role, or some other transition. Some people like the challenge and thrill of new opportunities, and other people like to wait until they feel confident, prepared, and ready to deal with whatever is ahead. In my research about reflective practices, participants were clear that there were many opportunities to engage with reflective practice, but they needed to make a conscious decision to engage with reflection or otherwise, it might pass by.

Engaging with reflection in the workplace was new for many participants in this case study. The first step for me to overcome was the notion that it was a 'social work' thing or that it was similar to counselling, therapy, or psychoanalysis. I framed critical reflection as a theory and a practice, and I connected with literature for those who were interested (Brookfield, 1995; Fook, 2002; Fook & Gardner, 2007; Hoyrup, 2004; Mezirow, 1990).

I introduced critical reflection as a way to introduce language about values, giving and hearing feedback, and a way to better understand oneself and the interactions with others. It's a structured way to deconstruct assumptions and to create an environment where people are open to hearing different points of view. In this context, most participants were not familiar with critical social theory (see Chapter 1 of this book for a more detailed explanation of the different theories, which inform the model). I needed to be clear that the 'critical' in critical reflection was not about focusing on the negative aspects of an experience but was based on critical theories of postmodernism. In essence, this means to me, that when a number of people are involved in the same situation they will understand and make sense of what happened in different ways. Importantly, critical reflection involves using a post-modern and post-structural lens (from a critical perspective) to explore the context of power. From this perspective, Fook (2002; 2012; 2016), Fook and Gardner (2007), and Morley (2004) argue that power can be disguised (especially in the use of language). Critical reflection involves deconstructing how power has been exercised in order to explore and challenge dominant power relations and structures and consider new ways of thinking. Critically reflective thinkers use postmodern and post-structural thinking to examine how binary thinking, dichotomous language use, and other discourses can limit thinking. This enables alternate perspectives to be developed.

I explained that critical reflection and reflective practices are used in a number of settings including health disciplines, education, universities, and business. Different disciplines may use different terms to conduct some activities, which may appear on the surface to be very similar to critically reflective activities. For example, critical reflection may also appear very similar to a type of evaluation. Or a critically reflective small group process may share some aspects of an action learning set. McLoughlin and McGilloway (2013, p. 18) note that the problem of terminology and how different meanings may be assigned to such central concepts as 'critical incidents' and 'assumptions', especially in a health context.

For everyone, except the other social worker, being reflective wasn't part of their practice, at least in a theoretical sense, although some talked about using reflection to think about their practice and how to integrate learning from previous experiences to 'learn from their mistakes'. Critical reflection adds another layer, where there needs to be an explicit focus through the lens of critical theory, to consciously explore assumptions about knowledge, power, and reflexivity (Fook, 2002; Fook & Askeland, 2006). This can be uncomfortable – it might involve sitting with uncertainty, being vulnerable, or perhaps recognising that the way that you reacted or responded was not great. In a leadership team in the workplace, there are additional complexities such as organisational culture, trust, hierarchical relationships, and, in some workplaces, it might not feel safe to be vulnerable, reveal personal weaknesses, or draw attention to something that didn't turn out well.

Introduction of critical reflection

At the next executive team meeting (meeting 2), I introduced the concept of reflective practices and critical reflection. I framed critical reflection within the context of postmodernism and connected these ideas to the literature, explaining that critical reflection writers suggest that we need to pay attention to three things to better understand how this works: knowledge, power, and reflexivity. As examples, I described:

Knowledge – what we know and how we came to know about it, e.g. how do we learn new things and what evidence do we need to be persuaded to change? What is unknown and uncertain?

Power – understanding the mechanisms of power in organisations, how people manage downwards and upwards, and how people in all parts of an organisation can act powerfully.

Reflexivity – is the awareness of ourselves and others and how people make sense of the things. Do I have a positive bias or a negative bias about things – e.g. do I assume that things will work out okay, or do I expect it will be terrible? How does my mood influence the way I interpret the interactions with me and how I use and respond to power?

I described some of the benefits of critical reflection as the opportunity to explore shared values and shared language, to explore how to improve communication and relationships, and to become more agile and responsive as we are more accepting of diverse views. We identified risks such as feeling vulnerable in being reflective and the importance of trust and feeling safe to try out new things. This connects with risks that have been identified in the literature about using critical reflection, such as that it can be a challenge to identify and name what is not being said and that taking criticism personally can lead to defensive reactions, which are not constructive or collaborative.

I spoke at the start of the meeting and used critical reflection questions as the meeting progressed to demonstrate ways to clarify assumptions and to deepen understandings. At the end of the meeting, we recapped the principles of critical reflection, some questions, and how they could be used to deepen understanding. I provided a two-page handout with an overview of critical reflection and examples of questions. After the meeting, there was ongoing interest from some of the managers who were curious about how critical reflection was similar and different to other reflective and management processes and where they could access additional writing or research. Over the next few weeks, I was frequently asked to provide examples of critically reflective questions that could be used to better deconstruct assumptions or to make sense of an experience.

I was encouraged that some of the managers were open to learning more about critical reflection and seemed interested in exploring and deconstructing their interactions with each other. Fook and Gardner (2007) warn that it can be a challenge for people who are learning about critical reflection to move past a more descriptive type of reflection (e.g. How did that go? What was my role? What could I do better next time?) and engage with reflection through the lens of critical theory. This involves thinking and examining organisational processes from different perspectives. In this case study, these are some of the questions that we used:

60 Helen Hickson

- Knowledge

  a   What assumptions and expectations do I have?
  b   What evidence is there? What evidence do I need? Why?
  c   What is the context? Are there alternative views?

- Power

  a   Who is making the decision? When? Why?
  b   What are we trying to achieve and how will we know if we have got it right?
  c   What are the opportunities to contribute to decision-making (e.g. consultation, negotiation, collaboration, and feedback)?

- Reflexivity

  a   What are my expectations about myself? What do others expect of me?
  b   How can I support other people to express their view or be heard?
  c   How am I seeing things? How might others see things differently?
  d   What is the 'mood' (e.g. Optimistic? Excited? Curious? Cautious?) Why?

I was optimistic that the value of critical reflection in this environment would be in exploring assumptions and using questions to share understanding and intentions about the topics of discussion amongst the members. At the following meeting (meeting 3) there was a presentation about future planning and innovation and the presenter described that she saw the value of innovation as a means of disruption of the status quo. An interesting conversation followed as participants spoke about how they define the word 'disruption' and how the word should be used. It became clear that the word 'disruption' meant different things to different people. For some people, disruption was seen as exciting, shaking things up, and looking for new ways to do things, but for other people, the word disruption was seen as something to be avoided – there were negative connotations about how the word was interpreted and whether disruption was a positive thing. This was a really useful, critically reflective conversation about how to use questions to deconstruct assumptions and to clarify the ways that people make meaning from their interactions and experiences.

Critical reflection in practice

At the following meeting (meeting 4), I recapped the principles of critical reflection and talked about some of the common questions that I had been asked and the follow-up resources that were available. I asked whether there were any thoughts about critical reflection or if anyone had used questions to explore assumptions or their understanding of an interaction or experience.

Two participants spoke about their experiences and provided illustrative examples that demonstrated the value of critical reflection to the executive team meeting. Robert spoke about a community meeting that he had attended where he delivered a presentation about the focus of the organisation and the plans for the future. Robert said that he was conscious about the words and language that he was using and much more aware of assumptions that the audience might have, particularly around meanings, knowledge, and power imbalances. He explicitly asked the audience to be interactive and ask questions to clarify their assumptions, challenging whether they were interpreting and understanding things in the way he intended. He reported that it was a very different conversation, and he was confident that the community members had a much clearer and more authentic understanding of the messages that he had intended to deliver.

Vashti's reflection was centred on her thoughts about reflexivity and how she found that it could be self-confirming, particularly when she was preparing to attend a meeting, training workshop, or even a party. Vashti described an event that she was attending on the weekend, which involved considerable effort and expense to attend. As they were driving to the airport, one of her children complained that it was going to be a boring weekend and Vashti replied that they had paid a lot of money to travel to this family gathering and everyone was going to have a great time. For the rest of the weekend, she looked for examples as evidence that supported the position that they were all having a great time. Vashti noted that if she was expecting a family gathering or a work activity to be awful and looked for evidence to support this, it is likely that she will find it. What you see is whatever you are looking for.

Analysis of the case study

Critical reflection is recognised as an advanced form of reflective practice that can be used to deepen understanding of a central issue (Brookfield, 1995; Fook & Gardner, 2007; Redmond, 2006), where participants explicitly pay attention to knowledge, power, and reflexivity. Brookfield (1995) argues that it is not enough to think about or reflect on an experience. The reflection needs to take into account the context and deconstruct how the personal experience is positioned within social and power arrangements.

Fook and Gardner (2007) provide some guidance for using critical reflection in organisational settings (Chapter 9) and as a framework for managers and supervisors to use for planning and review (p. 149). There is a complex relationship between the organisation and the individual, particularly in relation to leadership functions, organisational culture, strategic planning, and managing organisational change (Fook & Askeland, 2006). This connects with Fook and Gardner's (2007) writing about a critically reflective group culture, which they refer to as creating a climate of 'critical acceptance' (p. 78). Organisational culture is a defining aspect in creating a climate of acceptance because without this, people will not be able to articulate and discuss their interpretation, assumptions, and expectations for fear of being questioned, being challenged, or being wrong. In this case study, I noticed that some people did not contribute to conversations about what critical reflection is or how to use it. I sensed that there was discomfort with sitting with something that was new and unfamiliar in the context of a newly-formed leadership team who were jostling for positions in the organisation. Amidst the busyness of a startup company, it seemed that the organisational culture of the group was not robust enough to cope with the conflict and change, and individuals did not experience a context that felt safe to allow themselves to be vulnerable.

Understanding knowledge, power, and reflexivity

It is important to have an understanding of power, power dynamics, and how the mechanisms of power work in human service organisations. Exploring assumptions is a personal experience and requires courage and a commitment to learn and create the context for change and personal growth. This needs to sit within an organisational learning culture of a safe place to be vulnerable, make a mistake, be wrong, misunderstand, or misinterpret a situation. There is an element of vulnerability that is required for a person to concede, amongst their peers, subordinate staff, or direct supervisor that they don't know or aren't sure about something.

When critical reflection is introduced in an organisational context, some people may feel that there is a nonvoluntary requirement or obligation to reflect on their practice in nonvoluntary ways. If the organisational culture is primarily based on a hierarchy, people who are at the lower end of the hierarchy may feel powerless to object or reveal their shortcomings. Critical reflection can support the understanding of power dynamics in organisations and is a useful way to support people at the lower end of the hierarchy to recognise how power can be exercised by people at all levels in an organisation.

Evidence over time

Critical reflection was implemented over four months as a standing agenda item in the monthly executive team meeting, and there were frequent conversations and consultations outside the meeting environment. In the following three months, there were staffing changes and the momentum was lost. The dynamics of the meeting were different with new people attending the meeting and the critical reflection champions were not in attendance. Now, two years have passed and there are some elements of critical reflection that remain. The organisation has developed a shared language about 'exploring assumptions' and is more open to diverse ways of thinking. I notice that there is an increased focus on clarifying expectations – understanding what information is needed, where this needs to come from, and what evidence will be required to make a decision. The area where there is most noticeable legacy is that the participants of this group are more reflexive. I notice this when they talk about things like,

'Is that a fair assumption or are there other views?', or recognise that different opinions come from the way the other person understands the context or the objective. The discourse recognises postmodern ways of thinking, which includes the notion that there are different ways of approaching or responding to a situation, and diverse ideas are not necessarily right or wrong, just different. There is an enduring focus on explicitly asking questions to explore assumptions or to make sense of an interaction or experience.

Overall, critical reflection as a practice has not been embedded in the organisation. There are, perhaps, a few reasons for this. Firstly, I think that participants found it very challenging to sit with the uncertainty that comes from learning something new and the vulnerability about exploring their values and assumptions. The modern workplace is very busy and for people who are action-oriented and outcome-focused, it can seem counterintuitive to slow things down and value time to think about their interactions with other people. In addition, there has been staff turnover and some of the original champions have moved on, so the shared language and understanding has been gradually diluted. Critical reflection is occasionally referenced as a tool that was useful to support people to learn from their experiences and each other. There weren't any negatives, as such, with this case study. There were some benefits, but over time, the momentum was lost and champions moved on, and it would need significant engagement and effort to refresh the practice.

What makes it harder to embed in a human service organisation? In this case study, it was harder to work with participants who were not ready to engage with critical reflection, particularly when the organisational culture does not value reflection or time to be reflective. In addition, in a competitive workplace, it might be perceived as not safe to disclose a weakness, reveal that you have made a mistake, or identify a situation where something didn't turn out well.

Personal reflection

I enjoyed engaging with critical reflection in this context, as I am passionate about using critical reflection to explore assumptions, deconstruct experiences, and make meaning and to explicitly look for the mechanisms of power in organisations. Whilst I found it intellectually stimulating to introduce critical reflection to an executive team, I was frustrated that it was seen by some as a social work tool used mostly for supervision with social workers and social work students. In trying to understand this perspective, I heard participants describe their discomfort with uncertainty, vulnerability, and use of emotions, and their sense of incongruence with the busyness of their work schedules and investing time to reflect and share experiences. Perhaps because of this discomfort, it helped people who were not social workers to characterise critical reflection as something belonging to a profession, which they were not versed in. This might effectively excuse their discomfort. In the modern workplace, where outputs and outcomes are valued and we are accustomed to multi-tasking, I look forward to a time when critical reflection can be positioned more broadly as a key element of a vibrant organisational culture and as something which is needed by all professions.

Critical reflection is a valuable tool for the executive table. In my experience there were a few things that helped:

- Introducing critical reflection as a theory and a practice and providing practical examples that have been translated into the organisational context
- Demonstrating critically reflective questions at every opportunity so that it becomes part of the narrative of the organisation
- An organisational culture that values reflection and is safe for workers to explore uncertainty and vulnerability
- Explicitly identifying opportunities to look for multiple meaning and other perspectives
- Buy-in and support from senior staff are essential.
- Using questions to deconstruct assumptions, to clarify intent, and to come to a group understanding about meaning. For example:

  a   What does success look like?
  b   What matters most?
  c   What's the next step?
  d   Why? Yes, but why?
  e   Why are we doing it this way?
  f   How will we know when we have got it right?
  g   How will we know if we have gone offtrack?
  h   What's the outcome we are aiming for?

- Regular conversations across the organisation to influence the discourse and the culture in the organisation. It needs to be a standing agenda at meetings and be championed at every opportunity.

Conclusion

Critical reflection is both a theory and a practice and can be a useful technique to support human service organisations to make the best use of their most valuable resource: their staff. In this chapter, I have described my experience of introducing critical reflection to a team of managers and executives. I found that critical reflection was a useful and valuable tool to support an executive leadership team to deconstruct assumptions and make meaning from their interactions, but there are challenges with embedding it in the organisational culture. These challenges included the discomfort of sitting with uncertainty and being vulnerable in a competitive organisational environment, the power dynamics and mechanisms of power in a rapidly changing workplace, and the various stages of readiness of participants to engage in a new way of thinking and learning about their interactions with other people. Critical reflection was an engaging way to develop shared expectations and language, and I look forward to a time when critical reflection is recognised as a key element of a vibrant organisational culture.

References

Brookfield, S. (1995). *Becoming a critically reflective teacher*. San Francisco, CA: Jossey-Bass.

Fook, J. (2002). *Social work: Critical theory and practice*. London: SAGE.

Fook, J. (2012). *Social work: A critical approach to practice* (2nd ed.). London: SAGE.

Fook, J. (2016). *Social work: A critical approach to practice* (3rd ed.). London: SAGE.

Fook, J., & Askeland, G.A. (2006). The 'critical' in critical reflection. In S. White, J. Fook, & F. Gardner (Eds.), *Critical reflection in health and social care* (pp. 40–54). Maidenhead: Open University Press.

Fook, J., & Gardner, F. (2007). *Practicing critical reflection: A resource handbook*. Maidenhead: Open University Press.

Hickson, H. (2011). Critical reflection: Reflecting on learning to be reflective. *Reflective Practice*, 12(6), 829–839. doi:10.1080/14623943.2011.616687

Hickson, H. (2013). *Exploring how social workers learn and use reflection* (Unpublished doctoral dissertation). La Trobe University, Melbourne, Australia.

Hickson, H., Lehmann, J., & Gardner, F. (2016). Exploring the development of reflective capacity in young people. *Children Australia*, 41(2), 154–161. doi:10.1017/cha.2016.6

Hoyrup, S. (2004). Reflection as a core process in organisational learning. *Journal of Workplace Learning*, 16(8), 442–454. doi:10.1108/13665620410566414

McLoughlin, K., & McGilloway, S. (2013). Unsettling assumptions around death, dying and palliative care: A practical approach. In J. Fook & F. Gardner (Eds.), *Critical reflection in context: Applications in health and social care* (pp. 15–27). Oxford: Routledge.

Mezirow, J. (1990). How critical reflection triggers transformative learning. In J. Mezirow (Ed.), *Fostering critical reflection in adulthood: A guide to transformative and emancipatory learning* (pp. 1–20). San Francisco, CA: Jossey-Bass.

Morley, C. (2004). Critical reflection in social work: A response to globalisation? *International Journal of Social Welfare*, 13(4), 297–303. doi:10.1111/j.1468-2397.2004.00325.x

Redmond, B. (2006). *Reflection in action: Developing reflective practice in health and social services* (2nd ed.). Aldershot: Ashgate.

Yip, K. (2006). Self-reflection in reflective practice: A note of caution. *British Journal of Social Work*, 36(5), 777–788. doi:10.1093/bjsw/bch323

Section II

The changes made from the learning process

Chapter 6

From 'imperfect perfectionism' to 'compassionate conscientiousness'

Rebecca Donati

The term reflection has become conflated with a myriad of disparate understandings. Its overuse in common discourse has rendered a unitary definition seemingly improbable. The discipline and context in which it is employed are likely to influence the tenor of how it is intended. Nevertheless, reflection, in its simplest form, constitutes a nearly universal human experience. Consciousness and awareness engender a capacity to think about one's experience, a foremost facet of individual learning and growth. Clarà (2015) suggests, 'reflection can be defined as a thinking process which gives coherence to a situation which is initially incoherent and unclear' (p. 263). Though this definition adds some specificity, it negates an understanding of the broader social structures, which contribute to this process. Conversely, critical reflection situates personal experience within social, cultural, and structural frameworks to enable a transformative process of identifying ingrained assumptions (Fook & Askeland, 2007). Though this latter form of reflection often necessitates a more systematic and prescriptive approach, it can be invaluable in facilitating the emergence of new insights. It is this form of reflection that will be explored in the remainder of this chapter, specifically, Fook's model of critical reflection on practice (CRoP) as described in Chapter 1.

This chapter will focus on the individual learning that I accrued while learning to work with Fook's model and will also illuminate the depth to which I have been influenced by CRoP. In this account, I explore how the process of CRoP enabled the emergence of new personal and professional insights. Initially, I examine how the process of critical reflection led to the awareness of my perfectionistic tendencies. The remainder of the chapter vacillates between literary understandings of perfectionism and my personal experience of it. To conclude, I consider the implications of this new understanding and propose a nascent theory of practice.

Unpacking the incident: The impetus for continued exploration

As discussed in Chapter 1, CRoP is organised in two stages in which a critical incident is elucidated and analysed. Though analysed might appear too scientific a word, it is quite fitting of the thorough examination, which evolves within this process. The term 'critical' habitually connotes something that is negative or severe, however, in this instance it is meant to infer significance. An incident is, thus, critical if it somehow takes hold of the individual, possibly provoking contemplation, worry, or musing. Often, the cause of this fixation remains unknown and is the precise reason why further scrutiny might be beneficial. It is specifically this type of persistent pondering that led to the unpacking of my critical incident. The result of this introspection, through the process of critical reflection, is akin to an excerpt from one of Fook's (1996) earlier works:

> Adopting the deconstructive gaze of poststructuralism and turning a critical, deconstructive gaze on ourselves has a potentially liberating effect. Once we recognize that our world as we know and understand it is constructed by the framework (discourses) we ourselves have devised for knowing and understanding it, we can begin to change it by challenging the ways in which we have constructed, and continue to construct it.
>
> (as cited in Morley, 2004, p. 302)

To explicate this connection, a brief discussion of my critical incident will be provided as well as the learning, which emerged through the process.

In examining a critical incident from a social work practicum, it became apparent that what transpired in this occurrence was not an isolated event. Rather, a theme emerged, a single link in a continuous chain of happenings that connect to all spheres of my life. The critical reflection process allowed for an organised examination of an incident that, on the surface, appeared quite mundane. However, it was precisely this perception of normality that rendered me increasingly muddled. Why had this particular event stuck with me? It is something that continued to play in my mind like a series of fleeting snapshots as opposed to a coherent narrative.

The incident revolves around my experience of working with a client on budgeting skills while completing a student placement at a community counselling agency. From the outset, I believed neither myself nor the client was given much choice in the arrangement. Budgeting was not something I had previous experience in or prior knowledge of. Compounding this inexperience were immense feelings of guilt as the awareness of my own privilege became juxtaposed with the myriad of oppressions impacting the client. The client chose to conclude our work together much earlier than either I or my supervisor had anticipated. Feeling capable to work on these tasks independently, the client thanked me for the support and identified that they would no longer be needing assistance for this matter. I unquestioningly accepted this and offered that should they change their mind to please be in touch. Conversely, my supervisor thought that I should have been more insistent and directive in my approach. I wondered how our views on the situation could have been so opposite. It was this incongruence that prompted my desire to better understand the incident. As a social worker, it is imperative that I discern the implicit assumptions and the underlying reasons for my practice decisions.

The previously mentioned account is an abbreviated version of the original description I wrote of the incident, but the salient aspects remain. During stage 1, I began to ponder my thoughts about professionalism as well as the core values of the profession. Utilising a reflective approach, I considered what theories or assumptions were informing my practice and what the critical incident implied about my basic ideals and values. This self-examination led to a host of conclusions including that I believe client self-determination is paramount and that individuals who are seeking service of their own volition should be able to designate the quality and quantity of care they receive. This assumption was implicit in my account; however, it became explicit over the course of the first stage. It became apparent that a prior placement in the criminal justice sector might have influenced my thinking on this matter. Rigid guidelines and aspects of control limit client self-determination within the probation setting. Working in that sector provoked conflict between my own values and those necessitated by the system. In an effort to compensate, I may have corrected too far in the opposite direction resulting in an extreme view of what constitutes self-determination.

Over the course of questioning, I began to realise that my unwavering stance on client self-determination may also have been fulfilling a self-serving function. Something I was not conscious of at the time or was too afraid to admit was that I felt ill-equipped to help this client; I felt like an imposter. Supporting the client's choice effectively eliminated my personal responsibility by placing the onus for 'success' or 'failure' squarely on the client. In this way, I could both support self-determination and preserve my own feelings of worth as a practitioner. Fook & Gardner (2007) suggest that during CRoP it is not uncommon that individuals' 'fundamental beliefs become reaffirmed, . . . [however] what happens is they learn that there might be other ways to practise that will allow them to better enact these beliefs in different contexts' (p. 69). Through contemplation, I recognised that self-determination does not demand that the client have absolute independence. Rather, self-determination can be viewed along a spectrum wherein some situations might incite increased guidance from the practitioner in service of a client's best interest. Some researchers have attempted to understand how practitioners navigate this territory. A study by Rothman, Smith, Nakashima, Paterson, and Mustin (1996) suggests that practitioners demonstrate flexibility in their use of directiveness to respond to both a client's need and situational context and often employ a range of directive and nondirective approaches. Accordingly, my desire to uphold client self-determination has been reaffirmed albeit with fluidity for how it can be understood and applied in practice.

To return to a previous point, upholding client self-determination also served a selfish purpose. To place absolute responsibility in the client absolved me of the obligation to intervene. More importantly, if I did not take further action, I would not risk failure or ineffectiveness. In this sense, my passivity reflected my need to be seen as skilful and proficient in my role. This was a difficult and unsettling realisation, one that lay in opposition to my belief that I was acting in the best interest of the client. Typically, such a feeling of unease may have halted further contemplation. In this instance, both the encouragement of my group members as well as the level of trust that had been established in the classroom provided me the motivation to pursue the aetiology of this tendency. At this point, the theoretical framework of postmodernism and deconstruction played a vital role in helping to expound deeper meaning. Berlin (1990) identifies that our thought processes are often constituted by the construction of binary opposites. During stage 1, I posed the following question: It's interesting that I used the phrase 'right course of action,' because this implies there is a wrong course of action as well. I wonder why I have constructed this binary and its impact? Unknowingly, I had constructed false dichotomies, such as right versus wrong or pleased versus displeased, which limited my thinking and excluded alternate perspectives.

Upon further speculation, I began gathering all the pieces of information that had become unsettled: my need for control, my difficulty in accepting ambiguity, my need to pursue the right course of action, and so forth. It was as if each assumption represented a strand, and when woven together the relationship between these disparate parts could be exposed. This collective understanding is best summed up as a striving for perfectionism. I liken this development to how one experiences visual illusions; though the image is present in the background, it is concealed from view until such time that the appropriate conditions arise for it to be known. CRoP provided me this unique perspective and enabled the identification of my perfectionist inclination.

The idea of perfectionism is something I have long been aware of, though I have not given it serious consideration. Others have often described me as a perfectionist, yet I always assumed it to be in jest. I too have often masked certain tendencies with humour. It is likely that I have used whimsy to avoid meaningful introspection in this regard. Interestingly, it is only within my personal life, particularly academia, that I have briefly considered this notion. In my naivety, I had failed to consider the potentiality that these same tendencies could also influence my professional practice. Accordingly, through the critical reflection process, I have been motivated to pursue the idea of perfectionism and its impact on my personal and professional endeavours.

Perfectionism: Applying the literature to personal experience

Though there is an abundance of research and literature pertaining to perfectionism, there remains sufficient debate about its particularities. Contributing to this expanse is the myriad contexts in which it has been applied, including business, sports psychology, education, and so forth. While some authors link perfectionism to various personality dispositions (Hewitt & Flett, 1991) others perceive it as an 'energising force' (Hill, Hall, & Appleton, 2012, p. 353), a cognitive style (Burns & Fedewa, 2005), or a set of behaviours. Common to all approaches is a general understanding of perfectionism as 'characterised by exceedingly high standards of performance and concerns about making mistakes and the social consequences of not being perfect' (Damian, Stoeber, Negru-Subtirica, & Baban, 2016, p. 565). While perfectionistic tendencies can be a positive contributor in adjustment and are associated with higher performance and academic achievement, conscientiousness, problem-focused coping, and positive affect (Damian et al., 2016), it is also linked to both moderate and serious negative outcomes. Ashby, Slaney, Noble, Gnilka, and Rice (2012) review preceding research on adaptive and maladaptive forms of perfectionism and offer similar findings in their current study. These authors underscore the importance of understanding individualised definitions of perfectionism, unique manifestations of distress, and the level of worry associated with this tendency.

Though deliberation continues as to the positive and negative aspects of perfectionism, more recent works tend to focus on its adverse effects. Researchers have found associations between perfectionism and feelings of failure, distress, worry, guilt, procrastination, shame, and low self-esteem (Ashby et al., 2012; Pacht, 1984; Solomon & Rothblum, 1984; Sorotzkin, 1985). These are often categorised as more moderate outcomes; however, it is important to note that for some individuals the impact of such traits might be quite debilitating. Speaking from experience, I find that the accumulation of these feelings can be, at times, especially overwhelming. Drawing on previous research, Hewitt and Flett (1991) identify that more severe outcomes include various manifestations of 'psychopathology' (p. 456) such as alcoholism, anorexia, depression, and personality disorders. Difficulties in adjustment are thought to stem from a number of propensities including an overemphasis on failure, a drive to set and accomplish unrealistic goals, extreme maladaptive cognitive patterns, such as all-or-nothing thinking, and inflexible self-appraisals (Pacht, 1984). This information should be interpreted with caution, because although perfectionism is associated with such outcomes, cause cannot be attributed nor does it mean that these consequences are fixed. Since individuals are complex social beings, influenced by multiple elements that are constantly in flux, perfectionism should be understood within the larger narrative that is a person's life.

In reading through the literature, I was flooded with a swirl of memories, thoughts, and emotions. Each idea appeared as if a piece to a larger puzzle. I thought to myself, this could have been written for me; I do that, I think that. The experience was both validating and troubling. I have often felt an indescribable weight, a gnawing and pervasive pressure. I had not given much thought to these feelings, and I attributed it to a general sense of worry – a trait quite common in my family. Understanding these feelings within the context of perfectionism has given me clarity. Having a label for my experience is helpful, but it also brings with it a keen sense of reality that cannot easily be ignored. This is where it got troubling; I became saddened to think of its impact, to think of the many ways perfectionism has burdened me, and possibly those around me. Though I tend to perform well in most endeavours and excel academically, I also struggle with extremely high, near impossible expectations. I am fortunate that I have yet to experience the more serious outcomes associated with perfectionism. However, I am cognisant that the situation could worsen if I do not initiate change. In a similar manner to narrative therapy, I have chosen to externalise perfectionism. I do not view it as an inalterable trait but rather a highly entrenched cognitive style with corresponding emotions and behaviours. As such, I am positioning myself in such a way that I might begin to exert a level of control over it. Prior to engaging in a change effort, it is imperative that I understand how perfectionism develops.

Fook and Gardner (2007) identify that an antecedent for linking 'personal experience with social or cultural influences' (p. 91) is the normalisation of one's responses. I found comfort in the recognition that perfectionism appears to be a widespread phenomenon with interpersonal and social underpinnings. The development of perfectionism has been consistently studied throughout the years, but there remains divergence within the field. Consensus dictates that perfectionism does not follow a sequential process, and the paths that precede it are often varied and unpredictable. Damian et al. (2016) identify that a bulk of theory and research focuses on how parental factors contribute to the development of perfectionism. These authors also note the role of cultural influence and social discourse, related to achievement, performance, and success, in contributing to perfectionism. Flett, Hewitt, Oliver, and Macdonald (2002) suggest that the school environment, especially those focused on evaluation, grades, competition, and comparison, supports the growth, persistence, and intensification of perfectionism. It is likely that this relationship is compounded with each progressive year. It is further proposed that, paradoxically, as individuals experience academic success, their vulnerability to developing perfectionistic propensities also increases (Flett et al., 2002).

Connecting the personal with the social is an important part of CRoP. Hewitt and Flett (1991) make an important distinction between three manifestations of perfectionism: self-oriented perfectionism, other-oriented perfectionism, and socially prescribed perfectionism. As the name suggests, their paper describes self-oriented perfectionism as constituted by the expectation one places on themselves, motivated particularly by achieving perfection and evading failure. In contrast, the authors identify that other-oriented perfectionism is external, wherein individuals transfer their unrealistic expectations onto others. Their research indicates that this form of perfectionism may lead to blaming, lack of trust, or hostility and could be associated with loneliness, cynicism, and interpersonal difficulty. The third type is socially prescribed perfectionism, 'the perceived need to attain standards and expectations prescribed by significant others' (Hewitt & Flett, 1991, p. 457).

In contrast to the literature, I do not engage in other-oriented perfectionism. Rather, I find I am able to hold realistic expectations of others, to both rejoice in their successes and find opportunities for growth and learning in their challenges. I pride myself on the empathy, compassion, and understanding I demonstrate with others, both personally and professionally. In contrast, I adhere to self-oriented perfectionism, partially based on socially prescribed perfectionism. Though I hold unrealistic expectations for myself, I also erroneously believe that others, be it friends, teachers, supervisors, or family members, hold me to these same expectations. I use the word erroneously to highlight the falsity of this belief.

It is difficult to elucidate the antecedents of perfectionism in my own life. In contrast to the literature, my parents were not punitive nor did they set unrealistic expectations. Both my parents did not complete high school and have always been self-employed. Though they have been successful, I have observed the long hours, hard work, and stress inherent in operating a business. From a young age, I recall my parents telling my brothers and me that they wanted a better life for us. I began to internalise these messages and understand that the route to this 'better life', from their perspective, was through education. It is possible that I began to associate academic achievement with success and positive regard. In a way, I started to equate my own sense of worth with my ability to achieve. During adolescence, a time of identity formation and self-discovery, I garnered a sense of self from being perceived as intelligent. Damian et al. (2016) identify adolescence as a 'key period for investigating the factors that contribute to the development of perfectionism' (p. 566). I often struggled with body image issues and felt alienated as a result. Though I was not as pretty or as thin as my friends, I found solace in my academic ability. This provided me a means to compensate for my perceived inadequacies over which I believed I had no control. The more I exceled in school, the higher my expectations became. I was also highly motivated to avoid failure. It is quite telling that I can vividly recall the one instance, during the third grade, wherein I failed academically. At this moment, I remember the knot in the pit of my stomach, how red my cheeks were, and the feelings of disappointment that filled me. I can recall only a few other instances in my life where feelings of failure provoked a similar response. However, this also bears the question: In an attempt to avoid failure, have I been limiting the chances I take?

In the present, I have a much richer and more positive self-perception. I continue to be challenged by body image issues, but these moments are fleeting. I do not compare myself to my peers, and I have come to find beauty in my appearance. I no longer define myself by my achievements, yet the need to achieve persists. It is a confusing paradox and is likely reflective of the many years in which this inclination has become entrenched. In a way, perfectionism might have been a way of coping, a way to exert control at a time when I felt I had so little. Though I have grown in positive ways, in this regard, I remain stuck.

I have only begun to scratch the surface of the numerous ways that perfectionism influences my life. Within the scope of this chapter, a thorough examination of each would not be possible nor would I be equipped to tackle such an endeavour at this time. Slowly, I am beginning to unravel the intricacies of its grasp, but this is no easy task. I am finding that there are elements of perfectionism that I believe to be worthwhile and productive, while the majority are both limiting and harmful. Procrastination and fear of failure are two specific areas that cause me great difficulty. Lay (1986) defines procrastination as 'the tendency to postpone that which is necessary to reach some goal' (p. 475). Flett, Blankstein, Hewitt, and Koledin (1992) demonstrate an association between procrastination and both fear of failure and perfectionism, though further research is needed to better understand these relationships. I am reminded of a phenomenon I read about in a social psychology textbook. It most closely aligns with the idea that when an impending task is evaluative and intimidating, procrastination might be used as a type of barrier to mitigate the impact of a potentially negative outcome (Tice & Baumeister, 1997). Essentially, procrastination operates as a mechanism of self-preservation; if the individual does well on the task they are satisfied and if they do not perform well, they attribute this poor functioning to procrastination as opposed to a lack of inherent ability. This understanding might help explain why I engage in this type of behaviour. Regardless of the cause, it is absolutely essential that I begin to change my perfectionist tendencies, especially my striving toward unrealistic expectations, my fear of failure, and my tendency to procrastinate. As I move into my social work career, the need for this change becomes even more pronounced. The pace of the work, along with increasing caseloads, necessitates effective time management. Similarly, being so concerned with failure, to the point that I am rigid in my approach, will not serve the best interest of my clients and is likely to be detrimental to my professional growth.

Working toward a theory of practice

It has taken many years to develop perfectionism, and I would be remiss to think its dismantlement will happen overnight. CRoP helped to unsettle assumptions and move me in the direction of new learning, but I know this journey has just begun. During stage 2, I began considering the ways in which I can unburden myself of extreme forms of thinking and better integrate balance within my thoughts, feelings, and behaviour. In reflecting specifically on perfectionism, I have been considering a new theory of practice. I have chosen the phrase 'compassionate conscientiousness'. This is a metaphor for how I hope to retain my desire to achieve while also maintaining a healthy and productive outlook. I use the term compassionate because it denotes a level of concern and sympathy. It is my hope that I will one day be able to view myself compassionately, as I do others. Though I do not know how or when I will learn to view failure as growth or achievement as good enough, I am inspired to start on this path.

This chapter has outlined how my engagement in the learning process of CRoP empowered the development of new personal and professional understandings. The shared learning and openness exhibited amongst my peers, stemming from an empathic learning environment, engendered a willingness in me to explore difficult insights. My belief in the importance of client self-determination was affirmed; however, it also became clear that this tenet was similarly self-serving. It became evident that adherence to client self-determination, in this instance, concealed an underlying fear of failure or ineffectiveness. This realisation led me to examine the idea of perfectionism, including both literary understandings and my personal experience of its impact. Through this process, I have begun to consider an alternate way of being wherein perfectionism is not absolute. In speaking of perfectionism, Kelly (2015) writes, 'Such a life is riddled with fear and extreme caution. Creativity, joy, inspiration, and even productivity are stunted when perfection is the only option' (p. 3108). The idea of 'compassionate conscientiousness' is a cumulative representation of the growth I experienced through learning CRoP. The culture of trust that was established in the classroom, as well as the unwavering support I experienced from my group members, allowed me to be vulnerable and to be seen as imperfect. It is heartening to know that my most fruitful achievements may be yet to come. Importantly, I now consider it possible that such gains might only arise out of the missteps, failures, and defeats that are yet to challenge me.

References

Ashby, J.S., Slaney, R.B., Noble, C.M., Gnilka, P.B., & Rice, K.G. (2012). Differences between "normal" and "neurotic" perfectionists: Implications for mental health counselors. *Journal of Mental Health Counseling*, 34(4), 322–340. doi:10.17744/mehc.34.4.52h65w1n8l27r300

Berlin, S.B. (1990). Dichotomous and complex thinking. *Social Service Review*, 64(1), 46–59. Retrieved from www.jstor.org/stable/30012066

Burns, L.R., & Fedewa, B.A. (2005). Cognitive styles: Links with perfectionistic thinking. *Personality and Individual Differences*, 38(1), 103–113. doi:10.1016/j.paid.2004.03.012

Clarà, M. (2015). What is reflection? Looking for clarity in an ambiguous notion. *Journal of Teacher Education*, 66(3), 261–271. doi:10.1177/0022487114552028

Damian, L.E., Stoeber, J., Negru-Subtirica, O., & Baban, A. (2016). On the development of perfectionism: The longitudinal role of academic achievement and academic efficacy. *Journal of Personality*, 85(4), 565–577. doi:10.1111/jopy.12261

Flett, G. L., Blankstein, K. R., Hewitt, P. L., & Koledin, S. (1992). Components of perfectionism and procrastination in college students. *Social Behavior and Personality*, 20(2), 85–94. doi:10.2444/sbp.1992.20.2.85

Flett, G.L., Hewitt, P.L., Oliver, J.M., & Macdonald, S. (2002). Perfectionism in children and their parents: A developmental analysis. In G.L. Flett & P.L. Hewitt (Eds.), *Perfectionism: Theory, research, and treatment* (pp. 89–132). Washington, DC: American Psychological Association.

Fook, J., & Askeland, G.A. (2007). Challenges of critical reflection: 'Nothing ventured, nothing gained'. *Social Work Education*, 26(5), 520–533. doi:10.1080/02615470601118662

Fook, J., & Gardner, F. (2007). *Practising critical reflection: A resource handbook*. Maidenhead: Open University Press.

Hewitt, P.L., & Flett, G.L. (1991). Perfectionism in the self and social contexts: Conceptualization, assessment, and association with psychopathology. *Journal of Personality and Social Psychology*, 60(3), 456–470. doi:10.1037/0022-3514.60.3.456

Hill, A.P., Hall, H.K., & Appleton, P.R. (2012). An assessment of the similarities between a measure of positive perfectionism and a measure of conscientious achievement striving. *Psychology of Sport and Exercise*, 13(3), 353–359. doi:10.1016/j.psychsport.2011.09.003

Kelly, J.D. (2015). Your best life: Perfectionism – The bane of happiness. *Clinical Orthopaedics and Related Research*, 473(10), 3108–3111. doi:10.1007/s11999-015-4279-9

Lay, C.H. (1986). At last, my research article on procrastination. *Journal of Research in Personality*, 20(4), 474–495. doi:10.1016/0092-6566(86)90127-3

Morley, C. (2004). Critical reflection in social work: A response to globalisation? *International Journal of Social Welfare*, 13(4), 297–303. doi:10.1111/j.1468-2397.2004.00325.x

Pacht, A.R. (1984). Reflections on perfection. *American Psychologist*, 39(4), 386–390. doi:10.1037/0003-066X.39.4.386

Rothman, J., Smith, W., Nakashima, J., Paterson, M.A., & Mustin, J. (1996). Client self-determination and professional intervention: Striking a balance. *Social Work*, 41 (4), 396–405. Retrieved from http://go.galegroup.com.proxy1.lib.uwo.ca/ps/i.do?p=AONE&u=lond95336&id=GALE|A19138011&v=2.1&it=r&sid=summon

Solomon, L.J., & Rothblum, E.D. (1984). Academic procrastination: Frequency and cognitive-behavioral correlates. *Journal of Counseling Psychology*, 31(4), 503–509. doi:10.1037/0022-0167.31.4.503

Sorotzkin, B. (1985). The quest for perfection: Avoiding guilt or avoiding shame? *Psychotherapy: Theory, Research, Practice, Training*, 22(3), 564–571. doi:10.1037/h0085541

Tice, D.M., & Baumeister, R.F. (1997). Longitudinal study of procrastination, performance, stress, and health: The costs and benefits of dawdling. *Psychological Science*, 8 (6), 454–458. Retrieved from www.jstor.org.proxy1.lib.uwo.ca/stable/40063233

Chapter 7

Confronting the role of my identity as a mother in my social work practice

Jackie Schindler

In alignment with Fook's (2002) idea, which was further developed in Fook and Gardner (2007), that hidden assumptions need to be unsettled in a way that creates discomfort within a person for learning to occur, Critical Reflection on Practice (CRoP) has been, and continues to be, an uncomfortable and anxiety-producing experience for me. In spite of this, I have chosen to share my personal exploration of a critical incident using Fook's (2002) two-stage CRoP approach.

As a student in a Master of Social Work (MSW) programme, I was enrolled in a Critical Reflection of Practice course that required me to identify and share a critical incident I had previously experienced with a group of fellow classmates. The following chapter is in alignment with the structure and learning that occurred over the course of the semester. I will begin by detailing an unsettling incident that occurred that led me to question my professional suitability for social work. I will then take you through my experiences in applying Fook's (2002) two-stage CRoP model. While doing so, I will focus on some of the unsettled assumptions that were unearthed, and I will demonstrate how I was able to reach different outcomes. As I share my experience with you, I will highlight aspects of the learning process that allowed me to engage more authentically in the CRoP process. In my concluding thoughts, I will explain how my new understandings will inform my future practice and research.

The incident

Fook and Gardner (2007) describe the process of critical reflection as one that shakes up assumptions that are deliberately hidden. This idea resonated with me, as the incident I will detail is, in many ways, similar to other incidents I have experienced. The uncomfortable feelings that these incidents generated within me resulted in me hiding from my negative feelings and not sharing them with others. When I would attempt to reflect on my personal and professional choices, I was left with a sense of guilt and shame over what I believed my actions said about my professional self. Unlike my previous attempts, Fook's (2002) CRoP model provided me with a framework to better understand and locate the implicit assumptions and beliefs that were guiding my actions, which, in turn, allowed for different outcomes.

Despite the anxiety I had over sharing the incident with my fellow group members, I was willing to take the risk of being vulnerable because of the safe environment created within the classroom. The professor stressed the importance of safety and demonstrated vulnerability when she shared a critical incident allowing the whole class to assist her with unpacking the incident using Fook's (2002) CRoP framework. While engaging in the process, she was genuine; she demonstrated compassion towards herself and openly acknowledged that it was difficult, even for her, to be vulnerable. In addition to my professor's willingness to be vulnerable, a fellow student also shared a personal incident in front of the class. The professor stressed that the purpose of the exercise was to allow the individuals sharing to learn more about themselves and highlighted the importance of others not judging and/or trying to reach conclusions for other students. This allowed me to reach the level of safety I needed to share the following incident.

The incident I shared involves a teen boy I met while volunteering weekly with a youth group. To maintain confidentiality, I have changed the name of the teen and removed identifying information. The teens involved with the group were recruited from various social service agencies. Those selected were identified as being motivated and possessing strengths to overcome the difficult circumstances they were experiencing. Unlike the previous groups I had facilitated, this group lacked clear boundaries between the facilitators and the members. For example, personal rides were provided to teens, facilitators assisted teens outside of the group, and social nights took place at facilitators' homes.

As a volunteer, I started to give weekly rides to and from the meetings to a boy named 'Cole'. Cole was in his late teens and lived alone in a teen housing complex run by a local mental health agency. During our rides together, Cole shared a significant amount of personal information. These personal disclosures included his gender dysphoria, his being severely bullied for not conforming to gender expectations, his recovery from drug addiction, his struggles with mental health problems and frequent anxiety attacks, and his strained family relationships. He also shared that he does not have family or supports in the city.

When sharing, Cole would often ask for my advice as a 'mother', which was something other teens did during our meetings. I was the only mature woman/ mother in the group and many of the teens lived without, or had tenuous/ nonexistent relationships with, their mothers. I did not mind helping Cole when he asked, but I often felt like I was acting in a mother role. This caused me to feel a little anxious/guilty, as I felt I was crossing a professional boundary that could potentially lead to harm.

At the time of the incident, Cole was going through a significant transition in his life; he had just started his first year of postsecondary school. When he

Confronting the role of identity 81

came to the weekly meeting on the night prior to the incident, he was sick with a cold. In addition to being physically sick, Cole shared privately that he had been struggling with his mental health due to school demands. Cole also explained that he knew he should go to the doctors but was not going to go. He was terrified to learn bad news about his health, as he had not followed up on previous health-related concerns noted by his doctor. Cole believed strongly that the stress of going to the doctors would result in him experiencing another anxiety attack. When I took Cole home I was worried about him; he did not look well and from what he had shared I did not think that he was adequately taking care of himself. I could not help but compare Cole to my daughter, and I felt bad that he did not have the comforts/support that she did.

The next evening, I received a text from Cole saying he was in the emergency room alone. This upset me and without hesitation, I called him to ask if he wanted my support. I had assumed that the text was his way of reaching out to me for help, because he was scared. Cole responded, stating that he wanted me to be there, so I went. I was worried that if I was not there to support Cole the hospital staff would treat him badly due to his nonconformance to societal gender expectations and/or increase his anxiety. While sitting in the emergency room with Cole, I started to question whether I had made the right choice to be there. My anxiety and guilt over my choice worsened when my husband later said, 'You know that line? You didn't just step over it, you hurdled it'.

In Schön's (1994) research on educating professionals about how to locate implicit assumptions, he differentiates between 'reflection in action and reflection on action' (as cited in Hickson, 2011, p. 831). The incident I shared is one that stuck with me, as I had done both. I had reflected while in the situation, and I had continued to reflect upon my actions following the incident. I was aware during the incident of what I was thinking and feeling; yet, I made the conscious choice to act and ignore the negative feelings I was experiencing. When later reflecting on my actions, I knew that I would not have done anything differently despite my belief that I had acted unprofessionally. For this reason, I chose this incident to share and critically reflect upon despite feeling incredibly vulnerable and worrying my fellow group members would judge me.

CRoP: Stage one

The crisis in confidence in social work practice that is caused by social work theories not adequately meeting the complexity of practice situations is believed by Schön (1987) to be the starting point of reflective practice (as cited in Fook & Gardner, 2007, p. 24). This rings true in my experience with Cole. I used reflective practice theory to help identify the explicit assumptions and expose the implicit assumptions that were not immediately obvious to me. I did this by looking at the discrepancy between what I claimed was informing my practice and what I actually did; it became clear to me that there was a gap. I drew on my knowledge of professionalism and boundaries when thinking about the incident. I had internalised the belief that a professional social worker keeps a safe distance from their clients and does not act on or have intense emotions related to what their clients are experiencing. As a new social worker and in my role as a research assistant on a study assessing professional suitability and gatekeeping in social work, it is important to me that I am identified by others as being professionally suitable for practising social work. The need to be seen as a professional has been further instilled in me by my university's school of social work policies and focus on insisting students be mindful of how their personal lives will impact the public's opinion of professional social workers. Looking at the difference between what I said I valued and what the situation required allowed me to identify that the gap that existed was filled by theories on oppression, social justice, advocacy, and feminism, not by my desire to meet my own emotional needs of helping a child. I then asked myself what this said about me and what I value in society. I identified that I value fairness and people being treated with kindness and respect. I greatly value being supported by people when I need it, and I disagree with our society's approach of not standing up for vulnerable people. Through a variety of international experiences with collectivist cultures, I have come to disagree with our Western individualistic culture's preoccupation with assigning value to independence and seeing it as a sign of strength. Being dependent and receiving help from others is not only natural but also beneficial for the mental health of all the individuals in a society. As a feminist, I disagree with the artificial boundaries that have been created that separate me as a social worker from the people with whom I work. I also strongly value the traditional African practice of 'othermothers' (Collin, 1993), which takes a communal care approach to childrearing (as cited in Green, 2015, p. 202). I recognise that I cannot be everything to my daughter, and I do not want the burden that comes with trying to be. I want her to identify with and have opportunities to learn and be mothered by other women throughout her life.

The use of reflexivity within the CRoP model requires us to let go of our personal judgments and to ask ourselves what about me has me seeing the situation this way. It recognises that everything about who we are, and our contexts, will impact the way social workers and our clients create knowledge. Using this theoretical approach, I questioned what about me as a social worker and a mother had me see the situation the way I did. As a social worker, my awareness was drawn to the oppressive forces at play in Cole's life, his need for advocacy, and my need to maintain boundaries and act professionally. As a mother, I saw a child hurting that needed help, comfort, and support. My current middle-class social status, as well as my historical lower-class status, further influenced how I saw the situation. Growing up in, and having a family that still lives in, poverty, I have first-hand experience with how people treat you differently. My experiences of living both with and without power have resulted in my awareness of the power I now have and the many power imbalances that exist within our society.

When looking at my own personal experiences throughout my life that may have influenced the lens through which I saw the situation, I was drawn to my childhood experiences, to my experiences as an adult, and, specifically, to my father's resistance to accessing medical care and my role as advocate for him prior to his death. Throughout my childhood, my parents suffered from addiction and mental health problems, which meant they were not always able to provide me with the help, care, or support that I needed. Cole's experiences, feelings, and struggles were very similar to mine, and, as a result, I had increased empathy. Looking back on my teenage years, I recognised that I was able to get through difficult times because of the adults who helped me. For example, when I was homeless at 16, my boyfriend's mother gave me a place to live despite the discomfort she had over me living with her teenage son. My father's experiences with receiving healthcare additionally played a role in how I interpreted the risks associated with Cole's situation. My father did not seek needed medical attention and died earlier than he should have due to not wanting to be treated poorly by healthcare professionals. His addictions and lower-class status had resulted in him being judged and treated poorly by doctors and medical staff in the past. When my father was unable to walk and was forced to seek medical attention, I witnessed the stigmatising treatment he had feared. It was heartbreaking, and I continue to struggle with the anger I feel over what occurred. Throughout the six months of caring for my father before he died, I had to regularly advocate for him. Furthermore, I noticed that when I was with him, his anxiety decreased, and the medical staff treated him more respectfully.

When I reflected on whether the situation with Cole would have been different if he were not a teen, I realised it would not have been. In my other volunteer roles, as well as with my father, I provide similar care to people of all ages and genders. Although I had thought of my actions with Cole to be a form of mothering, I am now aware that the qualities within me that I associate with being a mother are ones that I use in all areas of my life and with people of all ages. When I care for people who are not children, I am not worried about mothering them; however, it has been insinuated that I am creating some kind of dependency on me and contributing to people's inability to care for themselves. When looking for different perspectives that may be missing, I wondered if I would be struggling with the feelings and choices I made regarding Cole if I were a man. I do not think I would. I would not be worried about being accused of mothering, and I would not be worried about others seeing my emotions as being unprofessional. Women who express emotions in the professional world are often treated as unstable, whereas men's status is often increased by expressing emotions. For example, when a woman cries over a family she is working with her ability to maintain professionalism is called into question; yet, if a man cries, he is applauded for being a caring person.

Using postmodernism and, specifically, skills of deconstruction, I looked at how I had constructed my identity in relation to others, what dominant discourses were present, and if I had created any binaries. With the help of my group members, I recognised that although I was acting in a volunteer position offering support to the youth group, I had constructed my identity as a social worker and a mother, not as a volunteer. I have become conscious of the fact that both of these identities are carried with me in everything that I do, although I believe they are each done for different reasons.

I have noticed that despite my feminist beliefs about mothers, I am perpetuating the dominant discourse that devalues the qualities typically associated with and attributed to mothers. I have internalised the patriarchal ideals of professionalism that do not value openness, caretaking, or the sharing of emotional states. Despite my beliefs about the value of mothers, I continue to feel that I am doing something wrong when I mother children that are not my own. It has become obvious to me that the beliefs I hold about who I am and how I believe I should practise are predominantly influenced by a feminist standpoint and are at odds with the beliefs I have internalised about boundaries and professionalism in social work. I struggle with the imposed boundaries, as I feel it separates me and gives me a power that I do not want and/or deserve. I question who has created the dominant discourse around boundaries and professionalism that exist within social work and who benefits from the power it creates.

When looking for the construction of binaries in my incident, I noticed that I had created a few. One binary I had created was related to my professionalism; I was either a professional who was maintaining boundaries or I was not. When I reflected on my experience with Cole, I was able to see many ways in which it was not an either/or situation. Although I had gone to the hospital to help Cole, I had still maintained some boundaries and professionalism with him. This was confirmed for me when I remembered that the hospital workers had identified me as his social worker. Another binary I created had to do with my identity. I saw my identity as either being a social worker or a mother. I did not leave room for both to coexist, creating the feeling that I was forced to choose one or the other. It has become obvious to me that although I feel obligated to carry my social work identity with me in almost everything I do, including volunteer roles, I do not feel the same way about my identity as a mother. I, instead, feel that I should disconnect from who I am as a mother as it may result in harming others.

The final theoretical perspective within the CRoP model, Critical Social Theory, led me to examine and understand the types of power that existed and how they influenced me. My personal experiences with poverty and with my father resulted in me seeing the hospital staff as having all the power and Cole not having any. I also saw myself as having a power that could positively influence the situation. Looking at my incident from a perspective of power, I am able to see that my beliefs about the power imbalance impacted my decision to go to the hospital. Although I had emotions related to Cole and his situation, it was his lack of power in the situation that caused me to go.

CRoP: Stage two

Prior to critically reflecting on my incident with Cole, I had worried that I would be viewed by my fellow group members as being unprofessional for acting as a mother to him. After initially completing stage one of the CRoP model, my perspective on professionalism and my views regarding the choices I made with Cole had changed. I was able to view my professionalism as existing on a continuum; it is not all or nothing and it should not be determined by a single action or feeling. Through the use of reflective practice theory and examining my implicit assumptions, I was able to recognise that I had not simply acted on my emotions and desire to mother Cole. Unbeknownst to me, I had drawn on a slew of social work knowledge and theories to inform my actions. Recognising this allowed me to see that the choices I made regarding Cole were professional decisions that align with social work values. I attribute the dynamics of my group to enabling me to engage more authentically in the process and reach the outcomes I did. Throughout the work we did together, my group members attempted to help me understand the reasons behind my decision to help Cole, and they asked questions in a way that made it obvious they were trying to help me unearth what I needed. Having their support and not feeling judged decreased the amount of anxiety I had, allowing me to engage more authentically than I had previously been willing to do.

Similar to Hickson's (2011) account of critical reflection, I was thankful for the time given between stage one and stage two, as I was able to continue ruminating over the incident and what had been uncovered. I was intrigued by what I had unearthed, but as I considered it, I came to the realisation that I had not gotten as far as I needed to. Despite recognising that legitimate social work theories had informed my actions, I still felt unprofessional as a result of my desire to mother Cole. I was continuing to hold the view that my identity as a mother needed to be separate from my identity as a social worker. Prior to moving on to stage two, I was encouraged by my professor to consider how my role as a volunteer and the blurred boundaries that had been created within the youth group may have impacted my decisions. When looking over the incident, I questioned the importance of those details and why I had chosen to include them. I realised that although those factors likely contributed to my actions, I believe I had included the information as a buffer to protect myself from fully acknowledging or disclosing what I knew to be true. Selecting an incident where I was acting in a volunteer role and providing others with the information about the blurred boundaries allowed me to not fully experience the anxiety and shame I felt over the belief that I was mothering social work clients. As I explored this further, I recognised that I was holding on to the belief that as a volunteer, I was allowed to be imperfect and, in some ways, I was allowed to be less than other social workers. I believed my fellow class-mates would not hold me accountable for my actions or judge me as harshly if they viewed me as a volunteer. Although I recognise that at the time I initially shared the incident I didn't fully feel safe yet with my group members, I believe the need to protect myself had more to do with the underlying belief that I am less than my professional counterparts. I suspect these feelings are related to my experiences of growing up in poverty, the resulting stigma I experienced, and the belief that I need to change and/or hide the socially devalued parts of who I am in order to be accepted within academia and the professional world.

While reflecting on this knowledge about myself, I attended a conference with Cole where he had the opportunity to present to a group of social service providers. Cole was sharing his personal story and the responses from the women in the participatory session following were groundbreaking for me. Not only had many of the women responded to him in a similar maternal way as I had, but one woman, in particular, had also shared during the discussion that she mothers the teens that she works with. The combination of the woman's disclosure and the sheer amount of confidence she possessed when she disclosed it, alongside witnessing the maternal behaviours of the other women, was significant for me; I no longer felt alone. Although this was initially very comforting, the realisation also created many questions that I could not answer. For example: If I am not alone in this, why do I hold these negative assumptions about mothering in practice? I have numerous social worker friends that are mothers, and if others utilise mothering in their work, why have I not heard about it before? Is it possible that my maternal identity and the qualities I attribute to it are actually valuable to social work practice? Is it possible that others do it but do not struggle with feeling unprofessional in the manner that I do?

To help answer these questions, I attempted to locate social work literature that would help me better understand what I, and likely other women, must be experiencing in their social work practice. After searching extensively and enlisting the help of a librarian at my university, I was disheartened when I did not come across anything that accurately reflected what I had identified and was experiencing. I did come across Donald Winnicott's (1971) theory on the 'good enough mother', and I was reminded that he and other object relations theorists had cast therapists as replacement mothers (as cited in Bueskens, 2014, p. 86). I was also reminded of the relational model's perspective that views collaboration, attunement, and the sharing of emotional states with clients as beneficial and necessary (Bueskens, 2014). I was struck by the realisation that not only had I been aware of these theories but I had also, on many occasions, claimed that my social work practice was informed by them. This created further confusion within me; if I ascribed to social work theories that allowed my maternal presence to be integrated in social work practice, why was I carrying fear, shame, and confusion over doing so?

Unable to find the answers I was looking for within social work literature, I decided to use a more feminist lens. This approach allowed me to not only draw conclusions about my feelings but also to establish a theory on why the literature related to my experience was virtually nonexistent. In Women in Context: Toward a Feminist Reconstruction of Psychotherapy, Irene Stiver (1994) writes about women's experiences at work. She states that many women experience internal 'conflict between their sense of self at work and their sense of self in their personal lives' (p. 434).

This not only verified for me that I was not alone in my struggle, but it also helped me realise that this was an issue that women had been struggling with for many years, as the book was published in 1994. To understand the issues that create this conflict, Stiver (1994) explains that we need to look at the many structures and forces at play within our society that impact women. I noticed that the qualities Stiver (1994) listed as being typically associated with women are the ones I have assigned to my maternal identity. These qualities include, but are not limited to, being accommodating, caring for others, being more person directed, and being emotionally expressive. Stiver (1994) highlights that our society's devaluation of these qualities has led to women feeling ashamed of who they are, experiencing self-doubt, and questioning their professionalism. Stiver (1994) draws awareness to how the 'female' designated qualities that are encouraged in childhood are later denounced by girls in adolescence when they learn they are not valued in society. At the same time, adolescent girls will attempt to distance themselves from their mothers as they view their mothers as the embodiment and source of these devalued qualities. The need to disconnect from and to overcome these 'female' qualities continues once they enter the professional world, as they are viewed as personal defects or signs of deficiency (Stiver, 1994). Recognising that I had likely been trying to disconnect from the mothering qualities I possessed since adolescence helped me understand why despite learning and identifying with theories that allowed my maternal presence, I had still carried guilt and shame.

The metaphorical male yardstick that is used to measure women and determine whether they are competent and professional is identified by Stiver (1994) as a source of women's struggle in the workplace. Women are taught to take power, to be competitive, and to act impersonally, which can interfere with a woman's ability to integrate who they are personally with who they are required to be professionally (Stiver, 1994). Women experience self-doubt about their competency, continually worry that they are behaving unprofessionally, and struggle to adapt to what they believe are the expectations of professional behaviour, as it often conflicts with their experiences, inclinations, and talents. This results in women feeling that their personal identity and qualities are bad and must be kept out of the workplace (Stiver, 1994). I had experienced the same emotions and done this very thing in my attempt to hide and separate my identity as a mother from my social work practice for fear I would be considered incompetent and/or unprofessional. I saw my emotions when working with Cole to be a sign that I could not be trusted to act competently. I had internalised that the presence of strong emotions suggested that I was out of control. Even after the recognition at the end of stage one that my emotions had not dictated my actions with Cole, I was still left with the fear that this may not always be the case. The very existence of these emotions suggested that I might not always be able to control them. I remained in fear of my emotions making me appear unprofessional, which was one of the factors prompting me to realise that I had not uncovered everything I needed to at the end of stage one.

In Mothering and Psychoanalysis: Clinical, Sociological, and Feminist Perspectives, Shaw and Breckenridge (2014) question how it is that a female dominated profession like psychoanalysis can be so invested in the image of a therapist as a blank screen that it lacks the capacity to explain the 'everyday messiness of working women in this field' (as cited in Bueskens, 2014, p. 155).

They further wonder how in 2012 it was possible to have so little research on the reciprocal influences of mothering and therapy and its impact on professional and personal development. Similarly, Bueskens (2014) and Botticelli (2014) both speak of psychotherapy as being a practice of care and tie the lack of the profession's recognition of this with gender (as cited in Bueskens, 2014). They believe that fully acknowledging psychotherapy as a practice of care would lead to its de-professionalisation and a tarnishing of the profession. The low value assigned to caretaking within our society is related to the fact that it is often performed by women and considered a feminine characteristic. Given the similarities between social work and psychotherapy, and the lack of social work research in this area, I cannot help but wonder if our profession is also purposively avoiding the issue for fear of tarnishing and devaluing our profession. While I believe gatekeeping to be an important part of research and necessary for practice, I cannot help but wonder how the dominant discourses and perspectives of those who are performing gatekeeping measures, such as universities, are perpetuating this movement away from valuing care.

Conclusion

In the chapter Melissa: Lost in a Fog: Or 'How Difficult is This Mommy Stuff Anyway', Sheehy (2014) writes, 'How little we understood the forces at work upon and within us. How we blamed ourselves for our own confusion and inability to find balance, thinking we had made so many choices. But did we?' (p. 216).

As I prepared to draw conclusions from this experience, Sheehy's words resonated with me, especially in regards to how I can integrate my maternal identity with my professional one. With society's continued devaluation of my qualities as a woman and as a mother, and the lack of research and theory available to help me move forward with integrating and bringing my maternal identity with me into my social work practice, I remain with the understanding that this has not been resolved for me. Although I am left with the awareness that I have not figured out how to fully integrate these two meaningful identities, I no longer feel alone in coping with this issue. Even more, I do not blame myself for my confusion or my inability to know how to move forward. Understanding that I am not responsible for this dilemma will allow me to feel less shame and guilt over the competing desires I experience. Knowing that this will be an ongoing struggle for me, I will continue to use the mantra 'I REFUSE to hide or feel guilty for the presence of my maternal identity in my social work practice.' I believe my mantra will help remind me of the value that exists in bringing my maternal identity with me into practice and that it will help me stand up to the dominant discourses that contribute to my shame.

As a final thought, I think it is important to note that although I did not address the impact of mothering on the clients that I work with, this is an area that significantly informed my thoughts and decisions in the past, and it will continue to do so in the future. I hope at some point to have the opportunity to research the impact of mothering on social work practice from the client's perspective.

References

Botticelli, S. (2014). Globalization, psychoanalysis, and the provision of care. In P. Bueskens (Ed.), *Mothering and psychoanalysis: Clinical, sociological, and feminist perspectives* (pp. 463–471). Bradford, Canada: Demeter Press.

Bueskens, P. (2014). Is therapy a form of paid mothering? In P. Bueskens (Ed.), *Mothering and psychoanalysis: Clinical, sociological, and feminist perspectives* (pp. 85–112). Bradford, Canada: Demeter Press.

Fook, J. (2002). *Social work: A critical approach to practice*. London: SAGE.

Fook, J., & Gardner, F. (2007). *Practicing critical reflection: A resource handbook*. Maidenhead: Open University Press.

Green, F. (2015). Re-conceptualizing motherhood: Reaching back to move forward . *Journal of Family Studies*, 21(3), 196–207. doi:10.1080/13229400.2015.1086666

Hickson, H. (2011). Critical reflection: Reflecting on learning to be reflective. *Reflective Practice*, 12(6), 829–839. doi:10.1080/14623943.2011.616687

Shaw, E., & Breckenridge, J. (2014). 'There is no longer room for me on your lap': How being pregnant and becoming a mother impacts the therapy relationship. In P. Bueskens (Ed.), *Mothering and psychoanalysis: Clinical, sociological and feminist perspectives* (pp. 139–160). Bradford, Canada: Demeter Press.

Sheehy, M. (2014). Melissa: Lost in a fog: Or 'How difficult is this mommy stuff anyway?' In P. Bueskens (Ed.), *Mothering and psychoanalysis: Clinical, sociological, and feminist perspectives* (pp. 213–218). Bradford, Canada: Demeter Press.

Stiver, P. (1994). Women's struggles in the workplace: A relational model. In M. Mirkin (Ed.), *Women in context: Toward a feminist reconstruction of psychotherapy* (pp. 433–452). New York: Guilford Press.

Chapter 8

Critical reflection on practice
Reflecting on confidence and group dynamic

Ashley Elsie-McKendrick

The Critical Reflection on Practice (CRoP) process felt both fulfilling and sometimes like a rollercoaster ride during my Master of Social Work (MSW) programme in Ontario, Canada. To illustrate this, I will describe my critical incident, my uncovered assumptions, and realisations. I will then describe my experience with the second Stage of the CRoP process both within my group and on my own. The process for Stages 1 and 2 differed in the richness and ease of practising each step.

During the MSW programme, learning about the CRoP process (Stage 1 in particular) was incredibly rewarding due to our instructor's (Laura Béres) teaching style and the course content. We began the course by learning the foundations of CRoP and practising Stage 1 with small groups. However, Stage 2 was challenging to apply, mostly due to my group's dynamic and to the overall short 13-week duration of the course. Other groups in my class formed organically, whereas ours did not. Our group's dynamic created difficulties that precluded the full CRoP process from unfolding. I completed Stage 1 with my group, and I obtained beneficial learning and insights. Unfortunately, Stage 2 did not unfold in our group for me: Only one group member completed it with the group, and I tackled parts on my own and with another group member. Critical reflection, combined with our challenging group dynamic, inspired me to gain new learning about myself and the CRoP process. After a jagged path of reflecting, I developed a mantra for practice that will hopefully cement my confidence for future challenges.

The outline of this chapter roughly follows the steps and flow of the CRoP process by beginning with the critical incident and flowing into Stages 1 and 2. Therefore, I will outline my critical incident, describe my learnings and insights from Stage 1, describe challenges I experienced with Stage 2, and conclude with important new insights about my overall experience of learning and practising CRoP. Finally, I describe how my confidence both as a social worker and professional has shifted due to engaging in the CRoP process.

My critical incident

My confidence during and following my Bachelor of Social Work (BSW) programme was lacking. I did not feel secure in my identity as a social worker. However, two years after graduating from the BSW programme, I secured my first social-work-related position. It was a full-time intake and administration position in a student support centre. When I was hired, I was excited to begin my social work career. My role involved triaging students to connect them to services related to their concerns. The centre included psychological counselling, academic support and accommodation, and other student support services. Each service had its own director, with one director overseeing all of them; except for psychological counselling. The head of psychological counselling was the director of the entire centre. Both I and the main psychological counselling intake worker reported to her. My colleague's position was permanent. Despite being hired on for full-time hours, I was not hired on a permanent basis. I was hired on a contract with the chance for permanency in a year, given that I was a new professional.

The centre responded to a variety of concerns with varying severity. The procedure for students presenting in crisis (e.g. suicidal thoughts) was that my supervisor (the centre's director) and the other psychological counsellors would be available for support for the student and intake staff. The centre closed at 4:30 pm. On the day of my critical incident, the main psychological counselling intake worker left early (at 4:00 pm). As he was leaving, a student arrived. I was alone in the front office with the student.

Things became complicated as the student disclosed that she had suicidal thoughts. I was afraid, because I had not done in-depth training on suicide intervention. After completing an assessment and building rapport with the student, I called the psychological counsellors to see if someone was still available to provide support. I could have called Campus Police but was previously told by my supervisor that that was the last resort. I felt I needed support so I approached my supervisor. I asked her if she would talk to the student while the student or I called a friend or family member to bring her to the nearest hospital. My supervisor said 'no' and wanted me to handle it. By that time, it was 5:00 pm and my husband was waiting for me outside to drive us home. I could not communicate with him without inappropriately disrupting the intervention with the student.

Defeated and frustrated, I returned to the student. The student seemed calm, but the situation was critical in my mind: I was afraid that she could escalate, hurt herself, or run. She called a friend who agreed to pick her up, so I waited with her. We explored why she was feeling suicidal and how we could help her feel safe. Another hour passed, and her friend arrived, so I texted my husband. He was worried about me, since I was not usually so late at work.

In the end, the student and I were safe. However, I felt dismissed by my supervisor's seeming incredulity that I would come to her instead of handling it on my own. While my time at the position was not *all* negative, this event marked the first of several difficult experiences that I have ruminated on ever since. Because this was the first event to stick out in my mind, I believed it to be suitable for further reflection and the overall CRoP process.

Stage 1: Reflection

When reflecting on the incident with my group I looked at this incident through the lens of the more painful experiences while working there. Because my experiences evoked unpleasant feelings, I never unpacked those feelings until the CRoP process. I resented the job, my supervisor, and my coworker, and did not feel comfortable reflecting on it until the course. As part of the in-class work, my group attempted to follow Fook's critical reflection on practice model as presented in Fook and Gardner (2007). Having our readings, class notes, and well-researched theories to aide us, Stage 1 became easier the more we engaged in it.

From Stage 1, I uncovered specific feelings, assumptions, and values that influenced my actions during and within the telling of the incident. My group asked me questions informed by the four theories inherent to CRoP: reflective practice, reflexivity, critical social theory, and postmodernism. We accessed the Fook and Gardner (2007) textbook many times to help shape our questions. Through these questions, I realised that I felt unqualified, scared, angry, and betrayed during my incident. Postmodernist and critical social theory questions helped me realise that my telling of the incident showed how unconfident I felt about my abilities and to whom I gave my power in the incident. How I told the incident shaped how I thought of myself and others in the situation. I was not secure in my social worker identity and felt alone, which made me nervous.

My nervousness also stemmed from the challenging of some of my implicit assumptions about the workplace throughout my incident. Regarding the CRoP process, Hickson (2011) explains that 'critical reflection occurs when the individual is able to understand and challenge the validity of their assumptions' (p. 831). I assumed all supervisors unconditionally support their staff. Reflexivity and reflective practice questions helped me realise the limitations of my assumption. I also realised that this assumption stemmed from my values of collaboration, relationship, and support. The incident contradicted my assumption. My supervisor described me as a competent social worker in conversation with others but did not support me when I came to her in need. The other intake worker was not there to support me either. My supervisor consistently supported that intake worker, despite that my supervisor perceived him as being competent.

I assumed I deserved support, which connects to my values of respect, safety, and being there for others. Examining how I formed these values made me reach into my history and how I have built my values. I grew up in an all-female family after my father passed away when I was seven years old. My mum was immensely supportive and hard-working. She expected my sister and me to work hard and would also help us whenever we needed or wanted. We had to be there for each other unconditionally. I admire my mum. My supervisor and my mother knew of each other long before I was hired. Stage 1 of the reflection process helped me realise that I assumed my supervisor would possess some of my mum's supportiveness because my mum held my supervisor in positive regard. The reality was not as simple as I made it seem in my incident, because my supervisor was sometimes supportive. For example, while my supervisor sometimes did not support my views, she supported me when I had personal struggles (illness, personal tragedy). Postmodernist questions encouraged me to see more than one perspective of my time during the position.

In addition to the aforementioned values, I value honesty, authenticity, transparency, and independence. My mum helped me to become the woman I am today. She fostered my independence from a nurturing place. That nurturing led me to social work in my early 20s, which shaped my values of collaboration, authenticity, and transparency. These values stem from the Ontario College of Social Workers and Social Service Workers values and ethics (OCSWSSW, 2008). Canadian social workers are required to challenge power imbalances within systems and between worker and client through collaboration. We are required to be transparent with clients about services and our scope of practice (OCSWSSW, 2008). Within CRoP, critical social theory echoes the OCSWSSW ethic of examining power dynamics when there is a potential imbalance of power.

Aside from cementing already established social work values and ethics, CRoP helped me to understand why certain values are important to me as a professional. For example, CRoP helped me to articulate why authenticity was important to me. Adamowich, Kumsa, Rego, Stoddart, and Vito (2014) state that our duty as reflective social workers is to be 'self-aware and take responsibility for our thoughts and actions' (p. 132). Learning the CRoP process helped me to expand on this notion of authenticity through looking at its origins in my life, how I define authenticity, and how I believe others to define authenticity. I realised how important it is to use authenticity to reduce bias and power differentials within systems and between worker and client. However, I saw myself as an inexperienced, incompetent social worker who was not prepared to help a suicidal client. I saw the rejection from my supervisor as a personal failure.

My group helped me realise that I did not fail and that I accessed skills, strengths-based values, and theoretical knowledge to help the student. After approaching my supervisor, I returned to the student with one important social work tool in mind: start where the client is. I tried to connect with the student on a human level. Instead of asking for information about a client, I got to know the young woman. I validated her feelings while upholding my ethical obligation to keep her safe (OCSWSSW, 2008). She called a friend who came to her aide. I supported her after all.

Did my supervisor know that I could help the client on my own or did she simply expect me to? I wondered if my asking her for help was a nuisance, because I should have known what to do. That is an unfair assumption that I never explored until the CRoP process both in class and with my group. Perhaps, she may have assumed too much, and I assumed too little about my capabilities. Yet, I held a 'how dare they' perspective, which disregarded the humanity and fallibility of myself, my supervisor, and colleague.

I held my supervisor and colleague to a high standard of practice, knowledge, and social skills because they were psychological counsellors with some combined 60-plus years of experience. I thought my being new meant they would support my learning. Instead, I felt devalued because I was new. The incident and ensuing experiences hurt, because my view of the job, the staff, and my supervisor shattered my assumptions about them. The job was supposed to be my first 'real' job after struggling to find one since graduating from my BSW. I heard great things about the agency, but my reality there was disappointing.

CRoP helped me realise that I maintained the power imbalance between my supervisor, colleague, and myself. I constructed myself as their subordinate. I was a new worker who was at the mercy of their wisdom and experience. I made myself a martyr from this incident. People I confided in told me that 'politics exist everywhere' and that 'every workplace has toxicity'. I held a contradiction in my mind that while workplaces may have toxicity, I did not believe they had to. My social work values made me strive for equality. I did not want to believe that I had to accept my position as a subordinate in a toxic environment. After some time in the position, I challenged the status quo and offered new ideas for process and services. They were shut down by my colleague and/or supervisor. The rejection became stressful. I left after two years, which ironically prolonged my stress. I struggled with leaving a well-paying job for reasons that seemed to be widespread and normal, according to everyone else.

My remaining time at the job was shaped by the sustained power imbalances between myself and both my colleague and supervisor. My group members' questions throughout stage 1 of the CRoP process helped me realise that my objections about the job were largely due to misplaced power. The supervisor had too much power in the organisation as she was the director of both one department within the organisation *and* the overall director. Resources and attention were given first to her department (over the others within the organisation). What pushed me to leave was that the future of my job depended on the other intake worker's job description. The agency let me down by keeping me on contract for two years when I was promised permanent (secure) work originally. They stalled my security because of delays in processing my colleague's job description. It seemed like my supervisor moved mountains for my colleague even if they were not fully ethical nor approved by relevant parties (e.g. human resources). However, she pushed for the changes to further his career, while my career was put on hold.

Through a critical social theory lens, I participated in my own 'domination', because I transferred my power to my supervisor and colleague (Fook & Gardner, 2007; p. 35). I felt powerless, but I had more power than I thought. After critically reflecting on the experience, I realised that I used my power to leave a distressing situation. I now feel less viscerally about the incident, because I now know what to do in the situation of a client presenting with suicidal ideation. The most important point is what I learned to do about the power imbalance and how to deal with potentially unsupportive future work environments. I value awareness of personal power and responsibility because of my history of loss. I have had to do things for myself and my family. The power imbalance between my supervisor and I rattled my internal sense of power and I easily gave it up, because I lacked confidence. 'What ifs' are not healthy but I wonder what would have happened if I had had more confidence and upheld my own power.

The fact that I could reflect this deeply and arrive at new ways of viewing my incident, means that Stage 1 unfolded well within my group and my understanding of the process was enriched by my learning in class. However, Stage 2 was a mess. Despite learning about both Stages in class and completing rich readings for both stages, Stage 2 became wrought with anxiety for myself and my group.

Stage 2: My own learning

Before I cover our group dynamic and how it affected the CRoP process, I will address my learning from Stage 2 that I completed with a fellow group member and on my own. The reflection process was exhausting. I am embarrassed by my initial reactions to my incident. I lumped my incident with every other negative experience that happened for the duration of the position. The job created health problems for me, which made it difficult to reflect until the CRoP course. I had tunnel vision with the incident. As Hickson (2011) states, 'what you see is whatever you are looking for' (p. 829). This rang true for me: Every aspect of the incident was proof of the negative views I had about my supervisor and colleague until I could critically reflect on it. The incident was not truly a tale of injustice: It was a learning opportunity.

The most profound learning I accomplished relates to my identity. I did not identify as a social worker during my incident, even though I was a registered social worker. After uncovering and naming my values from Stage 1, I realised that I acted on social work values that were already a part of my identity. I upheld key values inherent to social work. My identity as a social worker began to consolidate. During Stage 1, I thought that not being able to help the student on my own, being rejected by my supervisor, and later leaving my job meant that I was not an effective social worker. After critically reflecting, I learned that I satisfied my social work values by helping the student and respected my own dignity by eventually leaving the job. Leaving did not mean that I failed nor that I was weak.

I felt weak, because I left a well-paying job when I 'should' have stuck it out. Yet, I felt compelled to leave, because I was burnt out and my health was compromised. I wanted to discover if there was a connection between my distress and my job situation. I sought literature regarding temporary employment and the potential effects on worker health. In their study, Lewchuk, Clarke, and de Wolff (2008) found that a less secure employment situation is associated with negative health outcomes. At the time of the MSW CRoP course, I had not worked in social work since my BSW and was searching for secure employment. I wanted to gain experience in social work and help my husband with finances. The position was supposed to be permanent but that was not honoured. Given the employment climate in Canada, 'competitive pressures are leading employers to hold off on long-term commitments and save money by hiring short-term employees' (Immen, 2011). Leaving the job meant jumping into an abyss of insecure employment. I felt like I put myself and my husband at risk, so my reasons for leaving had to be salient and legitimate to make such a risky move.

Compared to those in long-term roles, precarious workers (those in repeated temporary, short-term contracts) are twice as likely to have mental health problems and to delay having children (Mojtehedzadeh & Monsebraaten, 2015). This finding disturbed me. I realised how much I was delaying my life goals for this job. I wanted a perfect, secure job, so I could afford to pursue my MSW and have children once I established myself as a social worker. I put so much hope into that job. Because I was on contract, I feared making a mistake or being thought of as stupid by colleagues. This fear informed my actions during my critical incident. It was validating to learn that my fear was partially founded in something external. While I value responsibility and inner power, it can be exhausting to put all responsibility and blame on myself. It is important to recognise social context and influences on one's construction of reality and identity. I allowed my identity to be prescribed by the job description while not recognising my own values, familial influences, and social context.

Stage 2 principles that focus on developing new techniques or theories of practice helped me realise that I possess tools that I could have used during my incident and can use in the future (Fook & Gardner, 2007). For example, because I do not think I clearly communicated my confusion and distress with my supervisor, I thought about how I communicate best. After reading Hickson's (2011) article on her own reflection process, I noticed that she mentioned using a journal as a method of reflection. A proverbial lightbulb went off in my head. I love to write prose, poetry, and to journal. I could have used my writing skills to communicate my concerns with my supervisor. The writing process helps me figure out what words and stories are informed by emotion or logic. Moreover, writing helps me to communicate in a calm and collected manner that uses the best of emotion and logic.

I thought about using a journal for future critical incidents and for reflecting, in general, during the MSW. Therefore, I decided to journal during my MSW placement. This process was valuable, uplifting, and validating. I usually prefer to process my emotions privately. Journaling allowed for a private outlet to reflect. However, I did not use my journal for critical reflection due to time constraints in the programme. I hope that future opportunities arise in my career for both private and group critical reflection. My experience with group critical reflection did not allow for safe exploration of vulnerable issues. Hence, a more positive and cohesive group CRoP experience could inspire an ongoing practice both on my own and with others.

Stage 2 interrupted: The group dynamic

Our MSW cohort struggled with cohesion. Our MSW orientation did not allow us to get to know each other except on a superficial level of learning each other's names and previous schools. In our CRoP class, some students sat with people they already knew and were comfortable with and formed natural groups. My group had a few members who were familiar but did not know each other well. We also had a couple of members who were even less known to the group. The lack of cohesion within the larger and smaller groups set the stage for a challenging environment within which to conduct an effective CRoP process. Safety and respect were not easily established within the group.

Stemming from clashing personalities and an incident involving one member invalidating another member's incident, our group culture and process suffered. According to Jan Fook and Fiona Gardner, 'group culture. . .is the most important aspect of critical reflection' (p. 79). The essence of a CRoP group culture involves building on 'safety and respect' and 'critical acceptance' (Fook & Gardner, 2007; pp. 78–79). Critical acceptance should breathe life into the person sharing their incident as the CRoP process unfolds. Critical acceptance posits that there is a democratic culture of respect, 'full disclosure' from each member, realisation that the focus must be on the incident and not 'past traumas', and a foundation of fostering 'further learning', 'exploration', and 'many "whys"' (Fook & Gardner, 2007; pp. 80–83). Our group understood an essential element of the CRoP process: what comprises a 'critical' incident. To question the validity of an incident being 'critical' to a group member is potentially damaging. Asserting that an incident is not 'critical' goes against the inquisitive, respectful, and postmodernist multi-perspective tenets of CRoP.

Upon sharing her critical incident, our group member was met with a challenge to the validity of her feelings about her incident and why it was 'critical' to her. While the purpose of the group is not to establish the validity of an incident, it is also imperative that a member of a critical reflection group will not be made to defend their incident, which she felt she had to do (Ruch, 2016; pp. 25–26). If a member wants to introduce new perspectives, they can do so from a place of 'exposing choice' instead of a place of attack (Fook & Gardner, 2007, p. 81). Given the invalidation from one member, my group did not possess the necessary ability to safely challenge the 'traditional assumptions about learning and professional practice' that can lead to rich growth and learning through CRoP (Fook & Gardner, 2007; p. 79).

Looking back on the process and that our group process could be a critical incident, it frustrates me that one interaction tainted my group's ability to feel safe in being vulnerable. It would have been valuable to engage in challenging learning and practice assumptions that we were experiencing in our MSW programme. For example, our MSW courses possessed a 'task-focused orientation', which focused on solving problems (Fook & Gardner, 2007; p. 79). Ironically, even though the CRoP course was part of the MSW programme, some of the other courses were in stark contrast to CRoP's main tenets. One course focused on objective, 'technical and rationally derided knowledge' so that we would become outcome-oriented social workers at the end of that course (Fook & Gardner, 2007; p. 79). The outcome-oriented focus of that course abides by 'procedural workplace cultures', wherein predictability and outcomes are paramount (Fook & Gardner, 2007; p. 79).

It is refreshing to be able to critically analyse hegemonic (or implicit, widely-accepted, potentially oppressive) assumptions about our MSW learning culture. However, to analyse and reflect on these assumptions requires 'trust and safety' (Fook & Gardner, 2007; p. 80). Our group lost our curiosity and became task-oriented so that we could complete our course requirements on time and without having to engage in conflict with each other. In addition, most of our group members were not confident with the CRoP process. No one wanted to take charge of the process, but certain voices overpowered others during group meetings. There was a power imbalance in that one group member often led group discussions and demanded attention. Because of his gender, age, and treatment of others, the group dynamic intensified. Our project became hijacked by the process of reflecting on only one incident while also having to complete a project together.

Similar to the dynamics within my incident, I was part of a power imbalance in my group. I was angry with myself for not intervening and feeling ineffective again. I did not speak up with our instructor until after the course. Reflecting on the CRoP process motivated me to examine why I dodged an opportunity to communicate my feelings both in my incident and within my group. I re-examined why I did not communicate clearly in my incident. For my group, I attribute not speaking up to a lack of confidence and an extreme lack of energy. Conflict and tension both require mental and emotional energy to effectively address and mediate. I experienced two great losses right before and during the MSW programme that, combined with my history of loss, caused burnout. Change and conflict became difficult for me to deal with during my MSW programme. I wanted to explore if this difficulty relates to my experiences of loss.

In her thought-provoking paper on grief and loss in social work, Goldsworthy (2005) explains that 'loss leaves people forever transformed' (p. 169). I lost my father suddenly as a child, I lost my closest friend suddenly a few months before my MSW, and I lost my beloved cat suddenly a few months into the MSW programme. These losses came as a surprise, and I felt like I lost vital parts of myself. During my MSW, I did not feel like the same person as the one in my critical incident: I would easily become irritable and angry whereas I did not use to prior to the MSW. During my incident, I became anxious in the face of uncertainty, but I had more energy to deal with conflict than I did during the MSW. Grief behaviourists posit that grieving individuals must choose where to exert energy, because grief becomes a 'stress response syndrome' that requires excess energy in order to cope (Goldsworthy, 2005, p. 172). I had to carefully direct my energy to my studies and self-care during the MSW. Group conflict was low on my priority list, especially when I felt exhausted and sad.

Quoted in Goldsworthy (2005), Lindemann (1944) points out that hostility can also be a part of grieving. The conflict in my group made me uncomfortable and angry. I did not feel hostile but I felt defensive of the group member who was invalidated. She did not want to raise the issue with the group or with our instructor, so it was not my right to do so on her behalf. That frustrated me, but I wanted to honour her. My downfall was focusing on her needs by keeping silent. I considered my well-being by thinking about how much energy to exert on the group process. Yet, I let myself down by not saying anything, because my CRoP process suffered. I completed a haphazard Stage 2, which went against my usual work ethic and values. I did not feel like myself and the group process emphasised that feeling.

Goldsworthy (2005) points out that people who are grieving experience a 'loss of normal patterns of behaviour' (p. 171). Who I was during the CRoP course was not the same person I was by the end of the programme. I did not want to shape my identity through negative and potentially destructive interactions with my peers. I appreciate the notion in Goldsworthy's (2005) article that it is important to integrate loss into one's identity instead of focusing solely on recovering from loss. In addition, Goldsworthy (2005) states that changes in our identity affect our connectedness with others, which was strained in my group. I had not truly integrated loss into my identity. I kept trying to 'get through' grief symptoms instead of owning my grief and deriving confidence from it. This realisation ties back to my critical incident: my lack of confidence in who I was affected my actions and how I processed the experience. The main lesson I have to learn from both my critical incident, my critical reflection group, and especially my group member who helped me complete Stage 2, is that 'I am more than my role'.

Conclusion

I tied my identity to how I was treated by my supervisor and my colleague and to feeling like a weak, nonvocal member of my critical reflection group. It is the same theme in a different package. I am a social worker with helpful skills and values. I can use my love of writing to help me process emotions related to uncomfortable power imbalances and to critically reflect in the future. I can also use writing to help me communicate more effectively with supervisors, coworkers, or group members. Further exploration is required of how I can build confidence and assertiveness to verbally communicate what I often feel more comfortable writing. I am more than my role. I am more than the pre-scriptions, pressures, and social influences in my workplaces and educational institutions. My identity is richer than 'subordinate', 'colleague', or 'group member'. I am more than my role. I plan on reciting that mantra from here forward: both in my personal and professional life.

Learning the CRoP process and implementing it with a group can be an enriching experience. If group conflict arises, participants must balance their own needs with those of the group. My group had to get through our course so we pushed through with our outcome-oriented tasks. However, we could have greatly benefitted from attempting the CRoP process with others we felt more comfortable with later in the MSW programme. Alternatively, using a journal to engage in the CRoP process could have been incredibly fulfilling. The grief that I was facing became one of the main interferences for engaging fully in the CRoP process. I sometimes wonder if I used it as an excuse to shy away from conflict. Regardless, I encourage those interested in CRoP to pay close attention to what is going on internally, what comes up during the CRoP process, and most importantly, to find someone safe to talk to about whatever does come up. My instructor's compassion, understanding, and wisdom rekin-dled my curiosity and interest in engaging in CRoP in some way (individually, with a group). If I could go back, I would confidently talk to her and ask for help with engaging in the CRoP process in a safer environment.

I am more than my role. I need to access my social work and professional values to engage in rich discourse with others, even if that means thinking outside the proverbial box of assigned roles such as 'group member' or 'worker'. I am satisfied with being a social worker, thanks to the CRoP pro-cess. There are many values and roles I ascribe to as a social worker, and I strive to do so each day since the MSW programme and CRoP course.

References

Adamovich, T., Kumsa, M.K., Rego, C., Stoddart, J., & Vito, R. (2014). Playing hide-and-seek: Searching for the use of self in reflective social work practice. *Reflective Practice*, 15(2), 131–143. doi:10.1080/14623943.2014.883312

Fook, J., & Gardner, F. (2007). *Practising critical reflection: A resource handbook*. Maiden-head: Open University Press.

Goldsworthy, K.K. (2005). Grief and loss theory in social work practice: All changes involve loss, just as all losses require change. *Australian Social Work*, 58(2), 167–178. doi:10.1111/j.1447-0748.2005.00201.x

Hickson, H. (2011). Critical reflection: Reflecting on learning to be reflective. *Reflective Practice*, 12(6), 829–839. doi:10.1080/14623943.2011.61687

Immen, W. (2011, May 17). Boxed in: The stifling effects of short-term contracts. *The Globe and Mail*. Retrieved from www.theglobeandmail.com/report-on-business/careers/career-advice/boxed-in-the-stifling-effects-of-short-term-contracts/article580315

Lewchuk, W., Clarke, M., & de Wolff, A. (2008). Working without commitments: Precarious employment and health. *Work, Employment, and Society*, 22(3), 387–406. doi:10.1177/0950017008093477

Mojtehedzadeh, S., & Monsebraaten, L. (2015, May 21). Precarious work is now the new norm, United Way report says. *The Star*. Retrieved from www.thestar.com/news/gta/2015/05/21/precarious-work-is-now-the-new-norm-united-way-report-says.html

Ontario College of Social Workers and Social Service Workers (2008). *Code of ethics and standards of practice handbook* (2nd ed.). Toronto, Canada: OCSWSSW.

Ruch, G. (2016). Relational practices of critical reflection: The role of communication and containment. In J. Fook, V. Collington, F. Ross, G. Ruch, & L. West (Eds.), *Researching critical reflection: Multidisciplinary perspectives* (pp. 23–33). London and New York: Routledge.

Chapter 9

Deconstructing 'pretty'

Jasmyne Lennox

This poem, 'Spoken Word Poetry' (www.youtube.com/watch?v=wXcVHjvLwRc), was not just created for an assignment but as a way to express the myriad of emotions that were evoked throughout the transformative process of critical reflection. I was required to submit an essay during the final (4th) year of my social work undergraduate degree programme in Australia, detailing an incident/situation and the subsequent critical reflection process I undertook. However, I did not feel that the words I had written on paper could express to the reader how confronting and challenging the task of a process like this is, whereby I was analysing my deeply entrenched implicit assumptions. Despite the empowering outcome, uncovering the way I interpreted the world was very unsettling, in realising that I was unknowingly influenced by imposed gender roles at a young age and helped maintained their power throughout my life. Therefore, I used spoken word poetry to showcase the raw emotions I experienced throughout my journey, in the hope that it would be something other women could resonate with and possibly empower them to question how they have constructed themselves as a woman. We were encouraged to use Fook's (2007) model of critical reflection, which focuses on deconstructive thinking through examining our implicit assumptions, particularly about power, to provide a means to reconstruct new ways of understanding ourselves, our practice, and our power. By using this model and postmodern theory, I was provided with the opportunity to transcend the fixed modernist theories of identity and power that were embedded in my thinking and reconstruct an alternative story – a story that aligned with a more fluid understanding of my identity, where I was a more active empowered agent within my social world instead of being a victim at the whim of patriarchy and structural inequalities.

In the poem, I highlighted that our thoughts and perceptions are constructed and can, therefore, be deconstructed, changed, and reconstructed (Fook, 2012). To further understand the background of the poem, this is a brief initial account of the critical incident, which was 'problem saturated' and emphasises the way in which my perception of the situation led to a sense of powerlessness and doubt within my ability to be a social worker.

The specific incident, which triggered my reflection, occurred one morning on placement. I was approached by a client who made a sexually inappropriate comment toward me. I didn't know how to respond, so I ignored him and went up to the office and disclosed my frustrations of these constant incidents to my task supervisor. This was met by a background comment from an older female staff member, 'How annoying to be called attractive every day'. Suddenly, out of nowhere, my frustration turned into tears alongside feelings of guilt, shame, embarrassment, and confusion. I felt like the older staff members looked down on me as if I was 'young and dumb' with nothing to offer other than a 'pretty face'. My outburst was a result of many conversations throughout my placement with both clients and staff members, which were solely focused on my physical appearance. The most harmful comments were made by my team leader, that I didn't look like the 'social work type' but more like a 'Gold Coast girl'. The Gold Coast is a beautiful city by the beach on the east coast of Australia, which has sadly been defined by the stereotype of image-obsessed, empty-headed narcissists with fake tans and silicon boobs. A part of me felt an injustice to be grouped into this stereotype. An assumption was made about me that did not require any actual knowledge of me but was assumed simply because I had blonde hair and wore makeup. However, another part of me, a big part, felt that it was my fault. My deeply felt complexity and uniqueness was diminished in the light of this stereotype, and it must have been something I had done. How could I be taken seriously if these were the opinions of me? I felt that my intelligence was ignored and that a combination of my appearance and my inability to respond effectively and assertively to inappropriate comments impacted my ability to be perceived as a professional social worker. The poem aims to portray this narrative as only one representation in one space in time of the many stories that exist. As Fook (1996, p. 4) states, it is an 'interpretation of reality rather than reality itself'. Therefore, knowing there are multiple constructed truths and that I participated in constructing my reality opened the possibility for me to change my disempowering narrative and thoughts around it by identifying what was distorted in my initial account of the incident.

The class I was taking was called 'Critical Reflection' where we used critical reflection models as a basis to be transformative in our practice to lead to some fundamental change in perspective through analysis of assumptions (Cranton, 1996, pp. 79–80). During the process of critical reflection and learning about it, we were alerted to the presence of dominant discourses that influence the construction of our perceived realities and, therefore, we were able to challenge them. My poem explored power and where it was located and the dominant discourse of patriarchy during the deconstruction phase. I utilised critical postmodern theory to identify how I constructed my own reality and to highlight the unintended disempowering elements of my analysis and the artificial dichotomies that limited the possibility for multiple potential interpretations/understandings of my identity. Postmodernism suggests the way we speak about things constructs the way we see and understand them – some things are left out in our stories and others are constructed as binary categories (Fook & Gardner, 2007, pp. 444–445). In my narrative, my physical appearance as a 'young pretty woman' was inextricably linked with not being perceived as professional or intelligent. I disregarded the fluidity and complexity of my identity in different contexts. I had constructed the binary of beauty versus intellect. I thought if my team leader perceived me as a 'Gold Coast girl' then that meant she thought I must not be intelligent and internalised that notion. However, through critical reflection, I realised that I was participating in and unintentionally supporting the dominant discourse of patriarchy, where there are distinct gender roles and the female body is valued based on its form (appearance) rather than its function (Morley & Macfarlane, 2011, p. 10) through the very language I was using in my story.

The next step was to unearth the origins of my recently discovered implicit assumptions – where did these ideas come from? Patriarchy can be perpetuated by important socialising agents such as parents (Featherstone & Fawcett, 1995, p. 30). One of my earliest memories is of my dad saying to me in a joking manner, 'You better grow up pretty because you aren't very smart', and my mother saying to me, 'Don't wear that, you have a brain'. I was given two distinct categories and two very different messages. You are either beautiful and dumb or smart and ugly.

For young girls, as we grow up, patriarchy reinforces the idea that our bodies are objects and are significant factors in how others will judge our overall value. We are socialised to act and respond to situations in certain ways defined by set gender roles. As this was overemphasised when I was growing up, it became apparent to me that throughout my life, I have been unconsciously seeking reassurance about my appearance to make sure I am socially accepted and not subject to ridicule or rejection (Featherstone & Fawcett, 1995, p. 30). At the same time, I was trying to 'prove' my intelligence, because I believed that beauty and intelligence cannot coexist in a patriarchal society. As a result, patriarchy retained its power over me by defining my experience. Through the reconstruction process of critical reflection, I was able to break down the fixed modernist notions of a woman's identity and role. I was able to embrace the complex contradictions that my identity embodies as an emerging female professional in our Western culture that holds traditional values of how women should act. I can assert myself in a professional setting and challenge the dominant discourse of what women 'should be like'.

The critical reflection process allowed me to make sense of my overwhelming self-doubt and my sensitivities to people's perceptions of me. It also changed my perspective. Through the process, I discovered that my initial construction of the incident was laden with fatalism, powerlessness, and artificial dichotomies. I constructed myself as unprofessional based on my appearance, which evoked feelings of powerlessness. I also held a strong belief that people commenting on my physical appearance meant my intelligence was disregarded, and I was not 'taken seriously'. Fortunately, I was able to expose and scrutinise my hidden assumptions that were upheld by patriarchy and, therefore, given the choice and power to change them. This reflection has highlighted the importance of reflecting on my positionality when working with people so that I do not create binaries of me (powerless) vs. them (powerful). My poem ends by asking for different perspectives on the incident, which subsequently provided me with multiple understandings of the incident. I will ensure to continue to question my underlying assumptions in my future practice.

References

Cranton, P. (1996). *Professional development as transformative learning*. San Francisco, CA: Jossey-Bass.

Featherstone, B., & Fawcett, B. (1995). Oh no! not more "isms": Feminism, post-modernism, poststructuralism and social work education. *Social Work Education*, 14(3), 25–43. doi:10.1080/02615479511220171

Fook, J. (Ed.). (1996). *The reflective researcher: Social workers' theories of practice research*. Sydney, Australia: Allen & Unwin.

Fook, J. (2007). Reflective practice and critical reflection. In J. Lishman (Ed.), *Handbook for practice learning in social work and social care: Knowledge and theory* (2nd ed., pp. 363–375). London: Jessica Kingsley Publishers.

Fook, J. (2012). *Social work: A critical approach to practice* (2nd ed.). London: SAGE.

Fook, J., & Gardner, F. (2007). *Practicing critical reflection: A resource handbook*. Berkshire: Open University Press.

Morley, C., & Macfarlane, S. (2011). The nexus between feminism and postmodernism: Implications for critical social work. *British Journal of Social Work*, 42(4), 687–705. doi:10.1093/bjsw/bcr107

Chapter 10

Social worker well-being and critical reflective practice

Fenix Cornejo

In this chapter, I will explore the role that critical reflective practice plays in well-being for social workers and what social workers learn from critical reflection. I conducted a small-scale research study in London, UK, to find out what social workers experience when learning to use the Fook model for critical reflection and to investigate whether it raised their awareness of well-being and supported professional self-care (Fook & Gardner, 2007). Given that recent literature suggests that a work/life balance has been a significant problem for social workers, this chapter hopes to offer a new perspective and raise awareness of how critical reflective practice can help social workers build well-being strategies to manage the challenges of the role. I will first look at the context of social work and social work organisations detailing how the context of social work is strained and how supervision is not all-encompassing. I will look at the issue of chronic stress among social workers and how this inevitably leads to burnout. I will then look to describe the research study and what social workers said about the power they hold and what aspects of critical reflection help with managing stress.

My experience of well-being is that it is not talked about among social work organisations or social workers. Organisations are not providing the right kind of supervision and support. The dominant culture is that of being busy in all aspects of life and work. Social workers are too busy to step back and see this. Workplace well-being schemes are usually about meeting performance targets or are reactive to presenting issues of hidden and negative chronic stress. I acknowledge that there are positive aspects to stress but my interest lies in what happens when chronic stress takes over the lives of social workers in a negative way, what social workers can do to manage this for themselves, and how a raised awareness can challenge the systems in which they practise.

In this chapter, I am sharing my experiences as I have a lived experience of both critically reflective practice (CRP) and an understanding of the lives of social workers and social work organisations. Combining both these perspectives can enrich and support the working experience of social workers. My social work career is international and varied. I obtained a joint Master's Degree in Social Work and Public Administration from the University of Southern

California. My experiences in Southern California taught me about the varied, diverse, and complex nature of families. Some years ago, I was recruited to come and work for a London local authority in England providing statutory direct services to adults living with learning disabilities and young people with care needs transitioning across from children's social care to adults' social care.

I was first introduced to critical reflection when I came into a macrosocial work role. I qualified with a specialism in community organising, planning, and administration, and I found my way to macrosocial work in the United Kingdom through training and organisational development and now social work education. I attended a London-wide critical reflective network group where the Fook model for critical reflection was introduced and practised. From this network, I understood that the experience of critical reflection and learning to critically reflect was crucial to consolidating learning and changing practice. Initially, learning the theories and the practice model was challenging, complex, and time-consuming. Though with ongoing practice and a clear learning plan, I realised they gave the learner a path to transformative learning. Armed with this knowledge, I introduced critical reflective practice groups to students, newly qualified social workers and the people managing them. I also introduced sessions to learn how to critically reflect for those managers.

You will have seen the definition of critical reflection in earlier chapters. I go further in defining the 'practice' aspect of critical reflection. I believe CRP becomes a professional capability and skill through ongoing practice. In my experience, CRP groups are good for changing practice, consolidating learning from experience, and enhancing well-being through learning from the group process and peers as well as unearthing new understandings of experiences. CRP is hugely beneficial to managing stress and building stress resilience. Being part of a consistent CRP group provides a means for ongoing transformational social work practice within statutory social work teams, improved outcomes for clients (those using services), and space for acknowledging, recognising, and moderating stress and burnout. I define this as an aspect of well-being and professional self-care. CRP is a professional way of being, which creates space to think, challenge, and transform practice thereby generating raised awareness for professional self-care and ultimately well-being.

The overall context

Social work is a sought after, rewarding, stressful, and challenging career. In the United Kingdom, social work is done in a variety of settings but mostly in statutory teams safeguarding the most vulnerable people in our community. In the current political environment and personal contexts that social workers practise in, it is important to find ways to manage the conflicting nature of the job (Hussein, 2018; Ravalier, 2018). Being in a neoliberal and managerialist environment within a statutory organisation leaves social workers in constant conflict (Morley & Macfarlane, 2014; Noble, 2004; Ravalier, 2018). They come into the field to make a difference with vulnerable families but find that it is riddled with statutory deadlines and performance targets, which mean more time is spent in the office than providing interventions with the families they support.

These statutory responsibilities mean social workers are doing jobs that are more challenging with fewer resources and support. Local authorities and large social care organisations use packages of support for social workers, which include line management supervision and group supervision. When these activities work well they are supportive, helping social workers deal with the emotional impact of their work (Gibbs, 2001). When they do not work well, social workers do not obtain support for processing and containing the emotional impact the work carries when managing risk in complex situations. This leads directly to a crisis in social work as a response to conflicting structural views, individual views, and the dominant office culture (Montano, 2012; Noble, 2004). Often, this conflict comes from the perceived power differential and the direction in which perceived power operates within the practice at the micro and macro level (Fook & Gardner, 2007). These conflicts leave social workers in a heightened state of mind feeling stressed, powerless, and, sometimes, helpless with their role and with their work with families.

The governing bodies for social work in the United Kingdom, the Health and Care Professions Council, the British Association of Social Worker's Professional Capabilities Framework, and the Chief Social Worker's Knowledge and Skills Statement all have guiding principles for how social workers should practise (BASW, 2017; DfE., 2016; HCPC, 2017). They all respond to the question of stress by stating that social workers should be more resilient. For example, the Knowledge and Skills Statement for child and family social work states that social workers should:

> Reflect on the emotional experience of working relationships with parents, carers and children, and consciously identify where personal triggers are affecting the quality of analysis or help. [Social workers should] identify strategies to build professional resilience and management of self.
>
> (DfE., 2016, p. 6)

There is little mention as to how to become resilient other than to be 'emotionally intelligent' and to 'use mechanisms such as peer supervision and group case consultation to help identify bias, shift thinking and the approach to casework to generate better outcomes for children and families' (DfE, 2015, p6). This research identified that learning to critically reflect and participating in critical reflective practice groups was one mechanism to do just that.

Well-being and self-care

There are many aspects to well-being and, overall, they fall into two categories depending on the activity: personal (lifestyle) or professional (workplace) approaches (Baker, 2011; Cox & Steiner, 2016; Lee & Miller, 2013; Singer,

2018). For social workers, the 'self' is the most important tool in the social work toolbox as building relationships and problem-solving are at the core of the work, and this includes who we are and what we bring (Lee & Miller, 2013). Professional self-care is based on the ethos of maintaining a commitment to and dedication for your work by taking care of your 'self'.

Self-care is an essential aspect of well-being that promotes ethical social work practice and is crucial for professional behaviour with clients who have complex needs (Grise-Owens, Miller, & Eaves, 2016; Lee & Miller, 2013; NASW, 2008). It is loosely defined by many helping professions as being influenced by the professions' 'knowledge, skills, values, and a holistic aspect of healthcare under individual control (Cox & Steiner, 2016). For social workers, well-being is the ability to refill and refuel in healthy and sustainable ways to provide care to the most vulnerable (Cox & Steiner, 2016). It is an essential, non-optional aspect of maintaining a professional role (Badali & Habra, 2003; Barnett, Baker, Elman, & Schoener, 2007; Grise-Owens et al., 2016). By valuing self-care as a core skill, social workers 'mirror the wellness they wish to create' and promote healthy, resilient, and long careers (Cox & Steiner, 2016, p. 14; Thompson, 2016).

Social workers must create 'goal-directed/problem-focused coping links' that support them in figuring out what is causing their stress and how to manage it (Collins, 2008, p. 262). The space CRP provides is a preventative and ongoing coping strategy (Barnett et al., 2007). Social workers are good at promoting self-care with the vulnerable families they work with but find it difficult to do it for themselves (DeAngelis, 2002). Social workers often attend work when sick, a phenomenon Ravalier (2018) calls 'presenteeism', and means social workers may provide worse care to their clients. They have continued to practise under stress without seeking help even though they know this impacts their personal and professional relationships (Barnett et al., 2007). This is due in part to the stigma of help-seeking, its association with vulnerability, and vulnerability being viewed negatively (Barnett et al., 2007; Brown, 2012).

Social Workers fail to ask for help and fail to engage in professional self-care for many reasons. There is a dominant idea in statutory organisations that social workers should be able to do more with less (Brookfield, 2016). In statutory organisations, social workers concede to this idea of working until exhaustion as it is accepted by the majority (Brookfield, 2016; Singer, 2018). They fall into the discourse of being busy and in 'a state of mind that suggests that they need to work nonstop' to be successful and achieve best outcomes for their clients (Badali & Habra, 2003; Jackson, 2014, p. 14). The harm comes from not giving time for reflection and professional self-care and as Bolton (2014, p. 15) puts it, 'yet the busier we are, the more vital reflection and reflexivity are to prevent missing significant issues and making mistakes'. Looking back at the research around professional self-care, it is important to note that supervisors and managers can do a lot in supporting awareness-raising for social workers including creating spaces for professional self-care, self-assessments, and plans that can be realistically implemented in the organisational context (Beer & Ashtana, 2016; Grise-Owens et al., 2016).

Learning to critically reflect and well-being

Critical reflection is important for responsible and ethical practice as it allows social workers to think about their actions, thoughts, and feelings and also reframes the impact of their work for transformational practice (Bolton, 2014). The underpinning principles that are key to this work are postmodern theory, the concept of reflexivity, and self-compassion. In its simplest form post-modernism allows an exploration of many, different, conflicting, and/or contradictory perspectives to issues coming up in practice. This allows social workers a way of holding, containing, and exploring alternative perspectives to their own. Reflexivity allows for an inward gaze in which social workers look to themselves and the aspects that they bring into the work they do (Fook & Gardner, 2007), and in this way, taking responsibility for the power they hold in each situation. Self-compassion encourages mindful awareness of thoughts and feelings, our common humanity in our work and ultimately being kind with ourselves and others when confronting difficult emotions within our work (Neff, 2015).

Through the creation of the culture of ethical and critical acceptance within groups, CRP can create a safe space. This safe space in the organisation allows social workers time to step back and think about their work. This enables them to rediscover who they are and remain curious about their own actions, values, and emotions to change implicit and explicit assumptions within their work. According to Thompson (2016), values are at the heart of social work practice and valuing reflection and what it brings makes us more ethical practitioners. Adopting professional values means social workers need to be aware of their own values, the values of others, the values of interacting systems and how they all interact. Ixer (2003) warns that if organisational values are too dissimilar to the social workers' own, then a discussion must take place to learn from this, otherwise it will create tension.

CRP is 're-examining personally experienced events to make new meaning of them in the light of other experiences' (Fook, Royes, & White, 2017, p. 118). The ongoing practice of critical reflection supports an inward gaze, a capacity to observe the self and how it manifests in personal and social lives to affect emotional and intellectual changes professionally (Birn-baum, 2008; Fook, 2012). The transformative effects are achieved by a recognition of the 'layers of assumption', which help build an understanding of how one creates knowledge and what sort of power individuals hold (Fook, 2017, p. 6). This is an aspect of professional well-being.

When understanding the effects of power, the social worker can develop alternative ways of thinking and actions, which question dominant ways of thinking, doing, and being (Mattsson, 2014). CRP allows for an exploration of the role of power, which looks at how your own values play a role in exercising judgement and making decisions in complex situations (Brookfield, 2016; Fook, 2017; Fook, Royes, & White, 2017). It is an intentional approach to be open to exploring assumptions within the practice and the power dynamics, which surround relationships (Bolton, 2014). Being able to focus on these assumptions, attitudes, and interactions, and how they may be all connected to emotions and common human experiences, potentially helps social workers to transform 'self-perception' and 'be kinder within their work' (Birnbaum, 2008, p. 847; Neff, 2015). CRP involves the experience of questioning, exploring, observing, analysing, and then reframing and/or replacing a dominant assumption that has been accepted by the individual and/or the majority (Brookfield, 2016).

Birnbaum (2008, p. 838) terms CRP groups the 'accompanying place' where social workers can get support and development in a 'non-evaluative way' and where the focus is on the emotional well-being of the social worker and not the client or the family. Here, social workers can reveal hidden values and reconcile any discrepant ones as they are discussed. This way, CRP becomes a complement to supervision not to take the place of it but to inform it. It is the transformative quality of CRP groups, which create the space for awareness of well-being through the 'accompanying space' (Birnbaum, 2008, p. 838; Thompson, 2016).

The research study

I conducted a small-scale research study using a qualitative approach of unstructured narrative interviews. The aims of the study were to explore the perspectives of social workers using the CRP model (on which very little research has been conducted) and make a case for its link to professional self-care. A snowball sampling method was used to obtain nine participants who took part in the study. The participants were all qualified social workers who came from a few different local authorities in London, UK, working in statutory children services, mental health, and adult social care settings. As a result, it is possible that the concept of 'space' is a precursor to professional self-care or an element of well-being in social workers.

Thematic analysis provided findings that showed that social workers used many group processes when learning to critically reflect, including the Fook model for CRP (Fook & Gardner, 2007). It also showed that social workers were overwhelmed with the 'busyness' of the work, that managers were overstretched, and that groups created much needed 'space'. A postmodern stance to the research allowed for multiple perspectives on an endemic issue already present in social work: chronic stress, and burnout. The principal conclusion was that the practice of CRP with groups creates space, which leads to aspects of reflection that help manage stress and improve well-being.

Social workers were asked to tell the researcher something about their experience of CRP professionally and personally. The common themes that emerged from the interviews were about stress and busyness, challenges of supervision, space, and impact of learning to critically reflect. Social workers described the 'busyness' of social work, stress, and the limited ability to find 'space' for reflection. One participant advised that there was no time to stop and think stating '[SW] constantly does feel like you're running on this wheel' (Cornejo, 2018, p. 43). Those that spoke about participating in CRP groups stated that they provided them with a way of 'stepping off the wheel' to take a breath and think about the work and its impact on the clients and themselves.

The research showed that social workers are indeed stressed. They are working in busy teams where there is an assumption that being stressed is good and that there is no alternative to stressful practice because being stressed means you are giving everything to your work. Often, being burnt out or at the point of being clinically stressed is seen as a badge of honour and as a commitment to their vocation (Brookfield, 2016; Singer, 2018; Smith, Stepanova, Venn, Carpenter, & Patsios, 2018). One participant stated, 'So, often what we do is, something happens, we're affected by it, there's no opportunity to unpick it or think about it, so we override it, but it doesn't go away' (Cornejo, 2018, p. 41).

This contradiction places limitations on the work. The emotional, physical, and sometimes depleting impact of the work is also a challenge as it results in high staff turnover from burnout, compassion fatigue, vicarious and secondary trauma, and professional depletion (Lee & Miller, 2013; Singer, 2018). A participant described the nature of the job: '[SW] is a very stressful job, and sometimes we're just going and going and going – we're not aware of perhaps how we're interacting with people or what we're actually doing' (Cornejo, 2018, p. 42).

In the current context, with the advent of technology and social media, everyone is expected to be busy. It is a current cultural phenomenon. This busy culture and the stress that results from it were reflected in the findings. Changes in regulations, restructures, and the negative media perception means social workers are balancing a delicate state for both themselves and the families with which they work. The assumption, from the participants interviewed, was that to do a good job you must do the job at the point of over-exhaustion. If the social worker is not exhausted at the end of the day, the assumption is that they have not given their all to the work and, by default, 'are not good enough' to do the work. This hegemonic assumption works against social workers in that they believe they need to get the work done no matter what it takes and they cannot say no and, by consequence, must take work home to complete no matter the cost on their well-being (Brookfield, 2016).

There was also an assumption with the social workers interviewed in the study that stress was not a controllable factor and that working with clinical levels of stress is normal. This is also an organisational and political assumption as managers, teams, and government reports function under the same guise. Social workers described being busy, which leads to stress but did not describe other ways of working. This echoes Lee & Miller's (2013) work on a framework for self-care. They indicated that well-being is not prioritised by regulatory bodies, employing organisations or professionals and, therefore, social workers are leaving it out of the discussion. Social workers are so busy that there is no space to stop and think about professional self-care or well-being. It needs to be a focus, and it needs to be a point of discussion at all levels.

Supervision is meant to be the protective factor that supports social workers to manage the challenges of the job. Participants in the study described good supervision as being reflective and dependent on the managers who delivered it. One participant stated, 'Because things have become so stretched and because perhaps supervisors, as well, have become so overstretched, I just think that finding the headspace for reflection, it's not there, because everyone's so busy' (Cornejo, 2018, p. 40).

The research findings show that, often, reflective and meaningful supervision is not happening. In its place is case management, performance-driven supervision, or no supervision at all, as managers are equally as busy, overstretched, and stressed. Many described the fact that there are huge demands on the manager that prevent good supervision from happening. In the current context, the neoliberal and managerial agendas have made statutory organisations punitive, overly regulated, and restrictive (Morely & Macfarlane, 2014; Ravalier, 2018). Without reflective supervision, social workers cannot find the space to stop, step back, and think about the impact the work has on their lives and the lives of others. Because the work is demanding, challenging, and sometimes dangerous, social workers need to find ways in which to speak up for themselves to sustain personal and professional health and well-being and good social work practice.

Social workers need to bring well-being to the foreground of the discussion to better understand it and the personal and professional protective factors offered by it (Grise-Owen et al., 2016; Lee & Miller, 2013). In the research, social workers discussed the idea of space, which mitigates the risks in the profession bringing about professional well-being (Monk, 2011). This space gave them the tools they needed to step back and think about cases that had been challenging and the impact of the work on their health and well-being.

Social workers discussed the importance of reflective groups including CRP as a way of learning and creating space, which leads to well-being. The social workers interviewed reported that space for reflection is valued. They stated that learning to critically reflect through CRP groups creates space (and permission) to find headspace personally and collectively. One participant added,

> So, something about that group is that I feel I can just put that down, and just be very honest about what I don't know and what I'm unsure about. And that's a sense of relief, and unburdening myself of my mask.
>
> (Cornejo, 2018, p. 48)

The social workers interviewed also stated that having this space in CRP groups 'creates practice efficiency and gives a way of looking after yourself in the best interest of the client' (Cornejo, 2018). They reported that learning to critically reflect creates a safe space within the context of the group and sometimes the team. This safe space is helped by the culture of critical and ethical acceptance from the Fook practice model as well as communicative spaces, which support and enhance learning from practice (Aspfors & Marit Valle, 2017; Fook & Gardner, 2007). Having a safe space was described as a relief from the busyness of practice and helped social workers to step off the wheel, which was described earlier with the concept of 'busyness'. This was important, and it showed that social workers valued CRP and reflective spaces to balance the pressure of the work.

Participants talked about the value of the CRP model in the areas of coming together (self and others), the influence of power, challenging self and others to think, looking at their own values and biases, getting to the heart of an issue, looking at different perspectives and acknowledging and recognising the emotional impact of the work (see Table 10.1). One participant stated, 'It's a really good way to share knowledge and information. And it's a good way to challenge yourself, and how you reflect, because sometimes the models of reflection are quite difficult, in my experience' (Cornejo, 2018, p. 47).

Social workers get better at looking at multiple perspectives related to an issue, task, or dilemma through developing skills in CRP groups. This opens the possibilities of understanding the work they do with clients and colleagues as well as building resilience. Another participant added, '[CRP] engages with your deeper thinking, which of course is there, and informs what you do, and the responses. So, it's about having that time to just peel back [the layers] a little bit' (Cornejo, 2018, p. 47).

In this respect, the findings show that CRP is a well-being and professional self-care practice tool, as it supports social workers to step back from the work and recognise the assumptions about the way they work. Through CRP groups, social workers learn how to raise their awareness about the challenges of the work and what they need to be healthy and have long careers in the profession. It is these aspects of reflection, which help social workers manage stress and provide a practical way to build resilience.

Table 10.1 Keywords and phrases related to learning critical reflection

Opportunity to put away paperwork
Gives space to slow down
Looks at different value systems
Allows for a wider look at all the systems
Helps unstick stuck cases
Supports self-challenge
Help to look at many perspectives
Helps to check in with feelings
Reflecting on social graces
Helps to find productive ways to work with the family

Social workers have permission to create space, practise critical reflection, and prioritise well-being as described throughout the documentation of the regulatory and professional bodies. Herein lies another assumption that came out of the findings: The reason social workers do not practise CRP or run CRP groups is that they often feel they cannot due to time or energy limitations. They have described feeling little power and influence over their role within the organisation. Social workers feel that the precedence goes to the churn of the casework, case notes, report writing, statutory regulations, timescales, and the busyness of the job. One participant stated, 'I think that we're so busy, and just flying all the time with whatever we've got going on' (Cornejo, 2018, p. 42). There is no priority given to well-being personally or organisationally.

The implication is that social workers and statutory organisations must be radical about this matter of creating space for well-being and professional self-care, as it helps to manage stress. Through a focus on learning to critically reflect and critical reflective practice groups to supplement supervision, organisations can support social workers to become better practitioners and keep them in a social work career for longer (Grise-Owen et al., 2016; Lee & Miller, 2013; Singer, 2018). Being radical means social workers take the permission from the registering and professional bodies to organise groups themselves, adding them to the diaries, demanding that time and priority is given to learning to critically reflect to meet continuing professional development and registration needs as a supplement to supervision.

To help social workers cope with the stress of the workplace, CRP provides a way to manage the conflicting values and can be used to further supplement supervision (Cox & Steiner, 2016). Social workers can aim for a culture of prioritising well-being through creating space. This leads to adding simple protective factors to their days such as CRP groups, reflective supervision, lunch breaks away from the desk, peer supervision groups, and leaving the office on time.

Reflexivity

Putting myself reflexively in the context of this research, I cast my mind back to how I have practised CRP and well-being in my own career. I think, often, social workers feel like they are going outside of their comfort zones by opening a conversation with their managers about their needs in supervision. This should not be the case, as there are learning agreements and supervision contracts that state as much. Sometimes, social workers themselves come from marginalised, disenfranchised cultures and family situations, which cause a lot of personal conflicts. This also impacts on the work and creates difficulty for social workers in how they practise.

Organisationally, I initiate supervision meetings with a new manager through an exercise of managing expectations for both myself and the manager. When I have asked for reflective practice in supervision and when there was none, I found like-minded colleagues to run my own reflective practice groups. For me, being a part of a reflective practice group allows me time to think about the challenges of the work. Through critical reflection, I can unpick the emotional impact of the work and give myself the same kindness and compassion I offer clients.

I was lucky to have positive role models who demonstrated how to prioritise well-being and self-care so that when it came time for me to ask for what I needed, I had a template I could use. Professionally, I managed self-care through proactively asking for what I needed. When I was not aware or unsure of what my needs were, I found that accessing workplace therapy schemes, mindfulness-based stress reduction, and mindful self-compassion programmes gave me the language and tools to find what I needed. I also found that working with a mentor helped to manage tricky areas of practice.

Conclusions

The research study discussed in this chapter highlighted that the dominant discourse in social work organisations is still about working under stressful conditions – professionally depleted and at the brink of burnout. As a result, I believe this requires a renewed focus on well-being to support social workers through more accessible, ongoing, and flexible CRP groups to supplement supervision. This chapter established that there are aspects of reflection within CRP groups, which help manage stress. One contradiction of this work is that although social workers value CRP and the space provided, they are not able to initiate these groups themselves.

Using CRP provides a space that social workers need to step back from their work and stop to breathe in order to be present for themselves and the clients. The use of CRP groups is indeed a professional way of being, which creates space to think, challenge, and transform practice thereby generating raised awareness for well-being. Social workers can combat the dominant discourses by dispelling the myth of 'busyness' and powerlessness through facilitating CRP groups and opening discussions in team meetings with students yet to come into the profession and with client groups. Individually, social workers can create more creative ways of finding space for well-being. A practical recommendation for organisations is to support the use of CRP groups more regularly to reduce stress, improve job satisfaction, and help social workers effectively manage difficult cases. In addition, if groups are supplementary to supervision, more regular groups could also help to clarify the expectations of supervision; thus, removing from supervisors some of the burdens of one-to-one supervision and allowing for good reflective spaces.

References

Aspfors, J., & Mantvalle, A. (2017). Designing communicative spaces - innovative perspectives on teacher education. *Education Inquiry*, 8(1), 1–16. doi:0.1080/20004508.2016/1275176

Badaldi, M.A., & Habra, M.E. (2003). Self-care for psychology students: Strategies for starting healthy and avoiding burn out. *Canada's Psychology Newspaper*, 25(4), 1–3. Retrieved from http://cpa.ca/cpasite/userfiles/documents/students/psynopsis25(4).pdf

Baker, E.K. (2011). *Caring for ourselves: A therapist guide to personal and professional well-been* (4th ed.). Washington, DC: American Psychological Association.

Barnett, J.E., Baker, E.K., Elman, N.S., & Schoener, G.R. (2007). In pursuit of wellness: The self-care imperative. *Professional Psychology: Research and Practice*, 38(6), 603–612. doi:10.1037/0735-7028.38.6.603

Beer, O., & Asthana, S. (2016). How stress impacts social workers – and how they are trying to cope. Retrieved from www.communitycare.co.uk/2016/09/28/stress-impacts-social-workers-theyre-trying-cope

Birnbaum, L. (2008). The use of mindfulness training to create an 'accompanying place' for social work students. *Social Work Education*, 27(8), 837–852. doi:10.1080/02615470701538330

Bolton, G. (2014). *Reflective practice: Writing and professional development* (4th ed.). London: SAGE Publications.

Brown, B. (2012). *Daring greatly: How the courage to be vulnerable transforms the way we live, love, parent, and lead*. London: Penguin Group.

British Association of Social Workers (2017). Professional capabilities framework – social work level. Retrieved from www.basw.co.uk/pcf/capabilities/?level=5

Brookfield, S. (2016). So exactly what is critical about critical reflection? In, J. Fook, V. Collington, F. Ross, G. Ruch, & L. West (Eds.), *Researching critical reflection and research: Multidisciplinary perspectives*. New York: Routledge.

Collins, S. (2008). Social workers, resilience, positive emotions and optimism. *Practice: Social Work in Action*, 19(4), 255–269. doi:10.1080/09503150701728186

Cornejo, F. (2018). *An exploration of social worker perspectives of critical reflective practice: A case for professional self-care* (Unpublished master's thesis). Goldsmiths University of London, London, England.

Cox, K., & Steiner, S. (2016). *Self-care in social work*. Washington, DC: NASW Press.

DeAngelis, T. (2002). Normalizing practitioners' stress: More psychologists recognize that self-care helps them be better caregivers. *APA Monitor on Psychology*, 33(7), 62. Retrieved from www.apa.org/monitor/julaug02/normalizing.aspx

Department for Education (2015). *Knowledge and skills statements for practice leaders and practice supervisors*. Retrieved from www.gov.uk/government/uploads/system/uploads/attachment_data/file/478111/Knowledge_and_skills_statements_for_practice_leaders_and_practice_supervisors.pdf

Department for Education (2016). *Knowledge and skills statement for child and family social work*. Retrieved from www.gov.uk/government/uploads/system/uploads/attachment_data/file/478111/Knowledge_and_skills_statements_for_practice_leaders_and_practice_supervisors.pdf

Fook, J. (2012). The challenges of creating critically reflective groups. *Social Work with Groups*, 35(3), 218–234. doi:10.1080/01609513.2011.624375

Fook, J. (2017). *The challenges of creating critically reflective spaces: The problem facing critical reflection*. Unpublished.

Fook, J., & Gardner, F. (2007). *Practising critical reflection: A resource handbook*. Maidenhead: Open University Press.

Fook, J., Royes, J., & White, A. (2017). Critical reflection. In M. Chambers (Ed.), *Psychiatric mental health nursing: The craft of caring* (3rd ed., pp. 117–124). London: Routledge.

Gibbs, J.A. (2001). Maintaining front-line workers in child protection: A case for refocusing supervision. *Child Abuse Review*, 10(5), 323–335. doi:10.1002/car.707

Grise-Owens, E., Miller, J., & Eaves, M. (2016). *The A-to-Z self-care handbook for social workers and other helping professionals*. Mechanicsburg, PA: The New Social Worker Press.

Health and Care Professions Council (2017). *Standards of proficiency: Social workers in England*. Retrieved from www.hcpc-uk.org/publications/standards/index.asp?id=569

Hussein, S. (2018). Work engagement, burnout and personal accomplishments among social workers: A comparison between those working in children and adults' services in England. *Administration and Policy in Mental Health and Mental Health Services Research*, 45(6), 911–923. doi:10.1007/s10488–018–0872-z

Ixer, G. (2003). Developing the relationship between reflective practice and social work values. *The Journal of Practice Teaching and Learning*, 5(1), 7–22. doi:10.1921/jpts.v5i1.304

Jackson, K. (2014). Social worker self-care – The overlooked core competency. *Social Work Today*, 14(3), 14. Retrieved from www.socialworktoday.com/archive/051214p14.shtml

Lee, J.J., & Miller, S.E. (2013). A self-care framework for social workers: Building a strong foundation for practice. *Families in Society*, 94(2), 96–103. doi:10.1606/1044-3894.4289

Mattsson, T. (2014). Intersectionality as a useful tool. Anti-oppressive social work and critical reflection. *Journal of Women and Social Work*, 29(1), 8–17. doi:10.1177/0886109913510659aff.sagepub.com

Monk, L. (2011). Self-care for social workers: A precious commodity, and ethical imperative. *Perspectives*, 1(3): 4–5, 7. Retrieved from www.bcasw.org/wp-content/uploads/2011/06/Perspectives-January-2011.pdf

Montaño, C. (2012). Social work theory-practice relationship: Challenges to overcoming positivist and postmodern fragmentation. *International Social Work*, 55(3), 306–319. doi:10.1177/0020872812437226

Morely, C., & Macfarlane, S. (2014). Critical social work as ethical social work: Using critical reflection to research students' resistance to neoliberalism. *Critical and Radical Social Work*, 2(3), 337–355. doi:10.1332/204986014X14096553281895

National Association of Social Workers (2008). Professional self-care and social work. In *Social Work Speaks* (8th ed., pp. 268–272). Washington, D.C.: NASW Press. Retrieved from www.compassionstrengths.com/uploads/NASW.ProfesionalSelf-Care.pdf

Neff, K. (2015). *Self-compassion: Stop beating yourself up and leave insecurity behind*. London: Yellow Kite Books.

Noble, C. (2004). Postmodern thinking: Where is it taking social work? *Journal of Social Work*, 4(3), 289–304. doi:10.1177/1468017304047747

Ravalier, J.M. (2018). Psycho-social working conditions and stress in UK social workers. *British Journal of Social Work*, 49(2): 371–390. doi:10.1093/bjsw/bcy023

Singer, J. (2018). The social work podcast: Self-care for social work. Retrieved from socialworkpodcast.blogspot.com

Smith, R., Stepanova, E., Venn, L., Carpenter, J., & Patsios, D. (2018). *Evaluation of step up to social work cohorts 1 and 2: 3-years and 5-years on research report. London. Department for Education.* Retrieved from https://assets.publishing.service.gov.uk/government/up loads/system/uploads/attachment_data/file/707085/Step_Up_to_Social_Work_eva luation-3_and_5_years_on.pdf

Thompson, V. (2016). Values-reflections on who I am and why I'm a social worker. In E. Grise-Owens, J. Miller, & M. Eaves (Eds.), *The A-to-Z self-care handbook for social workers and other helping professionals* (pp. 123–126). Harrisburg, PA: New Social Worker Press.

Section III

Research and reflections on learning and teaching critical reflection

Chapter 11

Reflections on learning as a teacher

Sharing vulnerability

Laura Béres

I have often mentioned to social work students in classes I have facilitated that I love finding and unsettling taken-for-granted assumptions that I have been holding. I find it exhilarating to learn afresh: I can sense goose bumps on my skin as I experience the 'aha' moment of realising something new about how I have been approaching the world. Although I continue to feel this way, this interest and willingness to be unsettled does involve an element of vulnerability when engaged in teaching and learning critical reflection as a form of 'co-research' (Fook, 2012, p. 233). In the future, I might say that I do not always 'love' it, but I always appreciate it. The unsettling and discovery of assumptions can be uncomfortable and cause a certain amount of anxiety, but I argue in this chapter that being willing to be vulnerable is an important aspect of transformative education.

This chapter may be of particular interest to people engaged in teaching, to those interested in a detailed description of how the critical reflection process can proceed in a journaling format, and to those curious about what might be going through a professor's mind as she is teaching. Teaching critical reflection certainly provided a transformative learning experience for students and for myself as their professor, and I hope to capture some of that sense of transformation in this chapter. I begin by describing and reflecting upon the process of learning how to teach critical reflection on practice for the first time in a Master of Social Work (MSW) programme in a Canadian university context and the resulting reflections on vulnerability and transformative learning. I conclude the chapter with some additional thoughts after teaching this same course for a second time. The second experience resulted in considerations regarding how I might, at times, need to balance vulnerability, and the associated 'attunement to students', with an awareness of what I require for a sense of 'self-protection'.

Although I was familiar with Fook's work on critical reflection (Fawcett, Featherstone, Fook, & Rossiter, 2000; Fook, 2002; Fook & Gardner, 2007; Hick, Fook, & Pozzuto, 2005) and had previously engaged in critical reflection on my own social work practice, I had not taught the model before. Adjusting the two-stage model from full-day sessions to cover a term of 13 weekly three-hour classes (11 weeks of teaching, one for an in-class test and one for presentations), for two required classes of 22 graduate students each, involved thought, planning, and willingness to adjust based on weekly feedback in the Critical Incident Questionnaires (CIQs) students completed each week (www. stephenbrookfield.com/ciq/; Brookfield, 2009). Having decided to conduct a research project regarding the teaching and learning of Fook's model of critical reflection on practice (CRoP), I decided, in addition to pre- and post-course questionnaires and weekly CIQs, which students were to complete, that I would use Fook's CRoP model to learn from any critical incidents that I experienced during the course. On two different occasions, I did experience what I felt were critical incidents, which occurred within the classroom setting and which stayed with me and worried me. I described each of these two incidents shortly after they occurred in a written journaling format and asked myself questions based on the four theories that inform the CRoP model as described by Fook and Gardner (2007). In this way, I was learning to teach CRoP but also learning how to use CRoP on my teaching practice at the same time. I was committed to modelling the CRoP stance and process, which then meant I also experienced some of the vulnerability that learners report experiencing when engaged in this process, since each time I reflected upon an incident, I also needed to decide how much of my experience I should share with the two classes I was teaching (see Chapters 2, 4, and 8 in particular for students' reflections on this vulnerability). Although at the time of writing the critical incidents I only completed stage 1 of the two-stage process, over time, as I went back to what I had written, and continued reflecting on what I had learned, I began to complete elements of stage 2. In presenting the descriptions of the process of critically reflecting upon these incidents in this chapter, I am providing an example of how to move beyond the idea of 'learning from students' or even the notion of 'the teacher as learner' and rather I am providing an example of 'transformative learning *with* students' as co-researchers of the CRoP process. It was through further discussions with Jan while completing this chapter that I was able to return to the learning from stage 1, link this to the literature, and complete stage 2 of the process.

Stage one

The first critical incident: Feeling unsettled, and not in a good way

A written description of the critical incident

I teach two sections of a CRoP course: My impression, after two weeks, is that the morning class seems to have more talkative students in it, while the afternoon class seems much quieter.

Last week, I started each class by opening up space for comments on the readings, reviewed Fook and Gardner's description of the culture required for critical reflection of practice, and then, because I had received feedback from the CIQs the first week that students were most engaged when involved in small group discussions rather than when I was lecturing with PowerPoint slides, I read a description of an incident from my clinical social work practice. With the class divided into four groups I asked each group to consider the impact of one of the four underlying theories of CRoP and to attempt to generate questions influenced by that theory: one group was to use the theory related to reflective practice, one the theory related to reflexivity, one postmodernism/deconstruction, and one critical social theory.

The morning class jumped into this exercise and, although one group, when I was checking on how they were doing related to time, mentioned they were surprised how hard it was to link the theory to the practice of asking relevant questions, everyone appeared engaged with the exercise. An interesting class discussion occurred following this, although I was somewhat worried that I had to cut off an otherwise useful conversation due to time.

In the afternoon class after asking the groups to begin attempting to link their assigned theory to the practice of asking questions to unpack the incident I had described, one group, in particular, expressed confusion, so I stayed with that group for a little while attempting to support the development of questions. One student, with what seemed to me to be a very stern-looking face, said it seemed straightforward, and so she was frustrated, because she then did not know what to do or how to link that with what I was asking. She crossly said, 'I don't get it!' I agreed that this exercise would actually uncover and highlight the difficulty of linking theory to practice and suggested that I could have taken more time lecturing on each theory, but there would probably still have been a gap between understanding the theory and actually putting it into the practice of asking questions. I think I probably sounded defensive and as if I was taking the comment personally, feeling blamed by her. Although some students said they had loved the exercise, and this seemed more in keeping with the majority of the students in the morning class, I was worried that the majority of the students in the afternoon class had found the exercise frustrating and distancing rather than engaging.

I carried on fretting about this. I imagined that the CIQs from the afternoon class would have highlighted lots of frustration. However, there was not as much of a difference in the comments on the CIQs as I expected. Both classes indicated learning from the difficulties inherent with coming up with questions (experiencing the gap between theory in practice through the act of trying to come up with questions). A handful of students in both classes indicated they felt they would have benefited from a little more description/recap of the theories and a clearer description of my expectations of them in the exercise prior to asking them to get started.

Reflective practice questions and responses

Were there any gaps between my explicit hopes (theory, expectations) for these classes and how they actually unfolded?

I hoped that instead of students, perhaps, disengaging as I lectured about the theories and the link to questions that they would be interested in the doing of it themselves – jumping into the practice of CRoP after the previous week of talking about the theory of it. However, this wasn't true for all of them. I think I overcompensated for my more natural style of engaging with the world by providing a learning experience that was overly suited for those who prefer to dive in the deep end. I was probably assuming I had a more 'traditional' learning preference whereas the younger social work students would want to be practising right away.

Does my account suggest anything about my underlying values or beliefs about teaching and learning?

Perhaps because I love to learn through having my ideas unsettled, I interact as if I expect everyone else to enjoy learning through having their ideas unsettled. Having discussed the culture and context needed for CRoP, I assumed we would all feel comfortable giving it a go.

Do any of those beliefs contradict my espoused/explicit descriptions of my beliefs about teaching and learning?

Although I love to learn through having my ideas unsettled, and discovering previously taken-for-granted ideas, it seems I can, unfortunately, take things personally and feel defensive if I feel blamed when someone is disengaged or frustrated. I guess I don't like that type of unsettling and assume frustration is bad somehow.

Reflexivity questions and responses

How did who I am affect the classroom interactions and my ongoing reflections on them?

Although I am always aiming to flatten any differences in power between myself, as a professor, and students, or myself, as a therapist, and service users, I wonder whether people may have felt uncomfortable asking for clarification because they might have thought I would have judged them negatively for not understanding what I expected right away.

I slip back and forth between two, perhaps, contradictory positions: I want to teach/facilitate in a manner which will be useful and so may slip into taking it personally and taking responsibility for something when it doesn't go as well as I had hoped and, on the other hand, especially at the graduate level, I expect students to take at least 50 percent of the responsibility for their engagement. I hope for them to take responsibility for asking questions, but maybe this is especially difficult when they don't know me well yet.

What emotions and physical reactions was I experiencing? How might I have dealt with them differently?

I think I felt my face tringle – as anger or frustration might show in someone's face. I did feel blamed and so then sounded defensive and as if I was taking it personally, although there may have been no intention to blame me. I could have brought the whole class back together and said that perhaps it might help if I go over everything briefly first and go over expectations more carefully. I still feel bad about this.

Postmodernism/deconstruction questions and responses

Looking back over the words I've used and how I have constructed the description of the narrative, what might I have missed in terms of setting up binaries or calling upon certain discourses?

I think for much of my description I have inadvertently set up binaries: One class is talkative, the other quieter; some were engaged, some were not; some would have liked more description/preparation for the exercise, some liked just jumping in; it was my fault/I could have done something better, the students could have asked for more direction. I only hint at more of the complexity when I say I was surprised that the CIQs were not all that different between the two classes and that even some of those who did enjoy the exercise would have liked a bit more direction to begin.

How might I have constructed myself and my role? What social discourses might have impacted me?

I wonder if I have attempted to position myself and create a role as co-learner in order to show respect for the knowledge and ability the students bring with them to the class, but then slip back into the role of more traditional professor/teacher when I fret about thinking I could/should have done it differently. There are always choices, and I chose to approach it one way. Just because it might have gone more smoothly if I had done it another/the other way doesn't mean I 'should' have done it another way.

Critical social theory questions and responses

Who has power in this incident? What social structures support the current distribution of power in this context?

I have power as a tenured professor who will be grading the students. Although I have indicated I am open to being flexible with the course outline and wish to share the power as much as I am able within the context of a university where I judge work and assign grades, I still have that power and can't give it away. As Giroux (1998; 2011) asks, how can I use power ethically and appropriately rather than merely sweep it under the carpet and pretend I don't have it?

The students have the power to point out anonymously in the CIQs what has been engaging and what has not been engaging and although they have the ability to ask and comment in class, they are still doing so within a particular context.

I can share these critical reflections of my teaching practice with them, or not. They are required to write up critical reflections as part of the course requirement. I can think about whether I will feel like I have become too vulnerable in sharing these reflections with the students and then not share them or adjust them so as to be 'safer'.

How are any personal experiences from my social context affecting this incident?

I am aware that as a female with power I may use power differently than male colleagues with power. As a feminist I may believe that the personal is political and that modelling and sharing examples of my reflections is a choice and, in some ways, a political choice, but I think I may also worry a little that this feminist position might be seen as too personal and, therefore, not respected or seen as professional.

Looking back on this first critical incident

As I was attempting to complete the CRoP process on the previously described incident by myself and was pressuring myself to decide how to address this incident in the next class, I can see with hindsight that I also inadvertently attempted a little 'problem-solving' at the same time. For people first learning this approach, this can become a barrier to asking the types of questions which truly will uncover underlying assumptions and beliefs. In this context, however, I believe I had already uncovered assumptions and, therefore, was able to move on to considering how to respond in the next class based upon my articulated values. I will say more about my overall learning after describing the second critical incident.

The second critical incident: Unsure as to how to manage classroom interactions

A written description of the critical incident

I had completed a short presentation regarding an article about 'human flourishing' (Gaye, 2010) and a chapter regarding 'spirituality and critical reflection' (Hunt, 2016) in the afternoon section of the course. I had given students about five minutes to talk in small groups about their reactions to the comments I had made and then invited people to share ideas and thoughts. Some students mentioned feeling this all made sense and resonated with their thoughts on spirituality and meaning-making. A couple suggested this was a new way of thinking and another that she did not find it especially helpful.

Julie (all names have been changed in this description) mentioned that although this resonated for her, she knew her partner would say he is an atheist and that he has not been influenced by spirituality or religion. Keith said that he thought we could not help but be influenced by these ideas and people would be naïve to think otherwise. Julie said that she did not think her husband would consider himself naïve. At this point, Keith and Liam were engaged in a brief private/side conversation, which resulted in some laughter. Julie and the other female students at her table all looked uncomfortable with the laughter and looked over to the table where Keith and Liam were sitting. Julie asked what they were laughing about. I heard Keith say that he had not been suggesting her husband was naïve. I asked Liam if he would comment. He looked somewhat uncomfortable, started to say something and then said, 'oh, never mind'.

Following this and during the time when small groups were working on starting the stage 2 process, I spent some time with Keith, Liam, and two female students, assisting them in starting the stage 2 process in their small group and asking questions of Liam regarding his critical incident. I then went to the table where Julie was working with four other female students in their group. She still looked somewhat upset, and I asked her if she wanted me to do anything regarding this incident. She told me they were adults and she didn't need me to do anything, but she also said she did not want to deal with them directly yet because she was still too angry and upset so didn't trust herself to deal with them appropriately. She also mentioned that they had a learning contract. I assumed she meant she had a learning contract with Liam and that she would follow-up with him because of that. When I read the CIQs, I saw that a handful of people commented on the 'uncomfortable situation' between Julie, Keith, and Liam, saying it affected their ability to focus in class, and one person wondered why I had not dealt with the males chuckling.

I was about to e-mail Julie to ask her how she had been doing, if she had dealt with the situation with Keith and Liam, and whether she would be comfortable with me raising it in class the next week. However, before I had a chance to e-mail her, I received an e-mail from her saying she had tried to meet with me in my office hour after class last week. I then called in to listen to my voicemail message and because she had left her phone number, I called her. I apologised for not having been there when she popped by to my office and for my oversight in not checking messages sooner. She presented her memories of how the incident unfolded and expressed her greater concerns with Liam's behaviour. She said she felt she and Keith could have had a decent conversation sharing their different points of view respectfully. She found the laughter problematic and she said that other students had told her that they heard Liam say to Keith that her husband was naïve. I mentioned to her that I had heard Keith say he had not been saying her husband was naïve and she said she wished she had heard that. She also said that she has been using the CRoP process with the other members of her group in order to reflect upon this situation. She said she recognises parts of herself in this but also thinks Keith and Liam should examine their male privilege. I told her that at the time I had given Keith and Liam the benefit of the doubt regarding not having intended anything hurtful but that Foucault would suggest we need to examine the effects of our behaviours rather than the intentions (Chambon, 1999), so I would raise the issue with them individually and in class. The conversation continued as we talked more generally about the class (how quiet it is usually), and the social work programme as a whole.

Reflection of practice questions and responses

What are my hopes for the classroom and do I see any gaps between what I hope for and what occurred – gaps particularly in relation to my skills/practices?

I want a class to feel safe enough to share ideas and be curious about new ways of thinking. The discussion in the first week about expectations of one another and the time we spent over the first few weeks talking about the necessary climate indicated that the class was open to the expression of differing points of view, but they also wanted a climate of acceptance and support. 'Critical acceptance,' as Fook and Gardner (2007) describe it, is perhaps not fully developed.

I am interested in people's different ideas and have attempted to model an acceptance of ideas that are different than my own. As one student looked a bit hesitant about saying she did not find the definition of spirituality particularly useful, that it didn't resonate for her, I did say it was okay to have different ideas.

I think if I had been angry with Keith and Liam's behaviour, I would have said something. I agree with Julie's follow-up comments that she imagines that she and Keith could have had a respectful and useful conversation, although she said she found the term 'naïve' had a judgmental quality to it, what really upset her was the laughter going on between the two of them. I also had a sense that Keith was actually interested in engaging in a conversation about a complex topic, but the laughter drew him away from it. I gave them both the benefit of the doubt and did not think they intended anything hurtful, and I was surprised that Liam did not take the opportunity to explain what he had said or what he was laughing about. It was the fact that I was surprised that someone who has otherwise been interested in engaging in conversation in class would leave this feeling hanging that threw me off. I was left not knowing whether to pursue it or let it drop. This was the 'gap'. When I spoke to Julie and she said they were adults, this reinforced the position I was coming from of not intervening in a situation between two adults, but when I see the CIQs, I see that this situation has affected more than just Julie.

Reflexivity questions and responses

What about me and my set of 'lenses' coloured how I handled/didn't handle the situation and how I look at it now?

I don't like conflict, although I will deal with it when necessary. I like all these students and just assume that they will be careful how they say things so as not to hurt one another. I also look for the good in them and assume none of them are intentionally meaning to hurt another.

It is certainly possible that because I like Keith and Liam, as well as Julie, that I saw their behaviour as perhaps insensitive but not as so totally inappropriate that I needed to challenge them on it or hold them accountable. I hoped that Keith saying that he didn't mean Julie's husband was naïve would have helped, but as I have said, I was really surprised by Liam's lack of response. I assumed learning and the classroom environment was important to him.

I have power in my role as a professor but prefer not to take on a position of power but rather respect my students as adults/equals. This also may have silenced me.

Postmodernism questions and reflections

What perspectives and views are missing? What are other ways of looking at it? Whose voice is missing or silenced?

I don't know Liam's point of view yet. I e-mailed Keith and have heard back from him and he shared his ideas. He indicated being somewhat worried that a conversation in class would end up being emotional. He said he would e-mail Julie and apologise. He said part of the problem was that both he and Liam were exhausted and sick but agreed the laughter and side conversation were not conducive to classroom discussion and he felt bad about that because open dialogue in university is important to him. I only have a few comments from a handful of other students so don't know what everyone else in the class is thinking and feeling about the situation.

In terms of other perspectives, it is possible Liam was feeling embarrassed by having been 'caught' less engaged in the whole classroom discussion than he would have liked to have been. Also, in writing about this incident, I've focused on the behaviours of three students but not the other 19 who were also present.

Has the language used in the description indicated any binaries?

I don't think I have set up any binaries. When I look at the language I have used to describe this incident I think I am mainly indicating how much I like and respect all the players. . .has this had an impact on how I responded and how I think about it now?

Despite liking them all I was left thinking, I would have liked to have responded differently when Liam said, 'never mind'.

Critical social theory questions and responses

What structures of power are at play in this situation?

I have the most power as professor although I am always attempting to share that as best I can in an appropriate manner. I don't see the two males as having more power than the female students in this classroom context where they are the minority, but I gather from CIQ comments and Julie's reflections when we spoke on the phone that they may be seen by the other students as having power and privilege as males. It is possible that the female students see me as colluding with the male students, as duped by them and unwilling to challenge what they see as their inappropriate laughter. I really don't think I would have

132   Laura Béres

handled this any differently if the laughter had been going on between two female students.

I think my bigger challenge is to follow along with Foucault's suggestion that we examine effects rather than intentions and that in giving people the benefit of the doubt regarding their intentions I end up not responding to the behaviours and the effects. I should perhaps use my power more rather than less.

Looking back on this second critical incident

In the follow-up class, I raised the fact that through reading the CIQs and talking with some of the students, I had come to realise that a classroom interaction the week before had upset several people. I explained that I had discussed the incident with the people directly involved and that I was also raising it in class so that it could be discussed more fully and so that I could apologise and take responsibility for the fact that I had not raised the issue at the time. Liam also apologised in class for his actions. In addition, I shared some of the learning I had gained through critically reflecting upon this incident. Interestingly, CIQs for this week showed some of the students 'felt bad' that I had apologised, stating they did not think of it as my fault and that they continued to feel Keith and Liam could have taken greater responsibility.

Stage two

What I have learned and what I will do differently the next time

Stage 2 of the CRoP process involves examining and summarising what has been learned through stage 1, asking further questions if necessary, and articulating any new theory of practice. The new learning can often be summed up in a 'mantra' as a reminder of the insights (Fook & Gardner, 2007). I have also found that it is in stage 2 that it is useful to review the literature that has already been published in related areas in order to link new learning to a broader theoretical base (see Béres [2017] for another example of this).

As I write this chapter, two years have passed since I first developed and began teaching the Critical Reflection and Appraisal of Practice course. Despite the two incidents, which I have described that worried me at the time, I had the overwhelming experience of this being a course which both the students and I found extremely engaging. The fact that the students found the course so stimulating and engaging both pleased but also surprised me to a certain degree. This was the context in which I completed stage 2 of the process and, as part of the process, decided how to approach teaching the course for the second time. However, having made my way through stage 1 through journaling, and not receiving input from anyone else as is usual in the CRoP process, I found it was particularly helpful to share my beginning stage 2 insights with a colleague (in this case, Jan) who was curious to hear a little more about what I meant by vulnerability. This encouraged me to pursue stage 2 in more detail and realise that the underlying element of the first two critical incidents was, indeed, vulnerability, which I could explore further.

What I have learned, or what has been reinforced that I already knew, about myself:

- I've always believed in the importance of congruence. My underlying values colour every area of my life: personal, teaching practice, and therapeutic practice. This is about walking the talk. If I am presenting the importance of CRoP, I am going to need to continue engaging in CRoP myself. This also means a certain amount of vulnerability, which I will discuss.
- I do not like conflict, but I do like talking things through and assisting people in trying to understand one another's point of view. Although, through critically reflecting upon the first incident, I came to the conclusion that I needed to stay focused on caring about students and their needs rather than feeling blamed if something did not go as well as I had hoped, learning from the second incident adds further nuance. Caring for and liking the students does not mean conflict will not occur. However, my stance of caring and respect may make it easier for students to 'hear' feedback on how some of their behaviours are being interpreted.

Specific learning related to teaching critical reflection:

- The importance of the culture of critical acceptance: I will spend more time on this in future courses and invited a former student, Nate, to come and speak about this also in the first class of the second course I taught. Fook (2012) describes 'critical acceptance' as being made up of 'acceptance' of the story being shared in the description of the critical incident, trusting the intent and perspective represented in the story while also maintaining a stance provided by the four theoretical frameworks, which will then allow for exploration of deeply held underlying assumptions (p. 223). It is the examination of these assumptions that can be unsettling for people, and I will strive to explain this more fully in the future. It means being able to talk about issues like 'spirituality', and those things that give people a sense of meaning and purpose, without judgement. (As described in Chapter 1, Jan has begun adding spirituality as a fifth theoretical framework to the CRoP process.)

Generalisable learning relevant to all courses I teach:

- The importance of vulnerability. I have never thought of vulnerability as a bad thing but realise many people do not like the idea of being vulnerable if they see it as being related to not being safe or protected. For me, it is more about being seen to be who I am, being authentic in my interactions, willing to show how I learn from my mistakes, and apologising when appropriate.

Further ideas about vulnerability

Rogers (2017), discussing availability and vulnerability as the guiding principles within her spiritual and professional practices, comments that vulnerability can take courage since it involves presenting oneself to others 'without the "false props" we often use to bolster our egos' (p. 151). She argues that this can engender hope in others, which I believe also came about in the CRoP classrooms. My willingness to share critical incidents from my teaching and therapeutic practice highlighted that I was able to share my limitations with students and continue to learn from reflecting upon them. This appeared to encourage students to also take a chance to talk about incidents from previous field placements about which they continued to be worried and even ashamed. Some of the students expressed that it was a relief to finally feel they no longer had to hide these previous experiences and so be able to learn from them and feel more hopeful and prepared for their next field placement assignments. In this way, we were able to create a place for shared vulnerability, which Osler and Becker (1997) argue relates to shared authority. This resonates with my reflections on my two critical incidents where I grappled with how to share my power and authority on the one hand and use it ethically and appropriately rather than abdicate it on the other hand.

Osler and Becker (1997), moving beyond the dichotomy of traditional versus progressive forms of teaching, argue that a 'different place' is found between these opposite points of the teaching continuum, which involves sharing both authority and vulnerability. They say teachers should open up their own imperfections so as to make room in the classroom for students also to show their imperfections. 'To share authority with our students requires that we become vulnerable. To do otherwise puts us back in one of the old places: the rock of unquestionable authority or the soft place of acquiesced authority' (Osler & Becker, 1997, p. 463). They conclude by pointing out that this does not mean teachers need to be embarrassed by their expertise and fearful of sharing their beliefs and knowledge, but they also can acknowledge their imperfections and encourage students to question them. Their descriptions of this 'different place' of teaching are reinforcing of my learning from my reflections and also congruent with the postmodern and critical social theory frameworks that are part of the CRoP process, as this moves away from dichotomous thinking about teaching positions and towards a transparent use and sharing of power.

Meyer, Le Fevre, and Robinson (2017) also hold a positive view of vulnerability, having conducted research with educational leaders, and found that being willing to admit their weaknesses facilitated the building of trust and thereby made it easier for their staff to also acknowledge difficulties. They argue, '[t]o be honest and open means to accept responsibility and expose one's own mistakes or weakness, in other words, to show vulnerability' (p. 222), which they admit is not for those who prefer to be seen as infallible. They go on to say that showing vulnerability can actually be seen as a strength, signalling a genuine desire to reflect on and inquire into one's own position (p. 223). Their data and resulting conclusions also show how leaders' disclosure of their own contribution to a concern 'fosters trust propensity in others as it signals leaders' truthfulness, benevolence and integrity [. . . and this] can encourage others to discuss mistakes and failures more openly' (p. 230). Although the critical incidents that students are asked to discuss in the CRoP process are not necessarily related to mistakes they have made, they often appear to feel worried and embarrassed about their incidents as though they thought they had done something wrong in the situation. Therefore, Meyer, Le Fevre, and Robinson's research findings provide me with further encouragement to continue to show my vulnerability and, thus, contribute to a sense of trust and willingness in students to also show vulnerability. It appears as though this sharing of vulnerability can further contribute to the transformative learning process where there is a movement away from traditional hierarchies and uses of power and knowledge.

Since these thoughts on vulnerability have contributed to the final aspect of my stage 2 of the CRoP process, they have also contributed to my creation of a mantra that can serve as a reminder of what has been learned: Transformative learning involves authenticity and vulnerability.

Continuing the critical reflection process: Balancing vulnerability with self-protection

Having completed teaching the Critical Reflection and Appraisal of Practice course for a second time, and through critically reflecting upon another incident that occurred during this second course, I made a slight alteration to my commitment to vulnerability and authenticity for transformative learning. I have reflected upon this incident in further detail in a chapter regarding 'practice wisdom' (Béres, 2019).

The term in which I taught the CRoP course for a second time was a particularly busy and emotionally draining four months for a variety of reasons. A colleague's sudden death required that I teach an extra course, and ongoing changes in the graduate programme resulted in one CRoP class size of 33 students rather than two sections of 22. I was committed to continuing to model vulnerability and authenticity for the students and was explicit about how I believed these qualities were tied to transformative learning. I also decided to continue using the CIQs to assist with attunement to students' experiences. Nonetheless, at the midpoint of teaching the course the second time, I discontinued the use of the CIQs. Using the CRoP lens of Reflexivity, I recognise that there are elements of my personality and social history that have positioned me to be hyper-aware of other's emotions and the dynamics between people, which means what I require for self-protection is probably quite different from what others would require. Possibly due to almost 30 years of experience as a clinical social worker/psychotherapist, I am already attuned to classroom dynamics and student engagement, and the anonymous comments made in the CIQs added what felt like an overload of emotional stimulation from the students this second year. Students could write about a reaction they were experiencing in the moment of writing, but this was not necessarily a lasting thought and often did not need to be addressed. Although Brookfield (2017) has stated that he continues to find CIQs exceptionally useful as a way to quickly become aware of, and respond to, any confusions, I found myself unwilling to continue using them this second time. I have found that Liechty's (2018) research regarding the 'use of self' provided me with a way of understanding how I 'used my "self"' and fine-tuned my commitment to my stance of vulnerability and authenticity for transformative learning during this more recent experience of teaching CRoP. Her research focused on social work educators' understanding of the role of the use of self in the therapeutic relationship, and the teaching of this to social work students, but I believe her findings are relevant to the learning relationship developed between professor and students also.

Liechty presents the themes that emerged from her analysis of focus group discussions within two different frameworks: the personal qualities and the professional capabilities required for appropriate use of self. The personal qualities that influence the use of self are described as openness, self-reflectiveness, attunement to others, commitment to social work, and emotional maturity. Openness is described as including elements of trust, curiosity and wonder, authenticity, willingness to share uncertainty, and courage. Attunement to others is described as including elements of caring and empathy, intuition, awareness of how others experience us, and emotional boundaries (Liechty, 2018). Her comments resonated with my own commitments to authenticity, vulnerability, and curiosity, contributing to considerations of how I am also engaging in the use of self as I teach. However, what was new and helpful for me was her description of the need to balance the awareness of how others experience us with the need for emotional boundaries. She reports one research participant as saying, "'[Use of self] includes an awareness and sensitivity to how others experience us." This sensitivity is desirable but can be overwhelming', while another participant added, "'At the same time we're trying to become empathetic, we become blind in the process, to tune out some of that, because it's too much stimulation." He noted, "There are really two processes – perceiving and protecting yourself simultaneously"' (Liechty, 2018, p. 154). She suggests this use of emotional boundaries is a form of self-protection.

This idea of needing to balance self-protection with an openness to others and willingness to be vulnerable provided me with an 'aha' moment. This has allowed me to move forward in my teaching, feeling much more comfortable with the notion that while vulnerability continues to be important to me in my commitment to transformative learning, since it involves attunement to others, it is also perfectly reasonable to set boundaries to protect myself from overstimulation through that attunement.

Conclusion

In presenting a detailed description of learning how to teach Fook's model of critical reflection, I hope I have demonstrated how useful the model is for examining our teaching practices. I have now used the model to critically reflect on teaching the Critical Reflection and Appraisal of Practice course twice within a university setting, showing how my learning process continues to evolve and is open to fine-tuning. Realising that my use of power, or authority, was related to feelings of vulnerability was the main element of learning from my critical incidents and an important step of stage 2 the first time I taught the course. This contributed to a further sense of there being a 'gap' in my understanding, which prompted a review of the literature regarding vulnerability. While teaching the course for the second time, and feeling overstimulated by the process, the critical reflection process provided a structure that led me to consider the impact of the use of self and self-protection. This provided me with the ability to conceptualise how these two commitments – one to vulnerability and authenticity and the other to self-protection – could be balanced and continue to develop the appropriate climate for transformative learning. No doubt, I will continue to learn more each year I facilitate this course.

References

Béres, L. (2017). Maintaining the ability to be unsettled and learn afresh: What philosophy contributes to our understanding of 'reflection' and 'experience'. *Reflective Practice: Multidisciplinary and International Perspectives*, 18(2), 280–290. doi:10.1080/14623943.2016.1269003

Béres, L. (2019). Valuing critical reflection and narratives of practice wisdom. In J. Higgs (Ed.), *Practice wisdom* (pp. 277–288). Leiden, Netherlands: Brill Sense.

Brookfield, S.D. (2009). The concept of critical reflection: Promises and contradictions. *European Journal of Social Work*, 12(3), 293–304. doi:10.1080/13691450902945215

Brookfield, S.D. (2017). *Becoming a critically reflective teacher* (2nd ed.). San Francisco, CA: Jossey-Bass.

Chambon, A.S. (1999). Foucault's approach: Making the familiar visible. In A.S. Chambon, A. Irving, & L. Epstein (Eds). *Reading Foucault for social work* (pp. 51–81). New York: Columbia University Press.

Fawcett, B., Featherstone, B., Fook, J., & Rossiter, A. (2000). *Practice and research in social work: Postmodern feminist perspectives*. London: Routledge.

Fook, J. (2002). *Social work: A critical approach to practice*. London: SAGE.

Fook, J. (2012). The challenge of creating critically reflective groups. *Social Work with Groups*, 35(3), 218–234. doi:10.1080/01609513.2011.624375

Fook, J., & Gardner, F. (2007). *Practising critical reflection: A resource handbook*. Maidenhead: Open University Press.

Gaye, T. (2010). In what ways can reflective practice enhance human flourishing? *Reflective Practice*, 11(1), 1–7. doi:10.1080/14623940903525132

Giroux, H.A. (1998). *Pedagogy and the politics of hope*. Boulder, CO: Westview.

Giroux, H.A. (2001). Pedagogy of the depressed: Beyond the new politics of cynicism. *College Literature*, 28(3), 1–32.

Hick, S., Fook, J., & Pozzuto, R. (2005). *Social work: A critical turn*. Toronto, Canada: Thompson Educational Publishing.

Hunt, C. (2016). Spiritual creatures? Exploring an interface between critical reflective practice and spirituality. In J. Fook, V. Collington, F. Ross, G. Ruch, & L. West (Eds.), *Researching critical reflection: Multidisciplinary perspectives* (pp. 34–47). London: Routledge.

Liechty, J. (2018). Exploring use of self: Moving beyond definitional challenges. *Journal of Social Work Education*, 54(1): 148–162. doi:10.1080/10437797.2017.1314836

Meyer, F., Le Fevre, D.M., & Robinson, V.M.J. (2017). How leaders communicate their vulnerability: Implications for trust building. *International Journal of Educational Management*, 31(2), 221–235. doi:10.1108/IJEM-11-2015-0150

Oyler, C., & Becker, J. (1997). Teaching beyond the progressive-traditional dichotomy: Sharing authority and sharing vulnerability. *Curriculum Inquiry*, 27(4), 453–467. doi:10.1111/0362-6784.00064

Rogers, M. (2017). Using availability and vulnerability to operationalize spirituality. In L. Béres (Ed.), *Practising spirituality: Reflections on meaning-making in personal and professional contexts* (pp. 145–164). London: Palgrave Macmillan.

Chapter 12

Researching the learning experience of critical reflection

Laura Béres and Jan Fook with Nate Meidinger and Tonya Salomons

As has been described in the introductory chapter and again in Chapter 11, the idea behind this book arose from the experience of teaching Jan Fook's Critical Reflection on Practice (CRoP) model for the first time in a 13-week academic term in a Canadian university. During the planning stages, prior to teaching the course, we decided to incorporate a research component into the course. In the last chapter, Laura described how she structured the course and presented her reflections that she engaged in during and after teaching the course, highlighting her process of learning how to teach critical reflection, and how to engage in transformative pedagogy more generally. In this chapter, we will report on the themes, which we have found through the process of analysing students' comments in questionnaires they were asked to complete prior to commencing the course and then five months following completion of the course. Although students also completed Critical Incident Questionnaires (CIQs) each week, we will not be reviewing the CIQs in this chapter due to space. However, five of the students who participated in this first course have added their detailed reflections regarding learning critical reflection in their own independent chapters within this book. Specifically, in this chapter, we will provide the rationale for this study and describe the methodological approach used, providing examples of themes within the data and describing our thoughts about those themes. The chapter ends with a discussion of the findings in relation to other claims made about critical reflection in the literature.

Rationale

As has been argued elsewhere, there is little systematic research on critical reflection, as it is a concept and practice, which has varying meanings and variously different ways of being practised (Fook et al., 2016). This means that it is difficult to amass cumulative 'evidence', from a range of settings, about what works. Given the alleged significance of critical reflection in contemporary professional education and practice, this is a major shortcoming. In particular, the outcomes of critical reflection have been under-researched (Fook et al., 2016) so that whilst there is resounding agreement about its value, there are few studies, which can attest unequivocally, through empirical research, to the sorts of positive outcomes, which are claimed for it (Fook, Psoinos, & Sartori, 2016). Whilst this chapter is not intended to be focused on outcomes, we believe one important way to add to a more systematic understanding of how critical reflection works is to document some of the overall patterns of learning, which occur for students. This will assist in guiding educators in planning and implementing courses, which both teach and use critical reflection. The bulk of the chapters in this book narrate the differing experiences of individual learners, aiming to give both a deep and a broad understanding of how and what different learners learn. This chapter, by contrast, aims to pull together the main themes and patterns regarding what and how students learned in Laura's initial course. In the following section, we describe in more detail our methods for collecting the data from students and also our approach to analysing students' responses.

Methodology

Braun and Clarke's (2006) descriptions of thematic analysis have guided our approach to this project, since they offer clear advice as to how to rigorously and deliberately conduct thematic analysis. They point out that one of the benefits of thematic analysis is how flexible it is, which means that it can be used in various ways but which also means it is crucial for researchers to be clear about how they particularly used it and engaged in the development and analysis of themes within their data. Unlike grounded theory analysis, which seeks to create new theory regarding a phenomenon described in the data, or interpretive phenomenological analysis (IPA), which seeks to provide rich and detailed descriptions of a small number of research participants' lived experience, 'thematic analysis can be a method that works both to reflect reality and to unpick and unravel the surface of the "reality"' (Braun & Clarke, 2006, p. 81). Braun and Clarke suggest it is important for researchers, therefore, to be transparent about their theoretical frameworks and assumptions, going on to describe the six phases of rigorous thematic analysis: familiarising oneself with the data; considering initial codes; searching for themes, reviewing themes; defining and naming themes; and producing the report. With their suggestions in mind, we present a description of our data and how we identified themes.

Participants

Forty-four Canadian Master of Social Work (MSW) students were registered and assigned to one of two 'Critical Reflection and Appraisal of Social Work' course sections in the School of Social Work within a small liberal arts university college in Ontario. The students ranged in age from their mid-twenties to mid-forties. All of them were Caucasian. The majority presented as women, with only two men in one section and three in the other section. In the first year of this course being offered, all students already had earned a Bachelor of Social Work degree (a four-year undergraduate honours university degree) and were, therefore, enrolled in this yearlong advanced standing MSW programme.

Procedure

One week prior to the course beginning, and following one of several presentations to students as part of the MSW Orientation Week activities, the research project that was to be conducted in relation to the course was explained and students were asked to complete a questionnaire about what they already knew about critical reflection and what their hopes for the course were. They were asked not to identify themselves on the questionnaire. All 44 students completed this pre-course questionnaire, which included the following questions: What do you feel you know already about critical reflection? How do you critically reflect and how does it help your practice? What are you hoping to get out of the Critical Reflection on Practice course?

We provided post-course questionnaires to students five months following the completion of the course at which point they had been in a social work field placement (internship) for four months. We waited five months before asking them to complete the post-course questionnaire, because we were interested not only in what students believed they had learned in the class but also in whether they found it was useful to their practice. Questionnaires were sent electronically to students, asking them to return the completed questionnaires to the Field Placement Coordinator, as someone not involved in the research project. We hoped that by offering this survey electronically and by ensuring we, as researchers, would not be able to identify respondents and connect survey comments to particular students, we would increase the chances of a higher rate of return. However, this resulted in only a 27 percent return rate (12 out of a possible 44), although this return rate is not unusual when conducting research surveys in this manner.

In the post-course questionnaire, we asked the following questions: Were your expectations of the Critical Reflection and Appraisal of Social Work course met? What sorts of things helped you learn Critical Reflection on Practice? Were there specific moments or experiences in class that stand out for you as you now look back at it? What do you think you learned about Critical Reflection on Practice; do you think your ideas changed at all? Have you been integrating Critical Reflection on Practice into your practicum experience; if so, has it been useful? What, if anything, do you think you will change about your ongoing practice as a result of what you learned about Critical Reflection on Practice? Could you please sum up what you think about Critical Reflection on Practice? If you had to tell someone who knew nothing about Critical Reflection on Practice, what would you say? These questions gathered a broad range of comments, which provided a detailed picture of what students believed had supported their learning, what they had learned from the course, and what the ongoing effects of that learning were in their practice.

Data analysis

Pre-course summary

Unsurprisingly, a review of the pre-course questionnaires showed a range of different levels of understanding of critical reflection. Answers suggested that students had all been taught in their undergraduate programmes that critical reflection was an important part of professional practice but that they did not remember having been taught what it was or how to engage in it. The following provides a summary (versus a thematic analysis) of the types of comments made in the pre-course survey regarding what they believed they already knew about critical reflection:

1   It is crucial.
2   It relates to self/growth/improvement/change.
3   It is linked to clinical practice improvement.
4   There is a psychodynamic influence, so it requires understanding our own background, triggers, as well as transference and countertransference issues.
5   I do not know much or anything about it.

In general, students thought critical reflection entailed reviewing emotions in relation to interactions with service users, and so it was to be done in supervision or in personal journaling. We reviewed these initial questionnaires for explicit content instead of latent or underlying themes (Braun & Clarke, 2006). The responses from students verified what Jan has usually experienced over the course of many years of facilitating critical reflection workshops and what we had expected as probable for these students also: students had been taught the importance of reflection, but they had not been taught a systematic approach to reflecting critically on their practice. The majority of them reported considering themselves as already engaging in reflection, since they said they did a lot of thinking and talking about their work. Jan has suggested that practitioners almost always indicate that they are already reflecting on their practice but usually have not been relying on a particular model to move the reflection beyond either a personal examination of emotions on the one hand or an overly rational attempt to problem solve on the other. Students also suggested they could see the benefit of the course and hoped to learn a new approach to reflection and, perhaps, increase their self-awareness. Jan's model of critical reflection was new to all of them, and so we planned to ask them, after completing the course, about their thoughts on this model and the process of learning it. We were, therefore, interested in completing a thorough thematic analysis of the post-course questionnaires with a focus on latent or underlying themes as well as the explicit comments.

Post-course thematic analysis

Before moving on to a description of our process of analysing themes in the data, it is important to mention that 22 of the 44 students also enrolled in a Narrative Therapy: Theory and Practice course that Laura also taught. Some of the comments made in the post-critical reflection course questionnaires made connections between the two courses and use language and turns of phrase that they would have learned in the narrative therapy course. We have mentioned in previous chapters that we also see ways in which critical reflection and narrative therapy draw upon similar theories and may also contribute to the further development of each. Interestingly, but also no doubt related to their involvement in this other course, students appeared to have shifted from making any comments about the link between reflection and psychodynamic theories in the pre-course questionnaire to making connections between critical reflection and narrative practice in the post-course questionnaire.

Nate and Tonya, as student participant-research assistants, as well as Jan and Laura, each read and reread the post-course questionnaire data separately, immersing ourselves in the rich descriptions offered, and making notes on our observations. Jan and Laura then met together and reread the data again, discussing the material and considering our initial reactions to what appeared to be most interesting: what jumped out at us or what was surprising or particularly eloquently described. Nate and Tonya had graduated by this point and were not able to meet with us again. Having been immersed in writing about and teaching critical reflection, we were clearly not removed sufficiently from the literature and theory to be engaged fully in an inductive analysis, but neither were we attempting to deductively analyse the data or fit it into preconceived categories. Laura then returned to the data, reviewing all the raw data again as well as the notes we had made together. Through this process, Laura coded the raw data manually using colour-coded highlighting. In this way, she highlighted comments made about the learning process with subcategories of those aspects that had supported or hindered learning in the class. She also highlighted comments made about whether or not students were integrating critical reflection in their practice with subcategories as to how they were doing that or whether they had future plans to do so. Finally, she highlighted what the students identified as being their learning, which had several different categories, ranging from having learned to be more politicised on the one hand to becoming more mindful on the other.

Having proceeded through the stages of reviewing the coded highlighted sections, Laura began to develop themes and then, following the Braun and Clarke (2006) model, returned to review the themes again until she had the sense that she was no longer seeing any further clarification of overarching themes. In returning to initial notes that we had made together, it was clear that the thematic analysis process had reaffirmed areas that we had begun to consider at that early stage of our immersion in the data. Finally, after both Jan and Laura reviewed themes again, Tonya and Nate read this chapter in order to check if these themes also resonated with their experiences and to ensure they were able to contribute their own reflections.

Results

We will focus on four themes in the data in this chapter: the development of empathy/compassion; becoming more politicised and aware of the need to transform action; the need for 'practice, practice, practice for learning'; and committing to the ongoing integration of critical reflection.

1 The development of empathy/compassion as a result of the critical reflection process

There were three explicit comments made in the data about the link between CRoP and empathy:

> CRoP helps individuals to practise and learn more empathy because it pulls away layers of bias and tunnel vision. It prompts individuals to be humble, curious, motivated, and inspired. CRoP offers growth on both professional and personal levels. Who could ask for anything more? (Student 'B')
>
> I will be more objective and less reactive and more empathetic, and I have gained a certain amount of wisdom from this process, which will continue to serve me well in the field. (Student 'F')
>
> CRoP is a set of theories that give one a solid foundation for knowing the world through different lenses – in different ways. And when one has that foundation, it can really help unpack incidents that challenge oneself in one's practice and, in doing so, one gets to see 'multiple truths' of a situation. And that grows empathy and perspective – which is what's really needed in the world right now. (Student 'K')

We were initially both drawn to these explicit comments about empathy and pleased to see that they were made by more than only one student. Through the thematic analysis process, it became clear that other students were also making comments that were related to this theme of empathy although not explicitly using the word 'empathy'. There was a sense of compassion for themselves also developing, since comments made the link between critical reflection, self-care, and the reduction of self-blame:

> It helps resolve feelings of responsibility and blame but can also lead to enhanced practice knowledge [. . .] I see CRoP as an important self-care tool, in that it enhances your ability to maintain control over your actions and to understand how the many social, cultural, and personal factors can influence practice decisions. (Student 'C')

Reflecting on my own biases and assumptions will allow me to practise from more of an open-minded and nonjudgmental position. [. . .] Ultimately, I believe critical reflection enhances one's interpersonal and intra-personal intelligence, which are both important elements of being a professional, ethical, and useful social worker. (Student 'J')

This same student also made the following comment about how critical reflection assisted her/him in working in a multicultural setting, which we believe also links to the sense of empathy, since it allows for understanding and compassion of people different from oneself:

I am in a multicultural setting for my practicum where I am often a minority (while I am used to being a part of the dominant population) and am working with people whose 'normal' or understanding of the world is different than my own. [. . .] Critical reflection has been extremely helpful in helping me [. . .] to constantly reflect on and address my own biases and assumptions while working with a different culture. (Student 'J')

2 More politicised and aware of the need to transform action as a result of critical reflection

In a similar vein to the last comment about working more sensitively and empathetically with multicultural groups, we saw a theme in the students' comments regarding having learned that critical reflection is linked to transformational action, thereby further politicising them.

Critical reflection on practice has helped me navigate to a preferred professional identity – one that includes taking the time to not only engage in critical reflection but to turn that reflection into critical action. To date, this course has been one of the most useful and practical in terms of developing my skills as a practitioner. (Student 'A')

I think what will stay with me throughout my practice is the importance of linking new ways of thinking with transformative actions. Knowing that awareness is a necessary first step that should be followed by a changed way of being. (Student 'I')

CRoP is a process that places responsibility on social workers to improve their practice by reflecting on incidents in their work. [. . .] and this reflection would be action focused. [It is] a method in which social workers go from reflecting on practice in a passive sense to an active dynamic approach. (Student 'E')

3 Practice, practice, practice for learning

Several students made comments about the structure of the course including the midterm test and final presentations and papers as all contributing to their learning. However, in terms of what assisted students in learning the most, they all pointed out that the fact that classroom time had been provided to them so that they could 'practice, practice, practice' was crucial. Some described feeling safe and able to comfortably engage in being vulnerable with their fellow group members, while others remarked on having experienced difficulties within their groups but having been able to learn through those challenges. One student remarked that she felt more attention should have been paid to group safety in this and other courses within the MSW programme:

> One disappointing thing that did happen in the CRoP course for me was when the group dynamics in my group suddenly became unsupportive of all members due to the inability of one member to hold the tension of the 'not-knowing' stance. [. . .] To be vulnerable one has to really trust other's intentions! (Student 'K')

This particular student went on to say that she 'really enjoyed the topic [she] wrote for [her] paper', which provided her with the chance of furthering her learning, despite what she had experienced as disappointing dynamics in her group.

Further comments regarding the theme of practice were as follows:

> The time to practice this technique was very helpful. It took a bit of time at first to process the whole concept but the practical piece of being able to apply the steps really helped consolidate the information. I also started to practice it outside of class in my own work, which helped. [. . .] The initial group work was uncomfortable as we tried to find our way into proper lines of questioning but also reinforced the right way to question and opened up a whole new way of thinking. . .we got better as we went along. Being able to have the space to practise what it was and wasn't really clarified the right process and the importance of this practice in our work. . .the key is – practice, practice, practice. Also watching it with the professor and a student was most helpful. (Student 'F')

> Working in the groups was helpful to learn critical reflection. It was also helpful to watch and participate in sessions that were done in front of the group. I found the midterm exam forced me to engage in the material more thoroughly, which led to a better ability to make use of it and apply it. (Student 'D')

> The atmosphere in the classroom appeared to be one of engagement. It was a safe place for discussion and trying new skills. The dedication to allowing space to practise the CRoP process with our own critical incidents was very beneficial – not just in terms of learning the process but also in terms of learning not to be afraid to engage in unsettling deeply held beliefs and assumptions. (Student 'A')

Having classroom 'workshops', where we were able to actually critically reflect and go through both stages of the model was helpful. [. . .] It was also helpful to have a demonstration at the front of the class. (Student 'C')

This student also provided an example from her group process when a group member moved from a position of self-criticism to a position of recognising a range of contributing factors in her critical incident. This provided a concrete example of how the practice in group assisted with learning. Nate has offered that by using classmates as a sounding board, CRoP helped them each to have the distance and support needed to sit with critical incidents. He said, in his own case, the ability to see others finding new meaning in their critical incidents was inspiring and provided information for his own exploration. He summed this up by suggesting exploration is contagious.

4 Committing to the ongoing integration of critical reflection

Although two of the 12 students reported that they had not integrated critical reflection into their field placement (internship) practice, those two both indicated wishing to do so when demands on their time lessened. A third student described being in a 'fast-paced organisation' where it was hard to incorporate it into her practice, but she did say that she and her supervisor were attempting different ways of integrating it so she hoped it would 'allow for a smoother transition once [she] enters the role of social worker'.

Nine of the 12 students indicated they were integrating critical reflection into their practice. This appeared to be accomplished for several of them by engaging in explicit negotiations with their supervisors about their wish to commit to this process. Others reported committing to the process of critical reflection by using the CRoP model in journaling formats or with a combination of journaling and supervision. One student also reported that her supervisor provided further readings about reflection and the need for reflection 'to facilitate effective therapy'.

If I get frustrated, stuck, or ruminate on an interaction with a client or coworker, I have been journaling about it, simply processing in my head, or discussing with my supervisor. [. . .] CRoP helps me to be a more ethical, unbiased practitioner and has beautifully complemented any Narrative work I do with clients/people coming to consult. CRoP truly helps me be more decentred and to strive to be less expert and MUCH more curious during each interaction. (Student 'B')

I included the process of CRoP in my learning contract and have received support in doing so from my field instructors. At the end of each practicum shift, as time and space allow, I have been trying to capture any thoughts or feelings I experienced throughout the day. This is usually done in the form of fast writing. (Student 'A')

I've been able to integrate it through examining moments with clients and other healthcare professionals when moments in my practice make me feel uneasy or my assumptions become unearthed. In past experiences, I would carry the emotional weight of these incidents through my practice without having a way to organise them and figure out how to move forward. (Student 'E')

Despite the fact nine of the 12 students described how they were continuing to incorporate critical reflection in their practice, they did comment about the demands on their time around which they had to consciously plan. This is consistent with Jan's experiences over many years of having heard practitioners explaining one of the major hurdles to critical reflection is their perception that it takes far too much time in their already extremely busy lives. Indeed, those three students who were not incorporating it indicated that it was because they were too busy. No doubt all the students were very busy, yet the other nine students were willing to commit to developing a way to integrate CRoP into their practice. The greater the perceived benefit of CRoP, the more probable it is that someone will make this commitment, yet merely knowing something is good for us and our practice, does not necessarily translate into its ongoing incorporation.

Participant research assistants' reflections

Nate comments that, as noted in the students' post-course questionnaires, CRoP provides a useful and systematic tool for students to explore and renew understandings gained from critical incidents. In my time of learning and implementing CRoP, I (Nate) have found the structure and theoretical leaning of the process to be helpful in providing a systematic and informative approach to explore critical incidents. In challenging professions, such as social work, the importance of having accessible tools to promote ongoing development and self-care is essential. Although the process of learning and implementing CRoP in a group environment presents its challenges, the ability to witness and experience the development of new understandings, articulations, and actions from critical incidents is both meaningful and inspiring. As we work with and rely on one another in work environments, it is fitting that we also work with and rely on one another in our professional development and self-care.

Tonya offers the following thoughts regarding empathy/compassion, group safety/dynamics, and ongoing reflection: I (Tonya) believe it is important to be explicit about 'practitioner empathy'. CRoP helped me unpack negative ideas I had about my subjectivity and how I felt it was something that I needed to suppress in my professional practice. In short, an exploration of our anthropology and worldview are necessary for understanding our professional practice and, by extension, our critical incidents.

Our group experienced some powerful cohesion although our previous experiences with one another would have suggested otherwise. While I (Tonya) did not feel unsafe, I understand the comments and expressed apprehension within the post-course questionnaires. However, 'safe' is not how I would describe any aspect of CRoP including the group dynamics. I know our group wrestled with the tension of vulnerability yet still wanted to go as deep as we could into our incidents in order to benefit from critical reflection. We were committed to the process and to creating space to accept each other as professionals, but I can see where other groups may have struggled with what Jan calls an atmosphere of critical acceptance. Perhaps a part lecture on the ideas of what an atmosphere of critical acceptance looks like could be useful in any CRoP course.

Finally, the demands of the workplace often dominate our practice and finding space and support to engage with CRoP is no doubt difficult. Recently, I (Tonya) have found that using the theory and practice of CRoP in my personal life has been of great benefit to me. It helps me recognise the critical incidents, which need unpacking and the process becomes more reflexive than reactive.

Discussion

What are some of the main issues which arise, which require further attention? Although much of the literature argues for the need for the right atmosphere of critical acceptance, which this small study supports, this study also has provided examples of how positive and transformative outcomes were possible despite some group members experiencing difficulties within their groups. This result of reporting transformative changes, especially changes which incorporated a more political awareness, is not something which can be taken for granted as an outcome of learning to critically reflect despite the fact that a critical perspective might imply this. For example, Lawrence-Wilkes and Ashmore (2014) report that a study of student teachers indicated that learners of reflective practice tended to be confined to the more instrumental or operational aspects of learning rather than the more fundamental social justice values, which might commonly be associated with a critical approach. Other literature, however, does indicate that some students do develop more thinking and skills related to empowerment (Lawrence-Wilkes & Ashmore, 2014, pp. 26–7; Fook & Askeland, 2006).

It is interesting to note, in response to Tonya's proposal mentioned previously that any course should include at least a partial lecture on the atmosphere of critical acceptance required for CRoP, that Laura did spend part of each of the first two classes talking about the need for critical acceptance in the course in which Tonya participated. However, Laura also had decided that it could be beneficial to spend more time discussing the importance of this the second time she taught the course and to stress it with the observations of a former student. Thus, she invited Nate as a guest lecturer to the first class of the second course so that he could share his experiences regarding the challenges related to group work and the need for critical acceptance. Despite Nate's contributions to these discussions about critical acceptance, there were again problems within two of the six groups created within the course. One student withdrew totally from her group and required course accommodations to proceed with the material individually. Another group appeared to not be as fully engaged with the process and this resulted in frustration for at least two of the group members, who either wrote about the problematic group process in a final paper or met with Laura to speak about their concerns individually.

It is possible that no matter how much care and attention we give to discussing this need for critical acceptance, there will always be the possibility of tensions and difficulties occurring when working in groups. Certainly, Brookfield (2017) argues that teachers' assumption that we can always ensure smooth functioning within classes is one of the many assumptions that need to be deconstructed through the process of critical reflection. Group work theories would suggest that difficulties and tensions are bound to be experienced as groups go through stages of 'forming, storming, norming, and performing' (Yalom, 1985) and it seems unrealistic to expect this to be any different when working through the critical reflection process in a group. Laura is considering that what she will stress in the future is that students should expect bumps along the way in working in a group and that developing ways to manage these challenges may be more important than attempting to avoid them altogether. Certainly, the ability to work better in teams, and especially across social differences, is a theme which emerges from this study and which is echoed in the literature (Chetcuti, Buhagiar, & Cardona, 2011; McDonald, Jackson, Wilkes, & Vickers, 2012). Indeed, the support generated by better relationships with colleagues is a major benefit of undertaking critical reflection (Fook & Gardner, 2007), and so, learning how to develop and maintain relationships through the critical reflection process may be an important skill that is nurtured and maintained.

As has been noted, it is difficult to generalise regarding the findings of studies, which seek to evaluate and identify the outcomes of critical reflection, given the very diverse range of definitions of critical reflection, the often disparate ways of practising it, and the many differing possibilities for researching it (Fook, Psoinos, & Sartori, 2016). How critical reflection is understood, taught, and evaluated is hugely divergent depending upon the profession, discipline, and research approach. What seems to be in common though are themes, which might be loosely grouped as contributing to 'human flourishing' (Ghaye, 2010). These relate to issues like developing increased empowerment (Attard & Armour, 2006) and being better able to deal with uncertainty, instability, and value conflict (Chi, 2010). The ability to deal with moral distress (Lawrence, 2011) and, indeed, stress itself (Stevens, Emil, & Yamashita, 2010) are both important aspects of human flourishing and support the theme of self-care, which has emerged from this study of student reflections on outcomes.

Is critical reflection transformative? In some ways, this is the 'million-dollar' question, which, in part, motivated this book. Students from this study certainly indicated that they were better able to connect their learning with political action and Tonya, in particular, notes how the use of critical reflection has extended into her personal life. Part of this question, of course, is tied up with the issue of how 'transformation' is itself defined. Without going into this detail, it is helpful to note that there is research, which makes the claim that learners have been transformed (Branch, 2010; Oyamada, 2012).

Fook and Askeland (2006) examined the question of 'transformation' from a 'critical' perspective, noting that 153 participants in critical reflection workshops claimed that they had developed:

- A broader and more complex view of their professional selves
- A more affirmed, empowered, and reflexive sense of themselves
- A reframed concept of power, which allowed them to feel more empowered and act in empowered ways
- A sense of being able to create new choices of how to interpret and how to act
- A better sense of themselves as players with agency in a context of working with others

These findings were broadened and strengthened by a larger study of over 400 workshop participants conducted by Fook and Gardner (2007).

The question of how and whether critical reflection helps people develop empathy and compassion remains one of the most crucial, along with the question of transformation. This, of course, is the ideal referred to in the quote from Socrates that the 'examined life' leads to 'ethical and compassionate engagement with the world and its dilemma's (quoted in Nussbaum, 1997). It was gratifying to note that students in this study noted this learning in particular. In some ways, it is possible to see compassion and empathy as part and parcel of human flourishing, but it is also interesting to note that a review of studies, which focused on outcomes of critical reflection, do not use these terms in particular within the outcomes, which learners themselves describe. One of the important contributions of this study, therefore, is this explicit link between critical reflection and the development of empathy.

Conclusion

This chapter traces the changes in thinking experienced by students in a 13-week course on critical reflection in an MSW programme in London, Canada. The study was conducted and has been included as a form of triangulation in that it provides another method for gaining an understanding of what changed for students alongside their more personal and in-depth accounts that can be found in five chapters within this book. We believed it was important to do this, as there is, unfortunately, very little research, which does detail the experiences of students in a more systematic way. This small study used pre and post questionnaires, asking students to comment on key aspects of their thinking about critical reflection.

Overall, whilst students initially demonstrated reasonably conventional thinking about critical reflection, their thinking by the end of the course was happily congruent with two of the major claims made about critical reflection: the growth in empathy and compassion and a more politicised outlook. Both these are aspects of a transformative learning experience.

References

Attard, K., & Armour, K. (2006). Reflecting on reflection: A case study of one teacher's early-career professional learning. *Physical Education and Sport Pedagogy*, 11(3): 209–229. doi:10.1080/17408980600986264

Branch, W. (2010). The road to professionalism: Reflective practice and reflective learning. *Patient Education and Counseling*, 80(3), 327–332. doi:10.1016/j.pec.2010.04.022

Braun, V., & Clarke, V. (2006). Using thematic analysis in psychology. *Qualitative Research in Psychology*, 3(2): 77–101. doi:10.1191/1478088706qp063oa

Brookfield, S.D. (2017). *Becoming a critically reflective teacher* (2nd ed.). San Francisco, CA: Jossey-Bass.

Chetcuti, D., Buhagiar, M.A., & Cardona, A. (2011). The professional development portfolio: Learning through reflection in the first year of teaching. *Reflective Practice: International and Multidisciplinary Perspectives*, 12(1), 61–72. doi:10.1080/14623943.2011.541095

Chi, F.M. (2010). Reflection as teaching inquiry: Examples from Taiwanese in-service teachers. *Reflective Practice: International and Multidisciplinary Perspectives*, 11(2), 171–183. doi:10.1080/14623941003672410

Fook, J., & Askeland, G. (2006). The 'critical' in critical reflection. In S. White, J. Fook, & F. Gardner (Eds.), *Critical reflection in health and social care* (pp. 40–53). Maidenhead: Open University Press.

Fook, J., & Gardner, F. (2007). *Practising critical reflection: A resource handbook*. Maidenhead: Open University Press.

Fook, J., Collington, V., Ross, F., Ruch, G., & West, L. (2016). The promise and problem of critical reflection. In J. Fook, V. Collington, F. Ross, G. Ruch &, L. West (Eds.), *Researching critical reflection: Multidisciplinary perspectives* (pp. 1–8). London: Routledge.

Fook, J., Psoinos, M., & Sartori, D. (2016). Evaluation studies of critical reflection. In J. Fook, V. Collington, F. Ross, G. Ruch &, L. West (Eds.), *Researching critical reflection: Multidisciplinary perspectives* (pp. 90–106). London: Routledge.

Ghaye, T. (2010). In what ways can reflective practices enhance human flourishing? *Reflective Practice: International and Multidisciplinary Perspectives*, 11(1), 1–7. doi:10.1080/14623940903525132

Lawrence, L.A. (2011). Work engagement, moral distress, education level, and critical Reflective practice in intensive care nurses. *Nursing Forum*, 46(4), 256–268. doi:10.1111/j.1744-6198.2011.00237.x

Lawrence-Wilks, L., & Ashmore, L. (2014). *The reflective practitioner in professional education*. London: Palgrave Macmillan.

McDonald, G., Jackson, D., Wilkes, L., & Vickers, M.H. (2012). A work-based educational intervention to support the development of personal resilience in nurses and midwives. *Nurse Education Today*, 32(4), 378–384. doi:10.1016/j.nedt.2011.04.012

Nussbaum, M. (1997). *Cultivating humanity: A classic defense of reform in liberal education*. Cambridge, MA: Harvard University Press.

Oyamada, K. (2012). Experiences of a critical reflection program for mid-career nurses. *Japan Journal of Nursing Science*, 9(1), 9–18. doi:10.1111/j.1742-7924.2011.00178.x

Stevens, D., Emil, S., & Yamashita, M. (2010). Mentoring through reflective journal writing: a qualitative study by a mentor/professor and two international graduate students. *Reflective Practice: International and Multidisciplinary Perspectives*, 11(3), 347–367. doi:10.1080/14623943.2010.490069

Yalom, I. (1985). *The theory and practice of group psychotherapy*. New York: Basic Books.

Chapter 13

Conclusion
Issues in teaching and learning critical reflection

Jan Fook and Laura Béres

In this chapter, we aim to summarise the themes covered within the various chapters of this book and also to clarify and expand upon the implications for teaching and learning that have emerged from these themes.

The experience of learning to critically reflect: A summary of the themes

The literature we reviewed in Chapter 1 indicates that the field of critical reflection is dogged by uncertainty and lack of clarity. The well-documented lack of consensus regarding understandings, definitions, and theoretical frameworks for critical reflection (Larivee, 2008) makes for a lack of clarity for students of critical reflection. In itself, this is not necessarily a bad thing. How critical reflection is theorised, and the different perspectives available on this, can mean a rich and complex array of interpreting and working with the concept, which allows for it to be understood and practised in many different ways, potentially addressing the differing needs and perspectives of many types of learners. Nonetheless, this can also be confusing and demotivating for students on their initial connection with critical reflection.

As we also stated in Chapter 1, there are both upsides and downsides of the experience of learning critical reflection. We made the point that perhaps it is oversimplistic to characterise the experience in such a polarised way, as, in fact, downsides might work to produce constructive outcomes as much of the literature on critical reflection indicates. The more positive and more negative aspects of learning are both perhaps integral to the experience of learning, since some unsettling of ideas and resulting discomfort may well be a necessary condition to the experience of change involved in learning. Much of the literature (and the chapters in this volume are no exception) attests to the very welcome fundamental and transformative changes, which the critical reflection process stimulates. However, the vulnerability involved in exposing personal experience and practice in order to critically reflect upon it, may, in fact, interact with the experience of risk and loss involved in having to question taken-for-granted beliefs, especially if these beliefs are integral to a sense of identity built up over time. Vulnerability might also be related to a heightened sense of attunement that can be experienced as overstimulation then potentially resulting in withdrawal from the process. The emotional side of learning critical reflection can, in fact, be a major, and unanticipated, factor in the learning experience as well. This is an aspect not always recognised in learning in higher education and can contribute to feelings of unpreparedness and even questioning of a learning process, which is not linear (as might be expected) but perhaps better understood as 'spiral' (Hickson, 2013). The problem with this is that since the learner has little idea of how this might work, at any point in what might seem like a downward spiral, a learner can lose confidence in the process. In addition, the risk involved in being critically reflective and personally vulnerable to others, and in contexts which do not support it, can take a great personal and political toll on professionals who are committed to it.

It is perhaps instructive here to return to, and indeed reaffirm, what conditions support the transformative learning process and in so doing, of course, to continue to understand how the transformation comes about. To do this, the work of Linden West (2016), as a psychoanalyst and academic within the field of education, is helpful. He acknowledges the role of the therapeutic aspects of critical reflection but, significantly (as has been emphasised elsewhere [Fook & Gardner, 2007]), states that it is *not* therapy: 'The work is not therapy, even if it can be therapeutic' (West, 2016, p. 129). Critical reflection involves learning at an emotional as well as an intellectual level, and in this sense, deep transformative learning involves a therapeutic aspect, perhaps in a similar way that therapy may also involve intellectual learning. Indeed, narrative therapists might describe the critical reflection process as involving 'transport' (White, 2007), as people are moved through the process from considering experiences in one way to reconsidering and reconceptualising them in another way that opens up new possible ways of living and working, which occurs in both therapy and critical reflection.

West also details aspects of critical reflection, used for research in his case, which mirror the framework of the model contributors have written about in this book. These include a containing space, stories developed over time, sensitivity to the emotional qualities of the encounter, a sense of control in having the choice about talking about personal matters, and offering but not imposing particular theoretical analyses (p. 129). Given an overall interest in human flourishing, he relies on the work of Winnicott, Freud, and Honneth with regard to 'connecting socio-cultural with inter- and intra-subjective understanding of human well-being and interaction' (p. 129). He emphasises how loving relationships can encourage the ability to take risks and 'engage fulsomely with the world [. . .] In feeling recognized, listened to, and really understood by a significant other, the capacity to take risks can be developed' (p. 130). This 'recognition' is located in group dynamics and encourages the development of self-respect. 'Respect can be more easily shown to others by acknowledging their rights' (p. 130). This is where the group climate and culture become important, as Dewey (1969) explains. Rigidity in groups can close down possibilities for learning. The need for democratic learning communities in which to critically reflect is, therefore, vital to developing meaningful professionalism (West, 2016, p. 131).

What do the chapters in this volume add to the picture we have previously outlined from existing literature? The chapters, not surprisingly, corroborate these themes clearly but also add more detail. The theme of the importance of a *supportive context* recurs. First, there is the necessity of an appropriate organisational culture, one which both supports and understands the culture of critical reflection. This is emphasised by Helen in Chapter 5, who worked to establish critical reflection in an executive team but saw it fade over time. Stephen, in Chapter 3, also notes the importance of having the organisational culture support the practice of critical reflection by having protected time to engage in it. Helen gives useful pointers as to how to keep the critically reflective organisational culture alive in different ways, ranging from ongoing communications at micro levels, to ensuring official buy-in from senior staff.

The chapters also point to the usefulness of establishing a conducive culture at a less structural level within learning groups. Nate, in Chapter 4, discusses challenges to group cohesion and suggests techniques form narrative therapy to help with this. Interestingly, he points out the manner in which group members might shut down the critical reflection process by becoming too focused on emotional safety and the offering of reassurances. Although he also recommends avoiding therapeutic approaches in the critical reflection process, he points out how particular narrative practices assist group members in creating the types of conversations which facilitate the deconstruction process. Specifically, he argues for incorporating the therapeutic posture of narrative therapy, the recognition of the importance of insider knowledge, and the technique of engaging in externalising conversations. Tonya, in Chapter 2, notes her surprise in how her learning group, about whom she was initially sceptical, developed a 'maturity', which allowed them to support each other. Jackie, in Chapter 7, recognises how the support of her group allowed her to deal with the anxiety and shame she initially experienced in exposing her practice experience.

The newness, or unfamiliarity, of the critical reflection learning process, and theories involved, is also an important factor in the learning experience. Helen notes how the language and concepts involved in critical reflection, especially regarding power and postmodern understandings of language, were difficult for her group and how she needed to acknowledge the similarity of other terms her group might be more familiar with. Stephen very appropriately points out how the critical reflection learning process challenges traditional linear ideas of learning and how he found this initially 'counterintuitive'.

The 'discomfort', 'stress', 'embarrassment', and even 'shame' are perhaps all aspects of the 'vulnerability', which learners experience in sharing their practice for critical reflection with group members. All the foregoing are terms, which authors have used in describing their initial feelings. Ashley speaks of the process as 'exhausting' and her embarrassment in her initial reactions to her incident. Much of these decreases as learners gradually transform their thinking to shift the 'blame' or judgements of themselves towards a greater appreciation of how their thinking is influenced by taken-for-granted professional or cultural assumptions. This can be experienced as reducing stress on the worker (see Stephen's Chapter 3) and may sometimes lead to an increased desire to research the issue raised by the critical reflection (as Jackie describes in Chapter 7), as opposed to continuing to see it as limited to a more personal issue. However, it is instructive to note that, sometimes, the discomfort experienced in sharing what may still be unresolved experiences can highlight further difficulties, which may need to be addressed. Several of the authors spoke of critically reflecting upon their own misgivings about sharing experiences and what this uncovered. Stephen, in particular, makes a very insightful observation that he realised how his difficulty in sharing unresolved experiences highlighted his own difficulties in power sharing.

In general, the chapters in the book also corroborate the overall outcome of the experience as transformative in the sense of refreshing and reenergising regarding their practice (Stephen in Chapter 3), being able to make sense of self-doubt (Jasmyne in Chapter 9), and, very movingly, of coming to an awareness that 'I am more than my role' (Ashley in Chapter 8). The transformative experience is also illuminated in several more specific ways: Stephen speaks of becoming more aware of what needs to be overcome in order to improve practice; Rebecca, in Chapter 6, usefully details different aspects of her transformative awareness of the self-serving function of her thinking regarding 'perfectionism'. She notes how she also found the experience of reading relevant literature (motivated by her breakthrough awareness) both validating and troubling and 'having a label for my experiences was helpful, but it also brings with it a keen sense of reality that cannot be ignored'. The critical reflection process helped begin a process of 'unraveling the intricacies of the grasp of "perfectionism", but this is no easy task', alluding to the various discoveries and emotions the process will elicit. Ashley speaks of her new awareness of the influence of the experience of loss in her life and how this was underpinned by 'not speaking up'. This awareness is what led to her realisation (previously) that she is 'more than her role'.

The experience might also be said to be transformative in the growing awareness of a new approach and capacity, which extends from it. Tonya words these nicely as: 'the honour, privilege and maturity to overcome conflicts' and ability to 'embrace the unknown'. Fenix, in Chapter 10, extends our understanding of the transformative aspect of critical reflection by enlarging on how the process can be used for self-care.

Nonvoluntary reflection

Whilst the bulk of the chapters are written by people who did not have a choice about whether to engage in learning critical reflection, this does not come across explicitly as an issue for them. However, it is useful to note what might be significant factors for learning when the critical reflection being required is perceived as nonvoluntary. One factor may be that when it is perceived that the critical reflection is required at an organisational level, or by the organisation (or managers), then the perception of it as nonvoluntary is increased and can be experienced as a threat. This might be exacerbated by a fear of experiencing vulnerability in such an environment, particularly because of the fear of what it might do to one's reputation or even potential for advancement in the organisation. This fear of vulnerability might also be further enhanced by the fear of personal and professional judgement. Tonya encapsulates this fear well when she notes her own scepticism and, indeed, fear of beginning the critical reflection process, not least because she already had some experiences with some group members, which made her doubt the group's ability to be supportive. Of course, in Tonya's case, as with the others who participated in Laura's university course, involvement was involuntary but with the slightly different set of complex power dynamics involved within a university setting. All the students had chosen to pursue their MSW and yet the critical reflection course was required. Their work was judged and graded. In Tonya's case, she also comments that her group members were all aware that they were developing professional identities and that their experiences with one another would be remembered and could potentially follow them in their careers.

What helps the critical reflection process?

Contributors make several helpful suggestions about how the critical reflection learning process can be enhanced and also the relative importance of several aspects. Both Nate and Helen provide practical suggestions: Nate incorporates several techniques from narrative therapy. Indeed, we have already discussed the therapeutic aspect of critical reflection, which contributes to transformative learning and so it is clearly important to continue to make the links and further develop how therapeutic techniques can be used appropriately in critical reflection sessions. Helen provides some concrete suggestions for creating and maintaining a critically reflective organisational culture (such as demonstrating how to ask critically reflective questions at every opportunity).

A resounding theme is one that has been touched on before – the importance of the learning environment. Specifically, this refers to the support and nonjudgemental attitude of other group learners (Jackie mentions this). Tonya expands this with her own five principles underlying 'critical acceptance'. These are 'courageous communication', 'staying outside the story', 'honouring professionalism', 'emotional safety', and 'vulnerability'. Rebecca refers to this environment as 'open': the openness of peers in creating an empathic learning environment and a willingness to explore emotionally difficult issues. Stephen's points about what also helps within the organisation (having protected time to

Conclusion 159

critically reflect) and, specifically, also helping to reframe the critical incident away from a person's professional weaknesses, can also facilitate the transformative learning.

And what if the environment created in the group is not conducive to learning? The answer might be quite simple: Ashley suggests that journaling might be used instead.

Implications for teaching and learning critical reflection

In this section, we will pull together some of the major directions, which have been suggested by the chapters in the book, and what they mean for teaching and learning critical reflection.

Creating a conducive learning environment

This has been almost a constant theme running through all the chapters. It is useful at this point to discuss the different types or levels of environments, which might come into play, the issues at each level, and some suggestions for possible ways of addressing these.

- At an organisational level. At an organisational level, it is vital to pay attention to the broader organisational context – the culture of learning, which is both explicitly and implicitly produced. Participants need to feel that the broader environment is one which will not exploit their vulnerability and one which does understand and appreciate what critical reflection is (both explicitly and implicitly). On an explicit basis, this might mean understanding (and giving time for and recognition of) exactly what is entailed in the concrete practice of critical reflection. It may also mean devising and enacting formalised learning and supervision policies, which include clear recognition of critical reflection. On an implicit basis, a conducive learning environment is one which supports and models a 'culture' of critical reflection, which respects vulnerability, models openness to learning from mistakes, and is not judgemental or blaming.
- At a small group or interpersonal level. At this level, it is easier to establish a smaller group environment based on the previously described principles. This may mean simply being explicit about what is involved in a critical reflection mindset and encouraging group members to develop what this means for them in a group context. It may also mean choosing group members and developing a group composition which will enhance these principles or, when this is not possible, spending initial time in developing a communal group culture. It also involves group members being vigilant of themselves to ensure they are attempting to act congruently with the values of a 'critically accepting' environment and developing nuanced ways to facilitate other group members to support this culture. However, there

also needs to be an acknowledgement of group processes and the very real possibility of a 'storming' phase (Yalom, 1985) so that group members do not feel like they have failed in the process if they experience difficulties. They can be encouraged to consider how they might respond to difficulties rather than expect to avoid them.

- At a personal level. On a more individualised, personal and emotional level, continued reflection on one's own behaviour and actions is helpful. The aim is to examine one's own thinking and feeling to understand the impact of these on actions (especially in the critical reflection group) and the hidden messages they might convey. This is particularly useful when these hidden messages appear to not be congruent with a critically accepting environment.

Preparation for vulnerability and unconventional ways of learning

Since vulnerability is a key theme, which has arisen from our chapters, it is appropriate to ask whether it is possible to prepare learners for what is essentially an unconventional way of learning. Is it better just to ask learners to experience a critically reflective way of learning, and to learn from it as they experience it, or is it better to help prepare them beforehand? The chapters appear to have answered this question quite clearly, and strongly. There is a call for more and perhaps better preparation in seeking to establish a critically accepting learning environment. In inducing any culture change, it is important to make explicit what the existing learning culture is and then to make explicit what the new culture is. Early time can usefully be spent, therefore, in having students reflect on what they have assumed about learning (what is good learning and how does it happen) and their own way of learning within this. One useful way to conceptualise critical reflection is that it is 'unlearning how to learn' and 'relearning how to learn'. Therefore, students need to develop their own explicit thinking about learning, in order to work on developing their learning process further. Students can be asked to reflect upon how they believe a learning culture is developed and maintained and what their own role in this is. Where do messages about how to learn come from, and how do we decide what messages we take on board? Initial exercises like these can both model a critically reflective way of thinking but will also assist in the group devising its own critically reflective learning environment. Groups can be encouraged to design their own learning environments through mutual discussion and agreement resulting from their reflections.

Laura's comments, in Chapter 11, regarding vulnerability within teaching, reinforce how important it is to leave an opening for others to participate and connect with the teacher's own learning process and how authority, as a teacher, can be shared through the process of demonstrating vulnerability. There is a pertinent story in the classic work by Belenky, Clinchy, Goldberger, and

Tarule (1986, p. 215) in which the authors relate how a colleague, early in her teaching career, struggled to do what she regarded as adequate preparation for each class. She wanted to demonstrate how much she knew and also give students all the relevant and important points involved in an analysis of a piece of literary work. When she presented the analysis to her students, she was puzzled as to why students did not interact and proffer their own ideas, particularly because she thought she had done such a thorough analysis. Then one day she was unable to prepare as much as she would have liked and so opened the discussion up to allow for more student input. To her surprise, they contributed enthusiastically. Whilst the point being made here is neither new, or even that surprising, what is surprising is how easy it is to forget to leave room for the contributions of others in the push to feel that, as teachers, we need to demonstrate our command and grasp of a situation or topic area. Creating a space for critical reflection reminds us that exposing our own 'not knowing', uncertainty, and personal vagaries may indeed open a space for mutual learning. However, Laura also points out in Chapter 11 that vulnerability does not only involve the *enactment* of being open within the classroom but also an *emotional* element related to attunement to others. She suggests that reflecting upon what is required for the balancing of vulnerability with self-protection may be useful for both teachers and learners of critical reflection to consider and should be discussed prior to beginning the critical reflection process.

Does critical reflection work for everyone?

Whilst most of the chapters conclude that their own critical reflection processes benefitted them greatly, there were, nonetheless, some chapters, which noted that their groups were not necessarily helpful and that the critical reflection process sometimes raises more uncertainties, thereby, leaving an ongoing sense of limbo. As we have stated repeatedly, having a conducive learning environment is vital to successful critical reflection. Clearly, it might not always be possible to carve this out in every context. It is important to be mindful about how much of the context you are able to shape as the teacher or co-learner and how well you are able to shape this. As also pointed out in Chapter 12, Brookfield (2017) argues that the teachers' assumption that we can always ensure smooth functioning within classes is one of the many assumptions that need to be deconstructed through the process of critical reflection. We may think we have much more control over the climate and process of a class than we actually have. We can do our best in a thoughtful and committed manner, but everyone involved will be bringing their own sense of agency, level of interest, and prior experiences, all of which will affect their experience of critical reflection.

It may be that some learners are more willing, or ready, to be vulnerable, depending perhaps on their past experiences. They may also be more capable of sitting with uncertainty or of resisting cultures, which appear judgemental or blaming. It is important in helping to facilitate critical reflection that the individual differences of learners are taken into account and that the process is supportive of people who may not be as open or ready as others to make potentially deep changes. For these reasons, it might be important to ensure that there are extra supportive mechanisms for learners who are undertaking critical reflection and perhaps also opportunities to 'opt out' if necessary. As Laura describes in Chapter 11, she was required to accommodate a student who was unable to continue her learning process within a group context the second time she taught the course. Certainly, within an Ontario university in a Canadian context, the implications of the Ontario Human Rights Commission (www.ohrc.on.ca/en/policy-accessible-education-studets-disabilities) are that educators should be considering what aspects of their courses are 'indispensable' and which of the 'procedural' and 'substantive' components can be accommodated for learning needs. Adjusting the structure of courses and the process of engaging with critical reflection may, indeed, need to occur for a variety of different reasons and will necessitate ongoing creativity and flexibility with course and workshop design.

There are two examples, which serve to illustrate consideration of the impact of past experiences on engagement with the critical reflection process. One is an example of an experienced social worker who also worked as a manager and provided counselling from a feminist perspective. She was deeply committed to the profession, her feminism, and her values. What was not apparent at the time of her entering a long-term critical reflection group was that she had experienced abuse as a child. There was absolutely no expectation, of course, that she reveals this in the group, and she did not (despite being a very active and enthusiastic participant). Nonetheless, about six weeks into the critical reflection process with the group, she asked to speak with the group organisers and said that she was considering not continuing. The process was raising too many sad and difficult emotions for her. The organisers listened empathically and talked it through with her in order to help her clarify what she wanted to do. After several weeks, she decided to continue and was able to complete some very challenging projects based on her initial reflections.

The second example also involves a feminist social worker who, at the time of being in a critical reflection group (run by Jan), was working in the family violence field and so, of course, did a lot of work with the police. She reflected really well and easily and said that she gained new insights from the experience and, in particular, that it enabled her to work better with the police (a big change for her as she had found this especially difficult before). A week later, she took me by surprise by emailing me and saying that she thought I would like to know that she had suffered abuse as a child (she did not raise this at all in the critical reflection process) and that now, for the first time, she had been able to let go of the grief she felt about this. She had reflected further and had been able to connect a lot of her assumptions to this ongoing grief. She had undergone quite a bit of therapy as well, but it was the critical reflection process, which had finally allowed her relief from this grief.

Whilst being gratified that I had inadvertently been able to help, my experience from both these stories emphasised to me that there is still a lot to learn about why critical reflection works (or not), what short- and long-term impact it has, and how, as teachers in the midst of this uncertainty, we can take some responsibility for assisting in the transformative process, whilst minimising the harm, which might be done.

Conclusion

Clearly, there is a need for much more reflection, much more research, much more sharing of experience, and much more openness to the learning process and what it means to contribute to human flourishing through critical reflection. However, in this chapter, we have summarised the themes, which have been highlighted by contributors of the chapters in this book, who each provided an in-depth critical reflection of their own learning process and some of the resulting effects. We have also explored the implications for ongoing teaching and learning of critical reflection that have arisen from the contributors' chapters as well as the small-scale study of a university-based critical reflection course.

Throughout this book, we have stressed the manner in which critical reflection, and specifically Fook's model of critical reflection, continues to evolve as it incorporates understandings from the study of spirituality on the one hand and techniques from narrative therapy on the other. It, perhaps, is a sign of health when a model like that of critical reflection is able to incorporate insights from those people who have been engaged in the process themselves, truly demonstrating the elements of openness and compassion that students have remarked upon. We are interested and excited to be involved as the reflections, research, and sharing of experiences continue.

References

Belenky, M.F., Clinchy, B.M., Goldberger, N.R., & Tarule, J.M. (1986). *Women's ways of knowing*. New York: Basic Books.

Brookfield, S.D. (2017). *Becoming a critically reflective teacher* (2nd ed.). San Francisco, CA: Jossey-Bass.

Dewey, J. (1969). The ethics of democracy. In J.A. Boydston (Ed.), *The early years of John Dewey* (pp. 227–249). Carbondale, IL: Southern Illinois University Press.

Fook, J., & Gardner, F. (2007). *Practising critical reflection: A resource handbook*. Maidenhead: Open University Press.

Hickson, H. (2013). Learning critical reflection for professional practice. In J. Fook & F. Gardner (Eds.), *Critical reflection in context: Applications in health and social care* (pp. 57–67). London: Routledge.

Larrivee, B. (2008). Development of a toll to assess teachers' level of reflective practice. *Reflective Practice: Multidisciplinary and International Perspective*, 9(3), 341–360. doi:10.1080/14623940802207451

West, L. (2016). Critical reflection? Autobiographical narrative enquiry and illuminating professional struggles in distressed communities. In J. Fook, V. Collington, F. Ross, G. Ruch, & L. West (Eds.), *Researching critical reflection: Multidisciplinary perspectives* (pp. 109–118). London: Routledge.

White, M. (2007). *Maps of narrative practice*. New York: W.W. Norton.

Yalom, I. (1985). *The theory and practice of group psychotherapy*. New York: Basic Books.

Chapter 14

Resources for learning and teaching critical reflection

Laura Béres and Jan Fook

Many books include suggestions for further learning at the end of each chapter. With this volume, we decided not to disturb the reflective flow, and the personal nature of the accounts by doing this. Instead, we have presented a collection of resources that we have developed over the years of facilitating critical reflection workshops and university-based courses. Since there are common themes, which link the chapters, we also felt it was more fitting to include further resources in a more collective way rather than to risk repeating ideas across the chapters. The resources presented here are intended to be applicable across a range of different teaching settings and may be adjusted to various learning contexts. For example, they could be used as facilitator reference material, provided as handouts or worksheets for participants, or reformatted into PowerPoint slides. We hope you find them useful.

Box 14.1 Exercise in developing critically reflective questions

Many students and educators wishing to use the critical reflection model used by the contributors in this volume have requested that a list of reflective questions be provided. We tend to resist this request, for several reasons.

- First, we have found that once someone truly understands the theoretical lenses, which inform this approach, they are able to have a much better grasp of the process and are then also able to generate appropriate questions.
- Secondly, questions to help participants delve beneath the surface of their stories, to uncover hidden deeper assumptions, must generally be asked in relation to the specific story of the experience being reflected upon. It is vitally important that people assisting someone to reflect develop the skills of listening, especially trying to listen underneath a story, to what is not expressed in so many words. If they just have in mind specific questions to ask, without thinking through how their question is relevant to what a person is saying, this can impede deep listening.

166 Laura Béres and Jan Fook

- Thirdly, the theoretical frameworks, which we outlined at the beginning of the book, are intended to provide a broad framework for questions. However, we have found that wording and framing these against the context of a story a person is trying to reflect upon can be quite difficult. Part of the skill of critically reflecting is being able to think through in more detail how the theories can inform analysis and questioning. This needs to be learnt over time. It is perhaps less well learnt if prescribed questions are provided beforehand.
- It is also important to remember that critically reflective questions are designed to foster two-way dialogue and should not seem like one-way interrogation. The flow is better if the reflective questions asked are clearly related to the responses given.

In the following list, we give an example of an exercise for developing critically reflective questions, which we have used in workshop training. The main aim of this exercise is two-fold:

- First, it aims to help people think through how to ask questions, which exemplify the principles of critical acceptance.
- Second, it aims to help people practise how to ask questions, which are relatively clear, so it is an exercise in good communication.

Broadly, the exercise consists first with telling the story of a brief critical incident and then the workshop participants are asked to observe five different questions and to think about/discuss them to rank them in order of least reflective to most reflective.

Step 1. First, we remind participants of some general principles, which guide the type of questions that might assist a person to reflect (we are indebted to participants in the London Critical Reflection Network for helping to formulate the questions in this way). These have been adapted from the points regarding the ethical learning climate of 'critical acceptance'.

For convenience, the points about an ethical learning climate are summarised in the following list. An ethical learning climate of critical acceptance (please see Chapter 1 for the full description of this learning climate) involves the following:

- Seeking deeper understanding through creating a safe space for enabling dialogue
- Acceptance, NOT affirmation
- Learning, not therapy, and right to draw limits
- Trust and respect
- Focus on the how/why of story construction
- Multiple and different perspectives
- Responsibility and agency, not blame

Resources for learning and teaching 167

General principles to guide questioning (based on principles of an ethical learning climate) are discussed. When doing this exercise, participants can be asked to try and think of examples of each of the types of questions before exploring the offered possibilities together.

- Questions, which do not imply judgement (an implication that the questioner dis/approves of what was done). The questions should be open and clearly convey that the intention is not to lead the person down a particular path of thinking, e.g. 'I'd like to hear more about why you think you did/thought that', NOT 'I don't think you should have done that' or 'I don't think that's what I would have done'.

- Questions, which leave room for disagreement and for openness, that is, questions, which might be transparent about the questioner's viewpoint but convey the message that, nevertheless, the questioner is genuinely interested in hearing the person's own perspective or interpretation, e.g. 'I think that if I'd been in the situation I might have thought. . .But I'm genuinely interested to hear if this is what you thought, or was it something quite different?'

- Curiosity questions, that is, questions, which invite the person to speak more about what the experience meant/means with the sole intention of trying to understand the meaning of the person's experience in more depth, e.g. 'I'm curious about what made you think that. . .can you say a bit more about this?'

- 'Reflexive' questions, that is, questions, which ask the person to reflect on who they are and how their own social position affects their perspective on their story, e.g. 'I wonder how the other people in the story perceived you and how this might have influenced the way they acted?', 'I wonder how you being a man/woman/young person/social worker influenced what happened?', 'What were you (or they) assuming about each of these types of people, which you think influenced what happened?', or 'What about your current location now do you think might be affecting how you are making sense of the memory and retelling of the situation?'.

- 'Directed feeling' questions, that is, questions, which ask about a feeling but also try to connect it with an underlying idea or assumption, e.g. 'You seem to be feeling frustrated/out of your depth/vulnerable, and I wonder what you were assuming about yourself/other people, which made you feel this?'

- Questions, which focus on the person's thinking, not making judgements or evaluations of other people in the story, e.g. 'Although you are implying that your supervisor did the wrong thing, I wonder what this says about your assumptions about supervision?'.

- Questions, which help the person to focus on their thinking, not necessarily what they should have done or could do better, e.g. 'I am aware that you feel you should not have done what you did, but rather than dwell on that, I wonder what you are assuming about yourself and what you should be capable of or what good work is?'.

168 Laura Béres and Jan Fook

Step 2. Secondly, we give a brief verbal presentation of an example of a critical incident. Here we provide an example incident from Jan's experience.

Context. This happened some years ago when I was starting a new job. I worked for a partnership between three organisations. About two months into the job, the first meeting to decide next year's strategy was held. There were 16 people present. All were senior managers in their organisations. My role was as an employee of the partnership to develop partnership projects.

Why critical for me? This sort of thing happens a lot, and I feel quite frustrated and annoyed at what seems like a waste of time!

The incident. Part way into the meeting, I couldn't follow what was happening. It did not seem like we were making decisions or following an agenda, and I couldn't see a strategic plan emerging. People were speaking and not necessarily referring to what each other was saying, and there was a negative tone despite the positive things being said. I stopped speaking/contributing. I left the meeting really frustrated, as it felt like a waste of a day.

Step 3. Ask the group to read the following questions (which are examples of what different groups, at different times, have asked to help me reflect on my critical incident) and, individually (or in pairs), try to rank them from the least to the most reflective.

1   What were you expecting to happen?
2   What do you believe is the purpose of meetings?
3   Why didn't you speak up?
4   Were you adequately prepared for the meeting?
5   Was the person chairing the meeting doing a good job?

Step 4. Go around the group and ask the individuals (or pairs) for their rankings, and discuss their reasons for ranking in the way they have. It might be easier to discuss each question in turn, and how different people have ranked it and why. Refer back to the principles in step 1 where necessary. Where possible, if the group decides a question is not very reflective, ask them to try different ways of making it more reflective.

For example, question no. 5 is not very reflective in that it shifts the gaze from the thinking of the person reflecting to making judgements of someone else (the chair of the meeting). Ask the group, 'How might this question be made more reflective?' or, 'How might you turn the focus back onto the person's thinking?'

Ask them to be as concrete as possible. For example, 'I wonder why you were assuming that the chair was not doing a good job? What would a good job have looked like?'

If helpful, you can make imaginary answers to the different questions to illustrate what each question might elicit.

Resources for learning and teaching 169

Box 14.2 Critical reflection 'cheat sheet': Pointers for facilitators

This is a summary of the stages of the critical reflection process and can be helpful for facilitators (especially new ones) as a checklist about the practical aspects of the process. It is important that facilitators try to model a critically accepting culture as much as possible. Sometimes it may be helpful for the facilitator to volunteer to present their own critical incident first and allow the group to 'practise' on them.

Preparation

Choose a critical incident (an incident [not a situation, issue, or case], which happened to you that you feel was significant to your professional learning and which you would like to learn from).

Write up to a ONE-page description covering the following:

* Why the incident was critical
* Background/context of the incident
* The actual incident

The incident should be a 'raw' description (not analysis or reflection) as much as possible and should be as concrete and brief as possible. Remember to respect confidentiality and to choose something you are prepared to discuss in the group. If need be, you may change major identifying details in order to respect confidentiality.

1 Stage 1 critical reflection

Present the incident to the group (either verbally and/or in writing).

The group begins discussion (assisting the person to reflect on their incident) by:

* Asking if there are any questions, which simply clarify the 'facts' of the critical incident (these are not questions which invite reflection but which are just about ensuring that members of the group are clear about what the incident is)
* Clarifying why the incident was chosen and is critical to the person (if this is not clear)

The group starts the critical reflection process:

* Begin the questions to help reflection (remember that the goal of this stage is to unearth fundamental assumptions – i.e. to try to get to the crux of the matter for the person). Remember the climate of 'critical acceptance' – a nonjudgemental atmosphere, which enables the person to feel free to put a range of assumptions/perspectives/interpretations 'on the table' for their own examination.

170 Laura Béres and Jan Fook

- Spend about half an hour or as long as it takes for the person to feel they have become aware of fundamental assumptions (this usually entails some change of thinking or new awareness) or feel that they have gotten to the crux of the meaning of the situation for them.
- Questions, which may help early on:

a 'Where does that come from?'
b 'Did you have any strong feelings (and what were they about)?'
c 'What was that about for you?'
d 'I wonder why you thought/interpreted. . .and not. . .?'
e 'I wonder why you chose to do. . .and not. . .?'
f 'What perspectives are missing from your account?'
g 'Do any assumptions about power/gender/class/culture have anything to do with the heart of the matter for you?'

End the process:

- After about half an hour, check in with the person by asking such questions as:

a 'Where has that gone for you?'
b 'Do you feel like this has gone anywhere for you?'
c 'Do you feel it has unearthed some fundamental assumptions that you would like to think about some more?'
d 'Do you feel you have gotten to the crux of the matter?'
e 'What would you say are the main assumptions, which have been unearthed for you?'

You may need to assist them to articulate some of the assumptions.

Then ask the person what they will be taking away to reflect further on, for further Stage 2 reflection later.

If the person still feels they are unsure about what has come out for them, the group may want to help by going back over some of the assumptions, which were raised, and helping the person to review if they think any of these are fundamental.

The aim at the end of Stage 1 is ideally for the person to feel that they have gotten to the crux of the matter and, at least, unearthed something they were not aware of before that will help them now think about what they have learnt/might want to change.

2 Stage 2 critical reflection

The overall aim of Stage 2 is to help the person repackage/relabel their learning as a new principle/guideline for action ('theory of practice'). In this sense, they are now trying to label the crux of how they want to both 'see and do' this aspect of their practice.

Before a Stage 2 presentation, they should think about the following:

- What was/were my main assumption/s (from Stage 1, although these might have changed after further reflection)?

Resources for learning and teaching 171

- How does my thinking need to change (as a result of becoming aware of these assumptions)?
- How does my practice need to change as a result of this changed thinking? ('What might I do differently if I found myself in the same situation [as my critical incident] again?')
- How would I label my new 'theory of practice' (guideline/principle for action)?

The person presents their preliminary thoughts to the group and the group assists them to respond to these questions. It is important to connect the responses to these questions with the reflections from Stage 1 (even if it is just to be aware of how the reflections might have moved further on). It is also important to use the person's own terms or language as much as possible for the new theory of practice.

It is important to pay attention to group size.

The ideal size for a critical reflection group is about five to six. If there are more than ten people, it may be useful to divide the group into two so that half the group engages in the reflection and half the group act as observers. You may ask one of the observers to act as a notetaker for the person reflecting (making note of the main questions asked and the main responses given). These should be given to the person reflecting for help when they are preparing their Stage 2 reflection.

Box 14.3 Possible critically reflective questions, which can be asked using different theoretical frameworks

Questions from a reflective practice framework

- What are my implicit assumptions and how do they differ from my explicit ones?
- How can I use this awareness to change my practice? (Stage 2 question)
- Examples: What fundamental values or beliefs are implied? What am I assuming about the nature of people, society, power, and conflict? What hidden ideas underlie what I did? Was I attempting to practise from a particular practice theory, which let me down? How did I fill the gap left in my theory to practise transmission with a gut instinct, creativity, or implicit knowledge? Did my profession's code of ethics influence my practice or did they not offer guidance? If not, how did I manage? If I was 'flying by the seat of my pants', what helped get me off the ground?

Questions from a reflexivity framework

- How do I influence what I see?
- How does what I am looking for influence what I find?

- Examples: Where do my assumptions come from? How does who I am affect socially what I see? How do my emotions affect my knowledge? What 'blind spots' do I have? How does who I am and how I behave affect other people's interpretations of me? If I was older or younger or a different gender, what might have been different?

Questions from a post-structural and postmodern narrative practice framework

- How does how I speak (my language) construct what I see?
- What social discourses are influencing my understanding and retelling of the incident?

- Examples: What words or terms do I use? Why have I chosen these? What language patterns do I use? What binaries exist? Have I used any polarised thinking? What other perspectives am I leaving out? Why did I choose to interpret it this way (and not other ways?) Where might I have been influenced to think in that way? Are there any other elements or events that occurred that I particularly chose not to mention that might offer other ways of thinking about it?

Questions from a critical perspectives framework

- What has this got to do with power? How do I participate in power? What are the connections between my personal experience and my social context? And how can I change my practice with this awareness?
- What were the broader social structures of power in play? Who else had access to power and how did they use their power?
- Examples: Do I have any self-defeating beliefs? Do I see myself as powerless? How do I see other people's power? How do I understand responsibility? What do I believe about how organisational and personal power is connected? Is anyone using resistance as a method of attempting to resist someone else's use of power?

Questions from a spirituality or meaning framework

- What is the significance or deeper meaning of this experience to me?
- How does it connect to my past experiences as well as my hopes and plans for the future?
- Examples: Where does this come from? What is it about for me? What is coming out about my fundamental values? What would I ideally like to happen? Are there any other experiences that would suggest a pattern and particular commitments in my work or life more generally? What motivates me to continue to be committed to this work? Does this feel meaningful?

Box 14.4 For a university setting: Clarifying what makes this *critical reflection* (usually using PowerPoint slides)

Begin by reviewing the two main strands of reflection:

- Analytic philosophy – closely related to empiricism – we must be rational and think logically – catch faulty logic – scientific experimentation.
- Pragmatism – an analysis of experience – always open to revising assumptions – the reflective cycle – always 'fiddling/experimenting' on practice but most importantly: 'Pragmatism is defined by its "calling into question any form of dogmatism" and its belief in a form of fallibilism, in which "every claim is open to revision"' (Brookfield, 2016, p. 15).

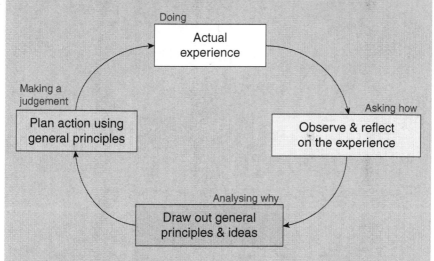

Figure 14.1 Simple reflection loop
This photo by unknown author is licensed under CC BY-NC (creativecommons.org/licenses/by-nc/3.0/creativecommons.org/licenses/by-nc/3.0)

Most students will be familiar with this form of reflection loop based on improving practice, but this does not incorporate Critical Social Theory.

- Reflection and critical reflection often 'conflated'
- Reflection and 'use of self' are not the same thing, but you do use 'your self' in reflection and critical reflection
- Reflection is not necessarily critical – could just be about improving practice effectiveness or making the agency more efficient
- 'Critical' isn't just 'deeper' or 'more profound' or 'negative', on the other hand

Critical Social Theory adds 'critical' to the reflection loop:

- The need to examine power and control, influenced by the Frankfurt School (Adorno, Marcuse, Habermas).
- Examine the minutiae of practice to find the embedded and unjust dominant ideologies and the 'struggles between unequal interests and groups that exist within the wider world'.
- Although seeming very 'open' (although not by everyone!), Western societies are full of economic inequity and various 'isms'.
- Dominant ideology convinces us this state of affairs/inequalities is normal and continues to reproduce these ways of being.
- We can't change this state of affairs without first understanding it.

I will often include a PowerPoint slide, which pictures someone looking into a mirror to represent 'reflection', and then compare this with a picture of someone standing in a hall of mirrors. Critical reflection of practice is more like a hall of mirrors allowing students to examine themselves from all kinds of angels. However, it can also be confusing and disconcerting.

The importance of understanding hegemony

- An important concept for Critical Reflection and Social Work as a whole
- Gramsci's concept, which describes the manner in which people who are subjugated by dominant ideologies 'buy into' the status quo. . .and make them seem normal/just the way things are

Examples

- Discourses that romanticise abuse
- Discourses of 'vocation' and 'perfectionism'
- Individualism within discourses of 'self-care'

The difference between domination and hegemony:
Certain understandings might shift over time from being imposed to being ingrained in taken-for-granted discourses and practices.

Figure 14.2 From domination to hegemony

Box 14.5 Considerations for a university course

There are pros and cons for both assigning students to working groups or having students develop their own groups. Consider carefully, which path to follow, and be clear to students as to why you have chosen the one you have.

Review 'critical acceptance' as a group requirement but also acknowledge stages of group work and the impossibility to guarantee a smooth process throughout.

Describe one of your own incidents to the class as a whole and have the class attempt to develop questions to ask you prior to the groups beginning the process themselves. It is also possible to interview one of the students in front of the whole class as to his or her incident to role model the process before they start it themselves. This can be done before Stage 1 and again before Stage 2.

Groups will be working on their own without a facilitator for much of the time if you need to divide your class into anywhere between four and six groups. Always bring the groups back together to debrief after working together. This will be especially important for those groups you have been unable to assist during that week's class.

Some students benefit from incorporating arts-based approaches to expressing their reactions to both Stage 1 and 2.

References

Brookfield, S. (2016). So what exactly is critical about critical reflection? In J. Fook, V. Collington, F. Ross, G. Ruch, & L. West (Eds.), *Researching critical reflection: Multidisciplinary perspectives* (pp. 11–22). Milton Park: Routledge.

Index

Note: page numbers in italic type refer to Figures; those in bold type refer to Tables.

'accompanying place' 111
Adamowich, T. 93
advice-giving approach 46, 48 49
'ambiguity of practice' (Fook and Gardner) 32
Ashby, J.S. 73
Ashmore, L. 149
Askeland, G.A. 49, 151
attunement 136, 155
authenticity 93

Baker, Jeffrey 3–4
Becker, J. 134
Bekas, S. 7
Belenky, M.F. 160–161
Béres, Laura: references to 8–9, 45, 90; chapters authored by 1–20, 123–138, 139–153, 154–164, 165–175; experiences of teaching Critical Reflection and Appraisal of Practice course 17, 123–137, 158
Berlin, S.B. 72
'binary opposites' 12, 35, 58
Birnbaum, L. 111
blame/blaming 8, 46, 50, 52
Blankstein, K.R. 76
Bolton, G. 109
Botticelli, S. 88
Braun, V. 140, 143
Breckenridge, J. 88
British Association of Social Workers, Professional Capabilities Framework 108
Broadhurst, K. 37–38
Brookfield, Stephen 4, 24, 27, 136, 150, 161
Bueskens, P. 88

burnout, in social workers 44, 98, 106, 107, 111, 112, 116; see also social worker well-being
'busyness' culture of social work 111–112, 113, 114, 115

Cairney, K. 8
Canada: employment climate 96; social work environment and context 44; see also Critical Reflection and Appraisal of Practice course
Canda, E.R. 14
change: challenges of 23; see also transformational action, development of as result of learning critical reflection; transformative learning
Chief Social Worker's Knowledge and Skills Statement 108
child protection services 8, 34–35, 37–38, 39, 40
CIQs (Critical Incident Questionnaires) 124, 125, 127, 131, 136, 139
Clarà, M. 69
Clark, M. 96
Clarke, V. 140, 143
client self-determination 71, 72
Clinchy, B.M. 160–161
collaborative group environments 45–46; see also critical acceptance; group culture/dynamics
community (Brookfield) 4
compassion, development of as result of learning critical reflection 144, 147–148, 152
'compassionate conscientiousness' 76, 77
Cook, C. 14

Cornejo, Fenix 106–119, 157
courageous communication, and critical acceptance 26–27, 158
critical acceptance 15, 24, 25–26, 45–46, 61, 97, 110, 114, 130, 133, 158; and courageous communication 26–27, 158; emotional safety 26, 29, 158; honouring professionalism 26, 28, 158; research finding of importance of 149–150; staying outside the story 26, 27–28, 158; and vulnerability 26, 27, 29–30, 158
Critical Incident Questionnaires see CIQs (Critical Incident Questionnaires)
critical incidents 16, 38; Béres' 124–125, 128–129; challenges to validity of 97–98; Donati's 70–71; Elsie-McKendrick's 91–92; emotional responses to 40, 50; Lawley's 38–39; Lennox's 103; resources for learning and teaching 169; Salomons' 19, 26, 30–32; Schindler's 79–81; teachers' sharing of 134
critical pedagogy 9
critical perspectives, in the integrated model of critical reflection 13
critical reflection 64–65; context of 7–8; 'definition of 2–3; differing needs of learners 161–163; executive leadership team case study 56–63; factors supportive of 158–159; implications for teaching and learning 159–160; importance of protected time for 39–41; nonvoluntary 157–158; preparation for learning 160; process for practising of 15–17; readiness for 57; resources for learning and teaching 165–175; safeguards in learning process 4; and social worker well-being 106–116; structure and process of learning 35–36; students' commitment to integration of 147–148; and supportive organisational environments 41–42; in a work-based training context 34–35; see also Critical Reflection and Appraisal of Practice course; CRoP (Critical Reflection on Practice)
Critical Reflection and Appraisal of Practice course 1; Béres' experiences of teaching 17, 123–137, 158; researching the learning experience 139–152; see also CRoP (Critical Reflection on Practice); Donati, Rebecca; Elsie-

McKendrick, Ashley; Meidinger, Nate; Salomons, Tonya; Schindler, Jackie
Critical Reflection on Practice see Critical Reflection and Appraisal of Practice course; CRoP (Critical Reflection on Practice)
critical social theory 13, 57, 84–85, 92, 93, 95, 127–128, 131–132; resources for learning and teaching 172, 174
critical theory 58
CRoP (Critical Reflection on Practice) 17, 45–47, 69–70, 76, 79–80, 124; distinguishing factors from therapy 49–50; group dynamics in 90, 97–99, 146, 148–149, 150; and NT (narrative therapy) 44–52; see also Critical Reflection and Appraisal of Practice course; stage 1 of critical reflection process; stage 2 of critical reflection process
'cultural suicide' (Brookfield) 4
cultures 58; as context for critical reflection 7–8; importance of supportive organisational environments 41–42; see also group culture/dynamics; organisational culture

Damian, L.E. 74, 75
'dark side' of critical reflection 4
D'Cruz, H. 40
de Wolff, A. 96
deconstruction 12–13, 57, 70, 72, 84; and critical acceptance 27; and physical attractiveness 103–105; in stage 1 of critical reflection process 16
deficit approach 31
Dewey, J. 3
disruption 60
Doherty, P. 37–38
Donati, Rebecca 69–78, 157
'double listening' 52

Elsie-McKendrick, Ashley 90–101, 156–157, 159
emotional aspects of critical reflection 5–6, 7, 63, 155, 156–157, 161; emotional safety, and critical acceptance 26, 29, 158
empathy, development of as result of learning critical reflection 144, 147–148, 152
Epston, David 47

178 Index

ethics: OCSWSSW (Ontario College of Social Workers and Social Service Workers) 93; and risk, in critical reflection 6; in social work practice 110

executive leadership team case study 56–58; analysis of 61–63; author's personal reflection on 63–64; critical reflection in practice 60–61; introduction of critical reflection 58–60

failure, feelings and narratives of 6, 49, 50, 51, 71, 72, 73, 74, 75, 76, 77, 93

fear, of critical reflection process 24

feminist perspective, and the mother role in social work practice 82, 84, 87

Ferguson, Harry 31

Ferguson, Y. 8

Finlay, L. 6–7

Flett, G.L. 73, 74, 76

Fook, Jan: approach to teaching and learning 9–10; chapters authored by 1–20, 139–153, 154–164, 165–175; references to 1–20, 24, 25–26, 27, 29, 32, 35, 44, 45, 46, 48–49, 55, 57, 58, 59, 60, 61, 69, 70, 71, 73, 74, 79–80, 92, 97, 103, 107, 111, 114, 123, 124, 130, 133, 139–153, 154–164, 165–175

'forced choices' 12

Foucault, M. 28, 129, 132

Freire, Paulo 9

Freud, S. 155

Gadamer, H.-G. 3

Gardner, Fiona 8, 24, 25–26, 27, 29, 32, 35, 45, 55, 57, 58, 59, 60, 61, 71, 74, 79, 92, 97, 124, 130, 151

gender: gender roles 102; and power 128, 131; stereotypes, and physical appearance 103–105

Gillingham, P. 40

Giroux, Henry 9, 127

Gnilka, P.B. 73

Goffman, E. 12

Goldberger, N.R. 160–161

Goldsworthy, K.K. 98, 99

'good enough mother' (Winnicott) 86

grief 98–99, 100, 162

grounded theory analysis 140

group culture/dynamics 90, 97–99, 146, 148–149, 150, 155–156, 159–160; collaborative group environments 45–46

Health and Care Professions Council 108

health impact of temporary employment 96

Heidegger, M. 3

Helyer, R. 8

Hewitt, P.L. 73, 74, 76

Hickson, Helen 5–6, 55–65, 85, 92, 95, 96, 156, 158

Holland, S. 40

Holt, K. 37–38

Honneth, A. 155

hostility, as element of grieving 99

Hunt, C. 14

identity 6, 7, 50, 95

'ideology critique' (Brookfield) 13

Immem, W. 96

'impostership'/imposter syndrome 4, 24, 50, 71

'inner managers' (Fook) 46

'inner victim' culture 46

insider knowledge, value of 47–48, 156

integrated model of critical reflection, overview of 10–15

IPA (interpretive phenomenological analysis) 140

Ixer, G. 110

journaling 124, 147; Béres' use of 123, 132–133; Elsie-McKendrick's use of 96–97, 99–100, 159; students' dislike of 8

judgements 8; nonjudgemental approach 38, 40, 158

Kelly, J.D. 77

King, Martin Luther, Jr. 51

knowledge 59, 60, 61, 62; construction of, and post-structural theory 12; insider knowledge 47–48, 156

Koledin, S. 76

Kumsa, M.K. 93

labels, internalising of 50

language 35, 156; and the critical incident 26–27; duality of meaning in 51; implicit assumptions and perspectives in 37; listening to 52; and post-structural thinking 11–13

Lawley, Stephen 34–43, 156, 157, 158–159

Lawrence-Wilkes, L. 149

Lay, C.H. 76

Le Fevre, D.M. 134–135
learning environments 8, 15; creation of conducive environment 159–160; importance of for critical reflection 158–159; preparation for unconventional ways of learning 160–161; *see also* critical acceptance
Lee, J.J. 112–113
Lennox, Jasmyne 102–105, 157
Lewchuk, W. 96
Liechty, J. 136
listening 15; 'double listening' 52
loss, in critical reflection 7, 98–99, 157
'lost innocence' (Brookfield) 4

Macdonald, S. 74
Madigan, S. 47
McGilloway, S. 58
McGregor, S.L.T. 7
McLoughlin, K. 58
Meidinger, Nate 12, 44–54, 143, 144, 147, 148, 150, 156, 158
Melendez, S. 40
Meyer, F. 134–135
Mezirow, J. 3
Miller, S.E. 112–113
Moon, J. 35–36
Morley, C. 58, 70
mother role in social work practice 80, 82–84, 85–86, 87, 88–89
Mustin, J. 71

Nakashima, J. 71
narratives: and post-structural thinking 11–12, 13; *see also* NT (narrative therapy)
Noble, C.M. 73
nonjudgemental approach 38, 40, 158
nonvoluntary critical reflection 157–158
NT (narrative therapy) 12, 44–45, 47, 143, 155, 156, 158; absent but implicit questioning 46, 51–52; externalising conversations 46, 50–51, 156; therapeutic posture of 46, 47–50

object relations theory 86
Oliver, J.M. 74
'one truth' 12, 45, 47
Ontario Human Rights Commission 162
openness 136
organisational culture 58, 61–62, 64, 156; 158; as context for critical reflection

7–8; importance of supportive organisational environments 41–42; and learning environments 159; in social work 106, 108, 112–113
Osler, C. 134
'othermothering' 82
other-oriented perfectionism 74, 75; *see also* perfectionism

parenting, and perfectionism 74
Paterson, M.A. 71
patriarchy, and gender role stereotypes 104
perfectionism 69, 72–76, 77, 157
physical appearance, and gender stereotypes 103–105
politicisation, development of as result of learning critical reflection 145, 152
postmodernism 11–12, 45, 47, 58–59, 63, 72, 92, 93, 103–104, 110, 127, 131, 156; resources for learning and teaching 172
post-structuralism 11–12, 58, 70; resources for learning and teaching 172
Powell, A. 14
power 28, 58, 59, 60, 61, 62, 93, 156; critical perspectives on 13; and gender 128, 131; and group dynamics 98; in social work contexts 108, 110–111; in teacher/student relations 127–128, 131–132, 158; and women's professional roles and identities 84–85; workplace imbalances 94–95
practice, importance of in learning critical reflection 145–157
'practice wisdom' 135
precarious employment, health impact of 96
'presenteeism' 109
problem-solving approach 36, 48–49, 128
procrastination 76
professionalism: honouring professionalism, and critical acceptance 26, 28, 158; and the mother role in social work practice 82, 83, 84, 85–86, 87–88
protected time, importance of for critical reflection 39–41
psychotherapy, and women's professional roles 87–88

questioning 37, 92, 93, 125; absent but implicit 46, 51–52; resources for learning and teaching 165–168, 171–172; 'right' questions 48

180 Index

racism, experience of by Fook 9
Ravalier, J.M. 109
readiness for critical reflection 57
'recognition,' in group dynamics 155
reconstruction 13; in stage 2 of critical reflection process 16
reflection 2–3, 130; definition of 69; learning experience and issues 3–8; space for in social work 113–114, **114**; students' perceptions of prior to course 142; value of 1
reflective dialogue 15
reflective practice 2, 3, 10–11; 92, 125–126; resources for learning and teaching 171
reflective questions 15
reflexivity 2, 59, 60, 61, 62, 92, 110, 126–127, 130–131, 135; in the integrated model of critical reflection 11; resources for learning and teaching 171–172; social worker well-being 115–116
Rego, C. 93
relational model 86
religion 14; *see also* spirituality
researching the learning experience of the Critical Reflection and Appraisal of Practice course 139–140, 151–152; data analysis 142–144; methodology 140; participant research assistants' reflections 148–151; participants 140–141; procedure 141; results 144–148
resilience 108, 114
resistance, in critical reflection 7
resources for learning and teaching critical reflection 165–175
Rice, K.G. 73
risk, in critical reflection 6–7, 59, 60
'road running' (Brookfield) 4
Robinson, V.M.J. 134–135
Rogers, M. 143
Rothman, J. 71
Ruch, Gillian 26, 30

safeguards in critical reflection learning process 4
Salomons, Tonya 23–33, 143, 144, 148–149, 156, 157, 158
Saric, M. 5, 6, 151
Schindler, Jackie 79–89, 156, 157, 158
Schön, Donald 3, 10, 81

self-care 109, 112–113; development of as result of learning critical reflection 144–145; *see also* social worker well-being
self-compassion 110
self-oriented perfectionism 74, 75; *see also* perfectionism
self-protection, and vulnerability 135–136
Shaw, E. 88
Sheehy, M. 88
Sheldrake, P. 14
Signs of Safety approach to child protection practice 38, 39
Simon, Roger 9
Sims, A. 14
skills development for critical reflection 36–39
Slaney, R.B. 73
Smith, W. 71
social beliefs 13
social inequalities 13
social justice 13; in Fook's approach to teaching and learning 9
social worker well-being 106–107, 108–109, 116; context 106, 107–108; and learning to critically reflect 110–111; London, UK, research study 106, 111–115, **114**; reflexivity 115–116
social workers: Hickson's critical reflection research study 56; and imposter syndrome 24; 'subject position' of (Heron) 28; vulnerability of 39; *see also* social worker well-being
socially prescribed perfectionism 74
Socrates 3, 151
'spiraling' (Hickson) 5, 155
spirituality 128; in the integrated model of critical reflection 14–15; resources for learning and teaching 172
stage 1 of critical reflection process 16, 17, 71; Elsie-McKendrick's experiences 90; resources for learning and teaching 169–170; Schindler's experiences 81–85
stage 2 of critical reflection process 16–17, 76; Elsie-McKendrick's experiences 90; resources for learning and teaching 170–171; Schindler's experiences 85–88
statutory responsibilities of social workers, UK 108
staying outside the story, and critical acceptance 26, 27–28, 158
Steh, B. 5, 6

Stiver, Irene 87
Stoddart, J. 93
stories 27; and post-structural thinking 11–12, 13; staying outside the story, and critical acceptance 26, 27–28, 158; *see also* NT (narrative therapy)
stress, in social workers 8, 31, 48, 94, 99, 106, 107, 108, 109, 111–112, 114, 115, 116, 150, 156, 157; *see also* social worker well-being
student support services context 91–92
'subject position' of social workers (Heron) 28
suicide intervention 91–92
supervision: Elsie-McKendrick's experiences 91–92, 93–94, 96, 99; and social worker well-being 109, 113, 115–116

Tarule, J,M, 161
team working 150; *see also* group dynamics
temporary employment, health impact of 96
thematic analysis 140
Thompson, V. 110
transformational action, development of as result of learning critical reflection 145
transformative learning 3, 5, 9, 29, 151, 152, 155–156, 157
Traverso-Yepez, M. 7
Tsang, A. 8

UK: social work context 106, 107–108; social work training programmes 34; statutory responsibilities of social workers 108

uncertainty 6, 9, 63
'unique outcomes' 12
'use of self' 136

values: OCSWSSW (Ontario College of Social Workers and Social Service Workers) 93; in social work practice 110
Vito, R. 93
vulnerability 6, 9, 59, 60, 63, 80, 154–155, 156–157; Béres' experiences of teaching the Critical Reflection and Appraisal of Practice course 124, 132–133, 134–136, 161; and critical acceptance 26, 27, 29–30, 158; and nonvoluntary critical reflection 158; preparation for 160–161; and self-protection 135–136; of social workers 39; within teaching 160–161

well-being *see* social worker well-being
West, Linden 155
White, Michael 12, 47, 50, 51
Winnicott, Donald 86, 155
women: gender roles 102; professional roles and identities 83, 84–85, 87–89; *see also* gender; mother role in social work practice
work environments, as context for critical reflection 7–8
work-based training context for critical reflection 34–35
worthlessness, feelings and narratives of 50, 51, 52

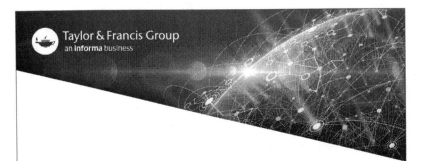